CENTRAL

UCO

Building Traditions, Educating Generations:

A HISTORY OF THE UNIVERSITY OF CENTRAL OKLAHOMA

BY
PATRICIA LOUGHLIN AND BOB BURKE

Oklahoma Horizons Series

SERIES EDITOR: GINI MOORE CAMPBELL

OKLAHOMA HERITAGE ASSOCIATION
OKLAHOMA CITY

Library of Congress
Card Catalog Number 2007929040

ISBN 978-1-885596-60-4

Printed in the United States of America

Jacket Design by Craig Beauchaw

Front Jacket Photo by Daniel Smith

Book Design by Kris Vculek

To the historians of Central history,
especially F.C. Oakes, Reba Collins and Stan Hoig

In Memory
Rev. Robert Anthony Burke, 1971-2006
University of Central Oklahoma graduate,
beloved son, brother, husband, father and friend

Central

CONTENTS

ACKNOWLEDGMENTS

Telling the story of the University of Central Oklahoma has been a rewarding and invigorating experience. So many people have such deep connections to Central – as a place of education and a place of opportunity – and our lives have changed in the process. Much gratitude and foresight goes to President Roger Webb, Don Betz and Kenny Brown for initiating a book-length history of the University of Central Oklahoma as the first public institution for higher education in Oklahoma Territory. Provost Bill Radke, Vice Provost Pat LaGrow, Executive Vice President Steve Kreidler, Vice President for Information Technology Cynthia Rolfe, and Assistant Vice President Dan Donaldson provided essential leadership, encouragement and support throughout the project. We extend a special thank you to Beverly Prosser and Linda Sharp in Academic Affairs for their attention to detail.

It is no small task to write the history of a university. And although the story begins in the 1890s and continues through the early 2000s, in no way is it meant to be comprehensive. Perhaps our most important contribution has been working with Carolyn Pool, Director of the Museum Studies Program, and history and museum studies students in developing an oral history project on campus in connection with the book. Beginning in 2004, Kim Penrod and Stephanie Fields, graduate students in the History/Museum Studies Program and directors of the oral history project, and student researchers in the Department of History and Geography, conducted over 60 oral history interviews with past presidents, faculty and staff, and alumni in partnership with Archives and Special Collections under the direction of Nicole Willard. The stories have been utilized throughout the book, helping to make the institutional history come to life. But the oral histories have another purpose. They have been deposited in Archives and Special Collections in the Max Chambers Library at UCO so that future generations of researchers may utilize them as they revisit the history of UCO. The Archives is a special treasure on campus, and Equlla M. Brothers, Annette Ryan, Diane Rice and Adrianna Schroeder shared their expertise with us and identified images and source material.

Generous grant support through Dean Pam Washington and the College of Liberal Arts and Dean S. Narasinga Rao, Associate Dean John Garic, Assistant Dean John Barthell in the Joe C. Jackson College of Graduate Studies and Research provided us with the opportunity to work with exceptional student researchers. Erica Johnson worked with the project in its infancy and conceptualized plans for the vignette contributors and topics. Other student researchers who were instrumental in the book project include: Julie Bennett-Jones, Melissa Brodt, Tim Cook, James Etzler, Jon Freeman, Felicia Harrison, Megan McGregor, Kathi Nehls and Greg Zornes. Tim Cook served as research assistant during the last phase of publication. Cook's attention to detail and technological expertise aided the book's completion. In addition, Kim Penrod and Jason Harris, created a historic walking tour of campus and the Laboratory of History Museum for students to gain a greater awareness and appreciation for their university and the wonderful anecdotes that accompany every building and program on campus. Exceptional individuals in Title III and Information Technology took interest in the project and provided invaluable support. We appreciate the good work of Toni Beller, Sandra Burkey, Gerry Cherry, Dale Knight, Julio Mata, Julio Pacheco and Barbara Reed.

University Relations, the UCO Foundation and the Alumni Association have been so important to this project and nurtured it along. Charlie Johnson and Gypsy Hogan always helped us share our progress with the university community. Most, if not all, of the beautiful color images in the book that document UCO history from the 1970s to today are the work of Dan Smith and more recently Jonathan Smith, campus photographers. Craig Beuchaw designed the cover. Anne Holzberlein and her staff at the UCO Foundation have provided consistent support. We extend a special thank you to Holly Henson-Murphy and Heather McCormick. And, of course, we appreciate our energetic UCO Alumni director, Stacy McNeiland, and her committed staff Cindy Gray, Wendy Lackmeyer, Juliane Morgan, and Lyndi Standefer.

We thank Stan Hoig, Virginia Peters, Kenny Brown, Holly Henson-Murphy, Jere Roberson, Donna Carlon and Paul Lehman for commenting on earlier drafts of the manuscript. We also appreciate the insight and encouragement of Lisa Antonelli, Jim Baker, Jim Bidlack, Janet Bellows, Nancy Busby, Candace Corollo, Ed Cunliff, Kristen Ford, Bob McGill, Mark Moore, Richard and Helen Peters, Royce Peterson, John Osburn, Pat McGinnis, Scott Monetti, Brad Morelli, Brenda Raimondi, Lucille Warrick, David Webb, Susan Wortham, Sue Youngberg.

We would like to thank President Shannon L. Nance of the Oklahoma Heritage Association for her continued efforts in promoting the publishing program of the Association and Gini Moore Campbell, Director of Publications & Education, for countless evenings and weekends editing and seeing this history through production. We have benefited from the talents of designer Kris Vculek creating the layout for this history from her Waukomis, Oklahoma, home office.

-Patricia Loughlin and Bob Burke, 2007

I would like to extend a personal thank you to Paul Randolph, one my first history professors at Pepperdine, who always offered smiles and encouragement to all students. My aunt and uncle, Kash and Ed McCaskey, continue to encourage and inspire me. As always, my husband Mike Logan, and sons, Owen and Bryce, remind me to strive for balance in my life.

-Patricia Loughlin

FOREWORD

By W. Roger Webb
President
The University of Central Oklahoma

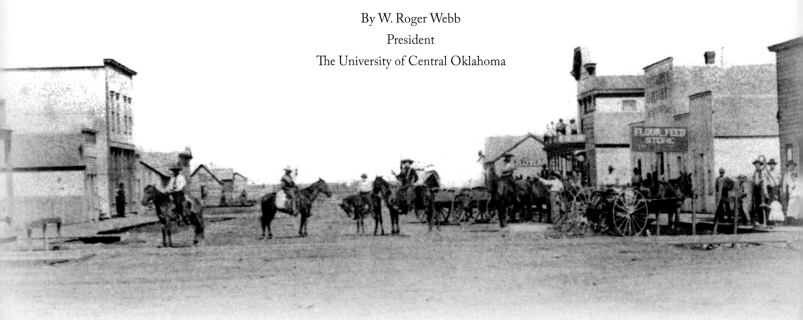

It is appropriate that in the Centennial Celebration year of our state that Dr. Patricia Loughlin, a distinguished UCO Professor of History, Bob Burke, Oklahoma's most prolific author and historian and a number of UCO's history students, have written an extensive history of the University of Central Oklahoma. I appreciate their invitation to write a few preliminary remarks for this important book which chronicles the building of a great University and a legacy of leadership for Oklahoma.

While reading through the manuscript, I have been reminded again and again how interwoven our campus history is with the lives and struggles and choices of the men and women who risked all to populate and nurture the prairies that would become Oklahoma Territory. They were a diverse group of men and women, strategically positioned on the borders of the Unassigned Lands on April 22, 1889. Some were positioned to run on foot, others were saddled on horseback, and still others perched in wagons with families, anxiously waiting for the rifle fire that would trumpet the signal that set off the greatest run for free land in the history of the Republic.

The terms and conditions for the Land Run of 1889 evolved from the Homestead Act of 1862 and the Indian Appropriation Act of March 2, 1889. According to President William McKinley's proclamation, no person was permitted to enter and occupy the land before the designated time, and anyone who violated this provision would be denied a right to the land.

From the very beginning of this settlement, there were issues of right and wrong, ownership and ethics, fairness and cheating. Those who violated the covenant and crossed the lines under cover of darkness to stake their claims early were known as Sooners. The Boomers, by contrast, patiently waited for the signal because those were the rules. But for both groups this moment seemed full of new possibilities spread out before them, full of risk and struggle, but also full of hopes for a better life.

By the time the dust had settled, the Territorial government in Guthrie was scrambling to bring order to this patchwork of overnight cities. Their mission was to provide a structure for the future of these new citizens and their children on the vast prairie that would become the new state of Oklahoma.

These were hard scrabble, down-on-their-luck folks. Few of them were educated or worldly, but their leaders were wise enough to know that their first order of business should be to establish a process of law and provide for a system of education. Perhaps because of the very hard knocks that had brought these pioneers together, they all wanted a better life for their children. Their next step was to create an institution to train teachers who would educate the boys and girls of this brand new land in its one-room schoolhouses. This was an assignment of enormous trust and responsibility, resulting in what is today the University of Central Oklahoma.

We were initially known as the Territorial Normal School of Oklahoma. The term "normal" was commonly used in the sense of being normative, setting the best examples for others to follow. Patterned after the latest and best thinking on education at the time, the school was designed in the manner of the first "normal schools" that had been established in Massachusetts by Horace Mann. Known as the "Father of American Education," Professor Mann had studied similar programs in France and Germany and he recognized the importance of developing colleges which taught teachers how to relate academic lessons to their children and the lives they would lead.

The new Territorial Normal School in Edmond expected its students to have a knowledge of the basic tenets of study, such as arithmetic, reading and writing, before they began teaching. But what made the Normal School so critical to the emergence of our young state was the fact that our graduates were more than teachers; they became models of ethical behavior and leadership for generations of students.

Another great American scholar and educator, Daniel Webster, reinforced the notion of values and character as the ultimate end of education when he said, "Make them intelligent, and they will be vigilant...give them the means of detecting wrong, and they will apply the remedy." John G. Mitchell, one of our early University Presidents, was a strong advocate for both scholarship and character. He observed that the "curriculum should be well balanced, for the future citizenship of our state is in the hands of our teachers." Clearly the knowledge and values both taught and modeled at the Territorial Normal School were replicated across Oklahoma through its graduates who became teachers, business and community leaders.

It is our honor today, at the University of Central Oklahoma, to be the guardians and keepers of that trust. It is our purpose in this book to document, narrate and celebrate the 117 years of history since our school's founding in 1890,

barely a year after the rifles fired to launch the Run of '89.

Like much of Oklahoma, the Territorial Normal School grew by fits and starts out of the red clay of Edmond. Political changes, both here and in Washington, combined with the labor pains of birthing a new state in 1907 to yield fairly rapid leadership changes. The school was fortunate to have a succession of early faculties and presidents with a sense of vision and character that established solid foundations.

That vision and character was sorely tested early in the twentieth century by the trials and demands in quick succession of the Great War, which drained the campus of male faculty and students; by the Great Depression, which drained the campus of funding; and by World War II, which threatened to drain the campus of its vitality. But the tradition of character that was established with our first cornerstones not only held the school together, it also managed to continue its mission, maintain hope, and even support the war effort. This demonstration of our values is symbolized by the Central tribute to those involved in World War II - the lovely wood, stained glass and graceful lines of the Y-Chapel of Song, an enduring structure which rose almost entirely from the volunteer efforts of our faculty and students.

The burgeoning growth of the Boomer generation after the war did even more for Central's growth than the impact of the first group of "Boomers" that had launched us 60 years earlier. The routing of Interstate 35 in the late 1960's and the construction of the Broadway Extension a decade later had an incredible impact on our home community of Edmond and contributed to a corresponding growth of the University.

The University and the city of Edmond have a long history of confronting challenges and opportunities together. When the first normal building began to emerge from the red Edmond clay, citizens of the town volunteered along with members of the school's faculty to carry brick and stone to the building site now known as Old North.

Through the years the University and the city found mutual benefit in joining together to promote and create such projects as the Edmond Economic Development Authority and the construction of the Edmond Chamber of Commerce office on University property. In that same spirit of partnership, city leaders worked with the University to bring the Oklahoma State Bureau of Investigation Forensic

Laboratory to Edmond and to create the Forensic Science Institute at UCO. There are few cities in America better suited than Edmond to be a nurturing community for an emerging university. Just as we have grown and grown up together over more than a century, the futures of UCO and Edmond remain inextricably tied together.

A glimpse of UCO today reveals a beautiful campus bursting with pride and optimism. We are a splendid blend of first-generation, legacy and traditional students from both urban and rural communities, returning adult students, international students, and those seeking to better themselves through professional and continuing education. They come to us from every county in the state, from across the nation, and from more than one hundred countries around the world. No longer the "commuter school" it once was, UCO has evolved into a dynamic, major metropolitan university. Our residential facilities and their amenities are attractive and new; our academic facilties are newly enhanced; our technology infrastructure is state-of-the-art, and our athletic programs are competitive and exciting. UCO's student government provides opportunities for leadership growth and encourages civic engagement. Our campus life offers diverse cultural events, popular student entertainment, and our performing arts programs are a magnet for the entire metropolitan area.

Yet with all these changes, incredible growth, dramatic beautification of our campus and remarkable technical innovation in delivering education, one thing has remained the same and always will: We are committed to being a place where great teaching is central to what we do, where character and civility and community are central to who we are, and where graduating the next generation of ethical leaders for Oklahoma is central to why we are here.

PREFACE

The University of Central Oklahoma's history began in Edmond, Oklahoma, in the early 1890s as a normal school, offering a curriculum designed to train public school teachers. Holding its first classes in November 1891, the Territorial Normal School of Oklahoma was the first public institution of higher education in Oklahoma Territory. Although three institutions – Central, the University of Oklahoma at Norman and the Agricultural and Mechanical College at Stillwater – can link their origins to the First Territorial Legislature and its selection of sites for higher education in the territory in 1890, Central was the first to conduct classes. The University of Oklahoma commenced classes in fall 1892, and the A&M opened in 1893. Significantly, the normal school opened first – ahead of both the university and the agricultural and mechanical college. Furthermore, the first building constructed for the purpose of higher education in Oklahoma Territory was the Normal Building, also called Old North, located on Central's campus in Edmond. Other institutions with normal school origins, including East Central, Southeastern and Northeastern, opened following statehood.

From simple beginnings as the normal school with Principal Richard Thatcher (1891-1893) instructing twenty-five students to today's university of approximately 400 full-time faculty and almost 16,000 students, Central has an exciting story to tell. The institution has experienced six name changes, most recently the transition from Central State University to the University of Central Oklahoma in 1991. In addition, nineteen presidents have guided Central's primary mission as a teaching institution.

Politics was inextricably linked to the development of higher education in Oklahoma. During the crucial early years of Central's existence, at a time when stable, consistent leadership would have been ideal, the school instead had six presidents in seventeen years. The troubling practice of dismissing college presidents and sometimes faculty with a change in governor continued during the early twentieth century. Politics continued, but during the 1950s, President Max Chambers halted mandatory political campaign solicitations from the faculty.

During the 1960s, Central State College transitioned from a teacher's college to a thriving, diversified commuter college. Triggered by the post-World War II era baby boom, students flocked to campus in record numbers. President Garland Godfrey (1960-1975) launched an ambitious building program to keep pace with projected enrollment. Dr. Joe Jackson (1951-1976), debate coach, dean of students and then vice president for academic affairs, worked in partnership with Godfrey during this time of transition. Presidents Bill Lillard (1975-1992), George Nigh (1992-1997) and W. Roger Webb (1997-) have continued to increase UCO's visibility throughout the state and nation, and have placed student learning and achievement first.

PHOTO BY VREELAND

CHAPTER ONE

Building Traditions

Territorial Normal School of Oklahoma (1891-1903)

The normal school opened its doors on November 9, 1891 — a significant date — because it opened before the university in Norman and the Agricultural and Mechanical College in Stillwater.
F.C. Oakes

From the beginning, the social life of the school has centered around its literary and cultural clubs and its athletic activities.
Stella Barton Fordice

Minnie Morton and the Legacy of Alumni

In 1892, officials at the Territorial Normal School made their first recommendation for a prospective teacher, Miss Minnie Morton. Although not yet a graduate of the program, Morton met the minimum qualifications for a position at a one-room school near her home west of Edmond. She rode her pony to the schoolhouse and received a monthly salary of $35.00, much of it bartered in meat and vegetables.

Minnie Morton Kibby was the first teacher from the Territorial Normal School appointed to a school house in 1892.
Courtesy Archives and Special Collections, UCO Library.

Her family took exceptional pride in her early successes, leading several generations of her descendants to earn degrees at the institution now known as the University of Central Oklahoma. In 2004, Anne Allbright, a history major, walked across the stage to receive her diploma, fully aware she was the fifth generation to follow her great-great-grandmother–Minnie Morton.

Beginning in 1891 with Morton and her classmates, students have benefited from the student-centered education at Central. Today enrollment consistently exceeds 15,000 students and the curriculum has surpassed the preparatory and normal school courses to include a variety of majors and graduate degrees. Throughout its history, the institution has emphasized the well being of its students and their preparation for life after graduation.

From the first classes in 1891 until 1904, when the institution became Central State Normal School, the founding leaders and teachers sought to emulate the national model of similar schools. They also struggled simply to survive. Politics sometimes disrupted the stability and collegiality of the institution. Likewise, pedagogical strategies and methods changed dramatically over the years, but these early educators formulated the primary goal that remained throughout Central's history—to serve and educate students.

Commercial rather than altruistic motives drove Edmond's political leaders to maneuver for the location of the normal school. The town was born in 1887 as a meager collection of buildings at a coaling and watering station on the Atchison, Topeka, and Santa Fe Railroad, which built through the Unassigned Lands of central Indian Territory during that year. Originally referred to as "Summit," the name changed to Edmond in 1889. That year, a few hundred settlers rushed to the town site on April 22 in the first of several land runs into what would become Oklahoma Territory.

Congress belatedly organized a territorial government in May, 1890, and the 400 residents of Edmond elected Democrat Dr. J.W. Howard as its representative to the new legislature. Fully aware that the small town's future might well depend on the economic stimulus of a governmental institution, Howard sought to locate a "prize" for Edmond.

The Edmond Santa Fe Depot grew more active following the opening of Oklahoma Territory in 1889. *Courtesy Archives and Special Collections, UCO Library.*

Howard and his fellow citizens considered several options. Milton J. Reynolds, a former politician and journalist from Kansas, and publisher of the *Edmond Sun*, hoped the village could acquire the territorial capital. His newspaper openly called for Edmond to become a county seat or the home of the university or normal school.

Unfortunately, representatives from other areas of the territory had similar designs to ensure the future of their settlements, resulting in a competition so intense that the legislators spent virtually all of the session late in 1890 trading votes and logrolling to acquire institutions. They gave the capital to Guthrie and, late at night on December 23, 1890, the legislature passed a bill granting the normal school to Edmond, the university to Norman, and the agricultural and mechanical college to Stillwater.

Immediately, the leaders of Edmond embraced their new institution. The bill creating the normal school had three conditions—the school had to be located in Edmond proper or within a mile of the town; forty acres of land had to be provided for the school, ten for the school itself and the rest to be platted into town lots; and the newly created County of Oklahoma, in which Edmond was located, would have to vote $5,000 in bonds for the school. Town leaders with ardent backing from local newspapers helped pass the bond issue in the county election on April 7, 1891.

Upon approval of the funding, a "locating committee" took the necessary steps to establish the school. H.J. Whitely of Oklahoma City chaired the committee, while John L. Mitch of Edmond served as secretary-treasurer and John F. Stone of Guthrie as a third member. After considering the offers of three citizens, the board chose Anton H. Classen's quarter section east of the town. Ten acres would provide

Downtown Broadway in Edmond during the 1890s. The Hotel DeHoss was an important establishment on Second Street and site for the first Thanksgiving community dinner, organized by the Ladies Aid Society. *Courtesy Archives and Special Collections, UCO Library.*

First Street in Edmond was the site of the Central Hotel, 1890. *Courtesy Archives and Special Collections, UCO Library.*

land for the campus and thirty acres would be divided into lots and sold to support the school. The people of Edmond enthusiastically supported their emerging institution and passed another $2,000 bond issue on August 4, 1891.

The vigor of support for education in the new Oklahoma Territory mirrored the values of their neighbors—the American Indian people of Indian Territory to the east. Beginning in the 1840s, the Five Tribes—Cherokee, Choctaw, Chickasaw, Creek, and Seminole—established mission schools, seminaries, and academies. The Cherokee Male and Female Seminaries, for example, began in 1846, and provided the elite members of the Cherokee Nation a strong liberal arts education to prepare them for the rigor of eastern colleges and then return to the Nation to serve as politicians, lawyers, physicians, and businesspeople.

Two institutions of higher education emerged in Indian Territory in the 1880s— Indian University, later Bacone College, established by Baptists at Muskogee and Galloway College, later Willie Halsell College, established by Methodists at Vinita.

The Oklahoma Territorial Legislature also established a public school system with a territorial superintendent and local county superintendents. Each county contained small school districts and an elected board. By 1891, 400 districts emerged to meet the educational needs of more than 22,000 students.

The demand for teachers was high in the bustling territory. More than 400 teachers, mostly settlers, worked in the territory's first public school system. Many of the early instructors had no more than an eighth-grade education, but the First Territorial Legislature was committed to providing a certification program for teachers. The initial certification program had three tracks and a temporary license. Prospective and returning teachers as young as 16 attended a two-week summer normal held in each territorial county, and upon successful examination received certification.

Richard Thatcher (1891-1893)

In Oklahoma Territory, the normal school became the first institution of its type to open. Plans for construction of a suitable building moved at a slow pace after the bond elections. Meanwhile, the newly organized Board of Regents moved to commence classes as soon as possible. In October, 1891, they chose Richard A. Thatcher as principal of the new institution.

Richard Thatcher left a government appointment in Washington, DC to become the first principal of the Territorial Normal School in 1891. During the Civil War, Thatcher joined the Union Army to be a "Drummer Boy" under General Sherman's command. *Courtesy Archives and Special Collections, UCO Library.*

The Territorial Normal School students met in the partially completed First Methodist Church, located on the southwest corner of Broadway and Hurd, for their first classes from fall 1891 until the completion of Old North in 1893. *Courtesy Archives and Special Collections, UCO Library.*

Members of the first class of the Territorial Normal School of Oklahoma at the First Methodist Church in Edmond in 1891. Principal Thatcher is standing fifth person from left in back row. *Courtesy Archives and Special Collections, UCO Library.*

Born in 1848, Thatcher had some education as a child before enlisting in the 111th Illinois Infantry as a drummer boy at age 15. Following his Union Army experience, Thatcher taught in one-room schools and served as a principal in Kansas before moving to Edmond in 1890 to purchase the Central Hotel. Shortly after arriving with his family, he received an appointment to work in the Census Office in Washington, DC. He returned to Edmond in the fall of 1891 to become the first principal of the Territorial Normal School.

With the building project still in the early planning stage, the school needed to find temporary quarters to conduct classes. Reverend Brooks offered rooms in the First Methodist Church, still under construction, on the southwest corner of Broadway and Hurd. Ongoing construction of the church delayed the opening until November 9, 1891, when Principal Thatcher and 25 students met at the church for the first day of school.

Still waiting for their furnishings to arrive, Principal Thatcher and others made temporary desks for students. Classes continued at the church for the 1891-1892 academic year.

With the headline in the *Edmond Sun* reading, "A Grand Opportunity, Opening of the Territorial Normal School at Edmond," Principal Thatcher announced his plans for the school. "The Normal School is designed to train you in the latest and most approved methods of school-teaching," Thatcher said. He discussed the need to specialize in teacher training as a distinct, professional skill, in many ways emulating other professional schools. "The medical schools train our physicians, the law schools, our lawyers, the theological schools, our ministers," he argued. "So the Normal Schools have the special function of furnishing trained teachers for the public schools and our legislature wisely provided that Oklahoma should have a Normal School, and located the same at Edmond."

The entering class was primarily women who lived in Edmond, most of them attending the preparatory grade, or eighth grade, and ranging in age from 13 to 21. Students could attend the Normal School tuition free if they declared their intent to teach school in Oklahoma Territory. As F.C. Oakes, an early English faculty member at Central and author of an unpublished manuscript on the early history of the institution, has maintained, most of the students were

Richard Thatcher

By Adrianna Schroeder, B.A. in History/Museum Studies, 2002, M.A. in History/Museum Studies, 2006; and Amanda Hudson, B.A. in History/Museum Studies, 2005

The first president of the University of Central Oklahoma had his own unique brush with history. At the tender age of 15, Richard D. Thatcher, consumed with patriotism, ignored his parents' wishes and on September 16, 1862, enlisted with H Company, 111th Illinois Volunteer Regiment. He served bravely as a drummer boy in the regimental band during the Civil War. Under the command of John "Black Jack Logan" Black, the company marched through Kentucky, Tennessee, Alabama, and Georgia, joining General Sherman's "March to the Sea."

After assaulting Confederate works at Kennesaw Mountain, the 111th marched on Atlanta and engaged in heavy fighting. During the melee, the rebels captured Thatcher on July 22, 1864, and sent him to Andersonville Prison. Fellow inmate Boston Corbett took pity on young Thatcher who had recently contracted tuberculosis and became gravely ill. Corbett nursed Thatcher back to health and literally saved his life. As president Thatcher always had a whiskey flask with him and occasionally took a nip to dull the pain that haunted him until his death. Under the ruse of a "prisoner exchange," the pair fell out of line and hid in some bushes during a forced march from Andersonville to South Carolina.

Thatcher recuperated and rejoined the army and served until his discharge on June 6, 1865. After the war, Thatcher returned to his boyhood home in Alton, Madison County, Illinois. Thatcher entered McKendree College, a private Methodist University, in Lebanon. He earned degrees in English and science, and a Doctorate of Divinity, with honors. He married Melissa Deford in 1869, and they had four daughters. Strangely, Thatcher's marriage to Deford brought him one step closer to his destiny in Edmond, and UCO.

Thatcher taught school in Illinois and served as superintendent of schools in Kansas. In 1890, he accepted appointment as a clerk in the Bureau of the Census in Washington, D.C. His wife and children moved to Edmond, Oklahoma Territory, where her brother, C.H. Deford, was an established merchant. Thatcher resigned his position in 1891, and reunited with his family in Edmond. He arrived at a most opportune time.

Thatcher was elected principal of the Territorial Normal School on October 15, 1891. He taught his first class of 25 students in the First Methodist Church at 19 North Broadway Avenue. Classes moved to Old North in January, 1893. Because of failing health, Thatcher resigned two years later. He taught at the school as professor of mathematics, however, until his death in 1909.

Thatcher has not been forgotten. The men's residence hall was dedicated as "Thatcher Hall" in 1935. Thatcher's presidential portrait still hangs in the building. In 1947, UCO dedicated a stained-glass window at Y-Chapel in honor of his patriotism. Memorabilia from his Civil War service and his days at Central are currently on display as part of the Thatcher Collection at UCO's campus museum.

At age 53, Thatcher succumbed to tuberculosis on the morning of November 26, 1909. Businesses closed and classes were suspended on the day of his funeral as the city paid its last respects to their pioneer educator. Thatcher left a lasting impression on Rubye Matthews, one of his former students. A half century after his death, Matthews said, "In the eyes of at least one little child, he was wonderful."

teachers "or those engaged in brushing up on the common branches to prepare to be examined for a third, or, maybe, a second grade county certificate to teach."

During the first year, the Normal School offered two 20-week semesters. The course of study included the preparatory department, or seventh and eighth grade, and two years of high school. More than half the students during the first two years of the Normal School were in the preparatory department. The preparatory department included five subjects—arithmetic, grammar, descriptive geography, reading, and orthography, commonly known as penmanship.

The normal department consisted of two terms work—for the first term, higher arithmetic, physical geography, elementary algebra, English analysis, United States history, and orthography—for the second term, higher algebra, civics, physiology, Lockwood's English, penmanship, and theory and practice.

Principal Thatcher was student centered. According to Oakes, Thatcher's former students often said that he was patient, engaging, and accessible. During the first year, Thatcher established a model school, a normal school literary society, later called the Philosophian Society, and encouraged the Board of Regents to consider building a dormitory for students. By early 1893, at Thatcher's request, the legislature made a normal school diploma legal as a five-year certificate to teach in Oklahoma Territory.

Construction of Normal School Building— Old North Tower

Two architects designed the plans for the Normal School Building in the early 1890s. Gall Whitely proposed the original design for the three-story structure with a basement in 1891, and J.G. Haskell added the clock tower and wings in 1894. Construction began immediately in late 1891 on the center portion of the structure. The Board of Regents took bids for building materials and soon contractors were bringing wagon loads of local stone samples to the Normal School site for inspection. Interestingly, the construction crew fired sandstone bricks for the Normal Building on the school site by using local clay from Captain Jackson's land a half-mile north of the school grounds.

The Board of Regents and Principal Thatcher had hoped the Normal Building would be completed in time for the school's second year, but heavy rains in May brought the project to a halt temporarily. By the end of June, 1892, the foundation and basement neared completion, "with massive rocks placed on solid foundations, stone work already above grade line, some window frames for the basement already set, and several arches up."

By the end of July, the exterior of the Normal Building looked impressive against the backdrop of gently rolling hills of the sparsely populated Edmond landscape. Though the roof had been secured and the brick walls were intact,

The Second Legislature of Oklahoma Territory appropriated funds to complete the original large sandstone structure called "Old North" in 1893. An announcement in the July 13, 1893, issue of the *Edmond Sun* stated that "an imposing tower and extended wings were to be added." *Courtesy Archives and Special Collections, UCO Library.*

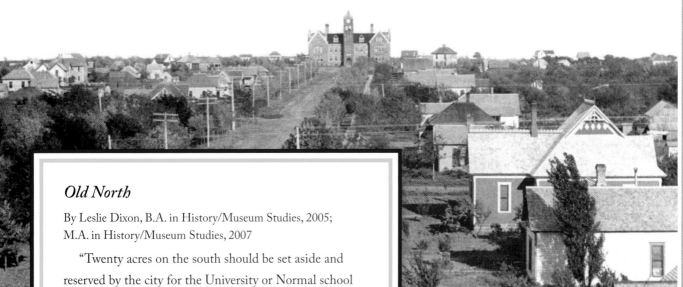

The view from Campbell Street in Edmond looking east through the residences and boardwalks to Old North, early 1900s. *Courtesy Archives and Special Collections, UCO Library.*

Old North

By Leslie Dixon, B.A. in History/Museum Studies, 2005; M.A. in History/Museum Studies, 2007

"Twenty acres on the south should be set aside and reserved by the city for the University or Normal school grounds. Now is the time to do it," stated Milton W. Reynolds, editor of the *Edmond Sun-Democrat*. The Normal School meant prosperity for the people of Edmond, an agricultural town of some 200 people. On April 7, 1891, the Normal School Bill allowed the Territorial Normal School of Oklahoma to be located in Edmond. Edmond citizens believed in educational opportunities for their children and their children's children through the Normal School. In addition, many more people settled in Edmond and created new business and employment opportunities because of the school.

Old North, originally known as the Normal School Building and later North Building, was the first building on campus and one of the oldest structures built for higher education in Oklahoma Territory. The citizens of Edmond contributed money and time to support the construction of the Normal School Building. Old North represented their hopes for the future of the city and state. Beginning in 1893 and until the completion in 1897, the construction of the Normal School Building brought delight to the people of Edmond.

In November, 1973, the Oklahoma Historical Society dedicated Old North, one of the largest existing native sandstone buildings in Oklahoma, as a historical site. In 2004, the renovations of the exterior of Old North were completed. Presently, Old North remains a symbol, "a magnificent structure," of an earlier era at Central.

the building still needed plaster floors, doors, and windows before the students could inhabit it. Waiting for the building's completion, classes met during the second school year in Central Hall, located on the north side of First Street opposite Central Hotel.

Instructors and students would not occupy the Normal Building until January, 1893. Even with the delays, the Normal Building was the first public building dedicated to higher education in Oklahoma Territory.

Faculty and Students

During the first year, Thatcher, a Republican and former Union soldier, served as principal and the only instructor. By 1892, he hired two more teachers and soon the faculty grew to five. Enrollment for 1893 totaled 114 students in a two-year teacher training program. The curriculum consisted of ten subjects in five departments—education, English, languages, mathematics, and science. Residents of Oklahoma Territory enrolled tuition-free, but paid an admission fee of $1.25 per term.

Thatcher struggled to balance the seemingly disparate duties of his position. How could he supervise the students as a popular principal and at the same time command their attention as a strict disciplinarian? Furthermore, how could he meet the direct daily needs of the school while promoting the school throughout the territory? This was no small task for one person. While his critics claimed he lacked discipline, as Oakes has recalled, Thatcher's students told him "they had a lot of fun in those first two years, and they revere the memory of Mr. Thatcher for it."

Within this context, some of Thatcher's critics argued that he had not "advertised" the Normal School enough to attract more students. At the time, Oklahoma Territory had a population of 60,000, with Oklahoma City and Guthrie each claiming more than 4,000, and Edmond remaining relatively small at 400. Roads were unimproved and the Normal School was difficult to access for out-of-town students. To compare, Stillwater had a population of 1,000 and attracted primarily local residents as well.

George Winans (1893-1894)

The early years of the Normal School did not meet expectations of many Edmond business leaders who had hoped the school would quickly provide a thriving economy and growth. In addition, the Panic of 1893, a nationwide economic depression, as well as a local drought spelled disaster for the fledgling school, the community. During his brief time at the Normal School, Principal then President George Winans published the first *Annual Catalogue*, which included a description of three different courses of instruction for a five-year renewable teaching certificate to teach in Oklahoma Territory and the student roster for 1893-1894. Winans articulated the school's mission as "neither a university nor a college. Its special function is to prepare teachers for our public schools." This mission continued to appear in the early issues of the *Annual Catalogue*. He split the Normal Literary Society into two new groups, the Lyceum and Pioneer Literary Societies. He altered the school week, declaring Monday a holiday and Saturday a school day.

With the transition from Thatcher to Winans, Thatcher was the only faculty member to remain at the Normal School. He taught mathematics and penmanship and was

George Winans, the former Superintendent of Public Instruction in Kansas, replaced Thatcher as principal in 1893. He served as principal—the title was changed to president in January, 1894—for one year but did not boost enrollment enough to satisfy Edmond citizens or the Board of Regents. *Courtesy Archives and Special Collections, UCO Library.*

also registrar and recorder. Winans taught history and the science of education, psychology, and school management and methods. The three other instructors were F.H. Umholtz, language, history, civics; J.O. Allen, natural science; and Mary L. Sloss, literature and rhetoric.

Politics continued to influence the granting of appointments and the termination of them. In May, 1894, Winans, Thatcher, and Umholtz, all Republicans were replaced by Democrats. College presidents and faculty shifted in and out of the territorial schools according to the political party of the territorial governor at the time. William C. Renfrow became Oklahoma Territory's only Democratic governor in 1893 and Democrats began to replace Republicans at Oklahoma's institutions of higher learning.

Pioneer and Lyceum

Central's first student clubs, the Lyceum and Pioneer, were established in 1893-1894. The clubs were an integral part of student life—the normal school required students to join one of them. The two clubs competed biannually against each other in debate, essays, parliamentary skills, dramatic art, and music. The winning club received the Regents Medal, a revolving prize housed by the winner until the next contest. The clubs charged admission to contests and raised $26 for books for the school's first library and reading room.

E.R. Williams (1894-1895)

In July, 1894, E. R. Williams, a Democrat from Texas, became the third president of the Territorial Normal School. Williams held the M.A. and taught professional work, Thatcher held the M.S., and James S. Buchanan held the B.S. and taught history and civics. After a brief stay at the Normal School, Buchanan took a position at the University of Oklahoma in 1895 and remained there for 35 years. The three women on the faculty did not hold degrees. In the summer of 1894, however, Vinnie Galbraith, Attorney General C.A. Galbraith's sister, secured a position at the Normal School to develop a department of music.

E.R. Williams, served as the third president of the Territorial Normal School for a one-year term. Williams was the first president to cite the educational degrees of his faculty in the *Annual Catalogue. Courtesy Archives and Special Collections, UCO Library.*

Providing safe residential accommodations for students in the Edmond community and supervising academic progress remained key priorities in the minds of the Normal School faculty. Living accommodations in Edmond were reasonable for students. A student could rent a room in the community for two to four dollars per month and board was about three dollars per week.

Admission to the Normal School was through examination. Each applicant needed to pass an examination in reading, penmanship, spelling, arithmetic, English grammar, geography, and American history. According to Oakes, the "nature of these examinations was very flexible and tolerant—sometimes oral, sometimes written; at other times, both. There is no record that any person was ever turned away because of having failed to 'pass' these examinations." But close supervision and training persisted, as Williams sent student progress reports home to parents.

Under Williams, enrollment increased from 116 to 161. During the early years of the school, instructors provided close supervision and moral direction to their students, or so the *Annual Catalogue* mandated, "All supervisors in charge should exercise a watchful guardianship over the morals of pupils at all times during their attendance." This type of moral guidance and supervision was part of the duties of instructors and continued into the 1950s at Central State.

President E.D. Murdaugh, the Territorial Normal School's fourth president. In 1937, Central erected a women's dorm and named it in honor of Murdaugh. *Courtesy Archives and Special Collections, UCO Library.*

E.D. Murdaugh (1895-1901)

In June, 1895, when Williams left his position as president at Central, E.D. Murdaugh, the Oklahoma A&M president, became the new president and served from 1895 to 1901. Williams was one of only three presidents in the early years who left the job voluntarily, finding the political environment in Oklahoma Territory "too foul" for his disposition.

Concerned that enrollment dipped to 156, five students less than the previous year, Murdaugh traveled throughout Oklahoma Territory giving talks and promoting the school. Oakes has described him as an eloquent speaker. By this time, the territory had established county institutes and, as Oakes has claimed, "kept would-be teachers at home for grade-making opportunities," rather than attending Central. Ever the innovator, Murdaugh created the Territorial Normal Institute, for three days in May 1895, for training instructors and conductors of the county normals of the territory during summer session.

Bronze and Blue

In 1895, Central became the first institution of higher education in Oklahoma Territory to adopt colors. The bronze and blue colors, the choice of President Murdaugh, were first worn and advertised by participant John Adams, Class of 1897, and other students at the first oratorical contest ever held in Oklahoma, the tri-college Oratorical Contest, featuring Central, OU, and A&M, at Guthrie in the spring of 1896. The colors have become tradition at Central, with bronze symbolizing the "burnished sun, the gentle light of intelligence" and blue as "the color of heaven's broad expanse, suggestive of depth, aspiration, hope, ideals."

In 1895, Central had 11 faculty members including—E.D. Murdaugh, President, Latin, psychology, and pedagogy; Richard Thatcher, mathematics, penmanship, and bookkeeping; J. Orlando Allen, natural and physical science; Mary Louise Sloss, English and literature; Nina Eugenie Johnson, form study, drawing, and physical training; Walter Lee Ross, history and civil government; and Mrs. Chas. York, voice training and music. Murdaugh added a music department and classes in higher mathematics, Latin, and physical culture.

The *Annual Catalogue* also provides a glimpse into the rules of decorum of the day for instructors and students. "Teachers," for example, "will be in their rooms five minutes before the ringing of the first bell. They are expected to remain in the building during the entire period of the session, and for at least five minutes after the close." Teachers were assigned a position in the hall to monitor student behavior and ensure proper conduct. Teachers were to use their class time wisely "for the benefit of their classes, and not for personal conferences or private business of any kind."

The *Catalogue* continued, "All supervisors in charge should exercise a watchful guardianship over the morals of pupils at all times during their attendance." Students, for their part, "must be diligent in work, faithful in the discharge of all duties, and exemplary in manners and conduct."

Students pursued five years of English, mathematics, voice training and music, drawing and physical training, and natural and physical science. Students also took three years of Latin, history, and pedagogy.

The question of denying admission at Central based upon the race of the applicant followed historical trends in the region. In 1895, an African American applicant was denied admission to Central Normal School a year after an African American woman was denied admission at the A&M College. During the same period, a black school opened in Edmond with Mattie Hamilton as the teacher.

Memorial for Three Students

A national depression in the early 1890s foreshadowed local concerns of economic stagnation. In addition, Edmond lost population as some of its citizens left to take advantage of new land openings. Where were the promises of prosperity due to the attraction of the Normal School, local residents wanted to know? By 1895, Central's enrollment hovered at 162, including the model school, and Edmond citizens grew increasingly concerned with the community's reliance on the larger, national economy.

To make matters worse, the Edmond community and the Normal School experienced several deaths during the year. J.H. Snyder, the mayor of Edmond, died in November, 1895, followed by the death of Major James Martin, an early pioneer, in January. On Arbor Day, 1896, Murdaugh, faculty, and students planted three evergreens in front of the newly constructed Normal Building to commemorate three Central students who had died during the year. Frederick Maxwell Stubblefield, took a bullet in his head in a shooting accident at the University of Oklahoma and died a few days later. A second student, Elbert White, died of inflammatory rheumatism, while William C. Belt's death is unknown. One of the three trees, a pine, served as Central's Christmas tree one year and as a symbol during the 50th anniversary.

The first five graduates of the Territorial Normal School of Oklahoma, from top, left to right, were John Adams, R. Mayburn Howard, Phronia S. Eckes, Ida W. Belt, and Rose M. Jackson. *Courtesy Archives and Special Collections, UCO Library.*

Graduates of 1897

By Erica Johnson, B.A. in History, 2005

In 1897, John Adams, Ida Belt, Phronia Eckes, Robert Howard, and Rose Jackson became the first five graduates from the Territorial Normal School of Oklahoma. The graduates experienced an elegant ceremony, with traditional Victorian attire and prestigious guests, including Oklahoma Territorial Governor Cassius Barnes. Other students from the school, such as Minnie Kibby in 1892, were recommended to teach in Oklahoma Territory because of the great need for teachers. However, the graduates of 1897 completed the entire program at the Normal School and received Life Certificates.

The first five graduates made many contributions to the school during their education at Edmond. Howard and Jackson started classes in 1892, and Adams joined them in 1894. All five of the students were members of the Pioneer Literary Society.

Despite their successes at the Normal School, the two men did not pursue careers in teaching. Adams received exemplary marks in arithmetic, penmanship, and physiology while in school, and received honors in the *Edmond News*. He was editor of the school newspaper, the *Normal Philomath*, and played third base for the Pioneer baseball team. Adams went on to earn his law degree from the University of Michigan

in 1900. Originally from Odin, Missouri, Adams chose to return to Oklahoma to practice law in Guthrie for more than 50 years. He also held the office of Superintendent of Logan County.

Howard, son of Edmond's representative in the territorial legislature, J.W. Howard, was admitted to the school in 1892 when he was only 14 years old, but went on to become valedictorian of the class of 1897. Howard earned his M.D. from the University of Michigan in 1901, and returned to Oklahoma City to open his private practice. He was chief of staff and attending surgeon at St. Anthony Hospital from 1912 to 1946, and taught at the University of Oklahoma College of Medicine from 1922 to 1946.

The three women took varying routes. Belt taught in Guthrie from 1897 to 1925. She returned to Central State Teacher's College to earn her bachelor's degree in education in 1926. She attended graduate school at OU and the University of Chicago. Eckes, formerly from Baker, Oklahoma, won the First Intercollegiate Oratorical Contest. She also was the victim of a murder attempt the year of her graduation by a jealous woman, Grace Allen, who loved the same man Eckes attracted. Eckes went on to marry William Gillman Smith, a graduate of the Normal School, and was active in the Women's Foreign Missionary Society in the Edmond Methodist Church. Jackson married Charles Gustason and emerged as a civic leader in Oklahoma City. Little else is known about her life after she moved to California.

Both Adams and Eckes returned to Central State College for the Golden Jubilee Celebration in 1947. Their faces appear in images across campus and in newspaper articles and scrapbooks. Each of the first five graduates achieved many successes, and their legacy lives on at UCO.

Phronia S. Eckes and the First Graduating Class (1897)

In January, 1897, "the greatest educational event in the history of the territory" occurred when the three territorial schools gathered for an oratorical contest at Oklahoma City. Phronia S. Eckes, soon to graduate from the Territorial Normal School, won the contest and $30 in gold coin for her lecture, "Humanity Against Itself."

In June, Eckes and four other students, John Adams, Ida W. Belt, R. Mayburn Howard, and Rose M. Jackson, represented the first graduating class at Central in a "momentous and gala occasion." With Governor C.M. Barnes attending the graduation ceremony, the women graduates wore white dresses and carried flowers and the men graduates wore formal attire. Adams and Belt returned to campus in 1947 for the golden anniversary of their class. Students at Central have established a longstanding tradition of attending their golden anniversary, beginning with the Class of 1897.

A strange thing happened to Phronia Eckes that summer. A "pretty young woman," Jessie Wiley arrived in Edmond looking for the Eckes family. Once at the Eckes residence, Wiley asked to stay with the family while she restored her health. Wiley claimed she needed the counsel of a "good Christian family" and Mr. Eckes was a minister. As author and historian Stan Hoig has described, "Miss Wiley appeared to be an intelligent, well educated, and refined young lady who had an apt poetical notation for almost every topic of conversation."

Wiley requested to sleep with Phronia Eckes that night. The next morning, Wiley prepared toast for Phronia and her mother. Reverend Eckes was tending to his stock when he heard a call from the house, "Come quick, Phronia is dying!" Her mother had also fallen ill to food poisoning. It turned out that Wiley was really Grace Allen of Altona, Kansas, a school teacher who had traveled to Oklahoma Territory to find Phronia Eckes and harm her. Apparently, a young farmer that Grace Allen had known in Kansas had recently moved to the Edmond area and was smitten with Eckes. The local authorities arrested Grace Allen and found "Rough-on-Rats" poison in her possession. She was ultimately released due to lack of evidence and returned to Kansas.

Territorial Normal School's first baseball team organized in 1896. Some accounts maintain the team won the conference crown for the most original uniforms, which ranged from long underwear to silk cravats. *Courtesy Archives and Special Collections, UCO Library.*

Normal Philomath, First School Paper

The school's first newspaper, the *Normal Philomath*, meaning "lover of learning," appeared in January, 1897, as a monthly publication. The first issue contained Phronia Eckes' award-winning lecture from the intercollegiate oratorical contest as well as the Normal's first yell:

> *"Karo, Karo, Kire, Kee*
> *Oklahoma Normal, Don't you see*
> *Hip! Hip! Who! Bronze and Blue;*
> *Oklahoma Normal, Hoo! Hoo! Hoo!"*

The *Normal Philomath* discussed campus activities, including athletics, and their connection to regional and national issues. For example, an article in the February issue of the *Normal Philomath* stated that college presidents in Kansas passed a resolution condemning football as a college game. Such sentiment helps to explain why Central did not offer a football program until 1903.

The athletic program always has been an integral part of educating Central students and fostering school spirit. President Murdaugh coached the baseball team and J.O. Allen, professor of physics and chemistry, launched the tennis teams for women and men.

Competition at Alva Normal

Central's unique role of educating teachers was altered in 1897 when the territorial legislature approved a second normal school to be established at Alva, Oklahoma. Edmond citizens had unsuccessfully opposed creating a competing institution. Central President Murdaugh served as acting president of the new normal until James E. Arment arrived.

Alva Normal, or Northwestern, demonstrated profound growth from its inception to 1902. The town of Alva was larger than Edmond and attracted the high school students in its community. In 1901, Alva enrolled 551 students and 600 students the following year.

To compete with Northwestern, Central altered its calendar from two 20-week semesters to three 12-week sessions. The restructuring attracted to Central teachers who had recently completed six months of teaching, the length of the common school term, and needed more course work for certification. In addition, with approval from the Board of Regents, Murdaugh kicked off a ten-week summer term in 1899, the first in normal school history.

The summer term offered more advanced courses than the earlier summer institutes. Again, the incentive was to attract students and provide course offerings and a flexible schedule. As far as the salary scale, Central paid its president $2,600 annually, the vice president received $1,200, and faculty salaries ranged from $500 to $1,000. During his presidency, Murdaugh hired the first assistant or secretary to the president, J.G. Imel, and his wife as the first librarian at the Normal School.

By 1898, Oklahoma Territory's system of higher education was off to a promising start. Central, the University of Oklahoma, the Agricultural and Mechanical College, and Langston Agricultural and Mechanical College served approximately 1,000 students. At the same time, Chilocco Indian School, an industrial boarding school for American Indian students north of Newkirk, had 500 students.

Central's *Annual Catalogue* for 1898-1899 also contains a category called "regulations" offering a glimpse into the code of conduct for faculty, staff, and students. If late to the school grounds, for example, faculty had to report their own tardiness to the president in writing.

Students had a more rigid code of conduct. As Oakes has pointed out, students needed continuous prompting about proper behavior in an academic setting. "Some of them would march boldly into corridors of the Normal," Oakes wrote, "singing, whistling, and dumping their quids of tobacco into all alcoves and corners that were not already overflowing with such extras." Moreover, loitering was not permitted in the halls or around the buildings at any time.

In keeping with his determination to cultivate proper etiquette in students, President Murdaugh instituted the first formal banquet in 1899, borrowing silver from prominent Edmond families for the occasion. The formal banquet became a popular annual event.

Model School

Murdaugh continued to lobby for the model school without success, calling it the most pressing need of the normal. Building on the model school originally envisioned by Thatcher, Murdaugh established the training program in the fall of 1897, hiring Lizzie Wooster as instructor. The program offered practice teaching and observation in the first two grades. With much success the first year in operation, Murdaugh encouraged the Board of Regents to consider expanding the program. After exploring the issue, the board decided that the Normal School was not ready for a larger program.

By the turn of the century, the Board of Regents became more confident with the national model school trend. In the catalogue of 1901, Murdaugh discussed the importance of the model school— "This department, so necessary for a Normal School, should be opened at the earliest opportunity." At the end of Murdaugh's term, all of the essentials were in place for the teacher training school, except the teacher training department.

The training school began in earnest in September, 1901. Emma Waite taught the beginning classes. A year later, Benjamin Franklin Nihart, Superintendent of Oklahoma City schools, served as the first director. Mary Brewer's kindergarten program was added in 1903.

When political power shifted from the Democrats to the Republicans in Washington, D.C. and Oklahoma Territory in the mid-1890s, Murdaugh's term as president of Central ended. In 1896, Republican President William McKinley appointed C. M. Barnes, a Republican and

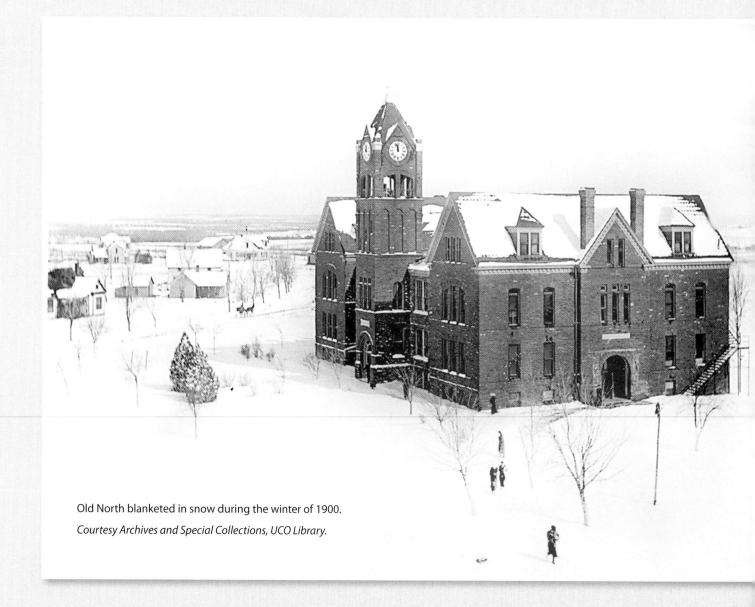

Old North blanketed in snow during the winter of 1900.
Courtesy Archives and Special Collections, UCO Library.

former Union soldier, as territorial governor. Barnes in turn appointed Republican L. W. Baxter, a faculty member under Murdaugh at Central for four years, as Territorial Superintendent. After assuming his post, Baxter named Frederick Howard Umholtz as president of Central.

In Oakes' unpublished manuscript on the history of Central, he has charted the political party of each faculty member and president with great care. During the early years at Central, faculty members needed to belong to the correct party. Oakes wrote, "Of the eight men on the faculty in 1900-1901, all but the president were Republicans. For the next year—1901-1902, of the ten men on the faculty, an even ten were Republicans. Much has been observed since Statehood (1907) concerning the large prevalence of Democrats on the School's faculty. Let it be stated here, lest it be forgotten later, that at no time since 1907 have all of the men members of the faculty belonged to the same party."

Oakes pointed out that when he applied for a position at Central in the fall of 1903, President Umholtz said he was glad that Oakes was a Democrat. According to Oakes, Umholtz then said that "since all the men on the faculty were Republicans, he wanted to employ some Democrats to keep down comment."

Following his service as president, Murdaugh became superintendent of Woodward schools for a year, then president of the State Normal School at Frostberg, Maryland, before returning to Oklahoma as president of the Oklahoma Military Academy at Claremore and president of Southeastern Normal at Durant. Later he returned to Central State College as a faculty member. Although historian L. David Norris has discussed Murdaugh's academic credentials, or lack thereof, as controversial at Southeastern, Oakes consistently offered a positive assessment of Murdaugh. "He maintained his great ability as a public speaker until long after his seventieth year," Oakes wrote of Murdaugh, "He was a princely character, always ranking much above his environment."

Frederick Howard Umholtz (1901–1906)

In 1901, Umholtz became Central's fifth president. Educated in Pennsylvania and experienced as a public school superintendent in Kansas and Oklahoma City, Umholtz, according to Oakes, "was the best educated and prepared man who had been elected president of Central up to this time."

Frederick H. Umholtz served as the fifth president in 1901. Prior to his appointment as president, Umholtz had been a professor at the Territorial Normal School in 1893-1894 and again from 1897-1901. *Courtesy Archives and Special Collections, UCO Library.*

When Umholtz became president, the faculty remained the same and, in fact, as an indication of the school's growth, acquired seven new instructors. Central housed nine departments—history, natural sciences, mathematics, physical science, English language, literature, ancient languages, modern languages, and pedagogy. The music program expanded as new instructors were hired to teach piano and orchestra. During faculty meetings, Umholtz created a formal environment and an opportunity to present faculty research. After a faculty member presented her work, the other members could ask questions, "the whole design of the program being to put each teacher in close touch with the work of others."

Student Clubs

Student clubs at Central began to flourish during the early twentieth century. The Lyceum and the Pioneer societies remained the center of student activities. In 1901, Nellie Gray Moore of the Pioneer Society won the oratorical contest. Other local clubs such as Sorosis, a women's music club, and the Royal American Knights, a secret debating society, were organized. In addition, national organizations including the YMCA and the YWCA

The 1902 graduating class posed for their graduation portrait in front of Old North. *Courtesy Archives and Special Collections, UCO Library.*

created chapters at Central. In June, 1902, graduates of the Territorial Normal School created the alumni association. The first officers included President John G. Imel (1900); Vice President Mary K. Harris (1902); Secretary Pearl Nihart (1902); and Treasurer Carrie M. Burks (1902).

Enrollment

The Territorial Normal School experienced an enrollment surge during the early twentieth century. The school even outpaced the University of Oklahoma's enrollment during the first seven years of the century. In 1901, enrollment climbed to 337. The majority of students attended the high school or preparatory program with a smaller percentage attending the two-year college program. Approximately 40 percent of the students were from Edmond. The remainder of the student body represented 95 other Oklahoma post offices.

Fifty-three students had graduated with a degree qualifying them to teach in the territory for five years. This policy was later revised so that a five-year certificate became a life certificate to teach. Later, during the 1904-05 term, the normal department contained 720 students and the model department had 175, for a total of 903. In contrast, enrollment at the University of Oklahoma for the same year was 475.

In the *Annual Catalogue* of 1902-1903, Umholtz outlined the mission of the normal school— "The special function of the Normal School is to prepare young men and women for the work of teaching. This must be accomplished, first, by thorough and liberal academic work; second, through the study of the child; third, through the study of the philosophy of teaching; and, fourth, through practice and training in the Model School. The work of the Normal School differs, therefore, from that of the college. A college aims to teach the different branches of knowledge to impart a general culture; the Normal School teaches not only the subject matter of the various branches of knowledge, but the resultant of these processes, and this aim is kept constantly before the student throughout his academic career as a learner. This fact distinguishes the Normal School from other institutions of learning, and determines the course of study as well as the distinctive methods by which the several branches of learning must be taught."

The total number of two-year college graduates with five-year teaching certificates was 112 at the end of the 1904-1905 school year. Among these were seven students with the Bachelor of Arts degree—the first B.A. year for the school—Minneoba Ballou, Mary Caroline Barrett, Isabel Bennett, Ober Elihu Haug, Otto William Jeffries, Pearl Elizabeth Nihart, and Anna Maude Swank.

South Building (1903)

With steady growth in student enrollment and the addition of the model school, the Territorial Normal School needed more room and received its second building, called the South Building, in 1903. The South Building contained the Assembly Hall, the registrar's office, and a balcony above Pioneer and Lyceum halls. For his part, Umholtz worked to increase the library holdings. The library was properly catalogued for the first time under Umholtz.

Other construction plans on campus included the addition of a new gymnasium in the south half of Old North Tower Hall. The gym provided floor space for 100 students, with ladders and ropes, horizontal and parallel bars, vaulting horses, and weights. A steam heating plant also was built about 200 feet away from the other buildings, "thus removing all danger from fire or explosion."

The Vista replaced the previous school newspaper, the Normal Philomath, first published in 1897. The Vista staff in 1903 (left to right): Alice Mann, Luther L. Dickerson, Lorena Hindes, Harvey O. Shuff, Kate Peters, Edward G. Klein, Laressa G. Cox McBurney and (not pictured) Roy Horace Jenkins. McBurney gave the newspaper its name in 1901. *Courtesy Archives and Special Collections, UCO Library.*

Governor T.B. Ferguson spoke at the dedication of the South Building, later known as Administration Hall. The new auditorium seated 800 and hosted Russell Conwell's "Acres of Diamonds" and musical performances. *Courtesy Archives and Special Collections, UCO Library.*

The Vista (1903)

Replacing the *Normal Philomath*, the senior class began publishing *The Vista* as a monthly literary magazine in November, 1903. Two English professors, C.R. Baskerville and F.C. Oakes, served as faculty advisors for the publication. Reba Collins, Central graduate and journalism professor, wrote in her master's thesis, "Starting with the very first volume *The Vista* reported elections and personal items about students, alumni and faculty. Progress of the school was lauded and athletics were promoted. The same news is being printed today. It varies only in quantity and treatment."

According to Collins, the senior class, led by class president Ira D. Griffin, published *The Vista* as a 6" by 8" sheet, printed on heavy paper and bound in blue. Subscription price was 50 cents per year, postage included, or ten cents for a single issue. Students selected the name "vista" meaning view, or viewing the present and the future. The initial editorial staff included Harvey O. Shuff, editor-in-chief; Alice Mann, associate editor; Roy Horace Jenkins, athletics; Lorena Hindes, local and alumni; Laressa G. Cox, college and exchange; Kate Peters, department; and Luther Dickerson and Edward G. Klein, business managers.

The first ten years of *The Vista* contained literary material, news, campus announcements, and humor. "The entire staff of these issues were made up of students," Collins has maintained. "Not even a sponsor's name was listed. Subscriptions and individual copies as well as advertising were sold to finance the printing that was done at the *Edmond Sun* plant. Early alumni of *The Vista* staff credit F.C. Oakes with aiding in the establishment of the publication, although in his manuscript on the history of Central, he does not take credit for assisting the paper in any way during the early years. Oakes supervised *The Vista* in many ways. As early as 1916, his name appeared on the masthead as editor and publisher. He continued to work with the staff until his retirement in 1937.

The Vista targeted students and alumni as their readership. Reba Collins indicated the purpose of the newspaper could be divided into five categories—promoting literary works, stimulating students, promoting the college, training the journalism student, and alumni coverage.

A broad aim of the newspaper was to "help to bind the students into one body in loyalty to the college." Content included news, athletics, gossip columns, editorials, images, and columns on proper student conduct and dress. During the early years of *The Vista*, nearly half the issues contained literary works. By the second year, several student essays and poems were included. The two literary societies, Lyceum and Pioneer, received coverage including programs and names of new officers. By February, 1906, *The Vista* solicited literary contributions from the entire school and the published entries from each class.

Athletics

"While some of the girls are playing tennis," *The Vista* reported in the fall of 1903, "basketball especially engaged their attention this season of the year and the grounds are crowded with players and onlookers every afternoon." When the women's team defeated Oklahoma City High School in an away game, they returned to campus and were greeted by "a large body of students who gave them an ovation and woke the town at the same time by vigorous yelling, 'Bowzer! Towzer! Razzle! Dazzle! Zip! Boom! Bah! Edmond Basketball-Rah! Rah! Rah!'"

Central encouraged students to participate in a host of athletic programs. By 1899, J. G. Imel, secretary to President Murdaugh, coached women's and men's basketball. In 1901, Central athletes competed in their first track meet held in Guthrie. Ira D. Griffen won the one-mile race and Otto Jeffries won the walking race. Two years later, Central held a track meet on campus between the women and men. Women wore bloomers and the men wore long skirts. During an intercollegiate meet at Oklahoma City in 1903, David Warner won Central's first gold medal for his victory in the one-mile bicycle race.

The unofficial beginning of football at Central came in 1903. In late October, President Umholtz received a call from the A&M College at Stillwater inviting Central to fill an open date for football on the Saturday before Thanksgiving. With only three weeks to assemble a team and practice, Professor C. B. Blake, vice president of Normal, accepted the challenge. Blake and his team of 13 players took the 5:00 a.m. train to Perry and then traveled on to Stillwater in "horse-drawn, livery stable rigs." The Central uniforms were homemade and they had "converted old shoes into football shoes by nailing leather pieces crosswise on the soles and heels." Playing on frozen ground, the Agricultural and Mechanical College defeated Central, 40-0.

Following this rather meager beginning, Umholtz established football in earnest in the fall of 1904. The first football coach was F.C. Oakes, athletic director and English professor.

RIGHT An early Central football squad poses for a team photograph before hitting the practice field. *Courtesy Archives and Special Collections, UCO Library.*

LEFT: Coached by President Murdaugh, baseball was one of the earliest competitive sports at Central, early 1900s. *Courtesy Archives and Special Collections, UCO Library.*

During the early years, the women were playing basketball outdoors, wearing sweaters, caps, and even gloves, and sometimes playing their games in a big tent. *Courtesy Archives and Special Collections, UCO Library.*

Chapter One Timeline

1889
- Eiffel Tower completed
- Oklahoma Land Run

1890
- National American Women's Suffrage Association formed
- George Washington Steele became governor of Oklahoma Territory
- First Territorial Legislature passed Council Bill #106 designating the Normal School at Edmond, the University at Norman, and the Mechanical and Agricultural School at Stillwater

1891
- Populist Party formed
- Governor Steele leaves office in disgust
- Richard Thatcher elected as first President of Territorial Normal School of Oklahoma (TNSO)
- TNSO first held classes in the Edmond Methodist Church
- Plans for North Building are drawn up by Architect Gall Whitely and work on the building begins the following summer

1892
- Grover Cleveland elected President of the United States
- Abraham Jefferson Seay became governor of Oklahoma Territory
- TNSO recommended Minnie Kibby as first teacher in Oklahoma Territory

1893
- New Zealand became the first country to grant women full voting rights
- National financial panic and depression
- William Cary Renfrow became governor of Oklahoma Territory
- George Winans replaced Thatcher as President of TNSO
- Completion of the Normal School building or Old North
- Oklahoma Territorial Legislature appropriates $15,000 to add tower and wings to North Building
- Architect J.G. Haskell is selected to design Old North tower and wings
- First school catalogue issued
- Central's first student clubs the Pioneer and Lyceum established

1894
- E.R. Williams appointed President of TNSO
- Entire exterior of Old North Building completed
- School's first library begins with $26 in purchased materials

1895
- Edmund D. Murdaugh became President of the TNSO
- Bronze and Blue became the TNSO school colors

1896
- Jewish Zionist Movement founded
- Tennis teams established at TNSO
- William McKinley elected President of the United States
- Plessy v. Ferguson upheld "separate but equal" public accommodations
- TSNO first baseball team formed

1897
- Cassius McDonald Barnes became governor of Oklahoma Territory
- First five students graduated from TNSO
- TSNO first school newspaper the *Philomath*, is published
- Central's Model Training School opened in the fall and Lizzie Wooster appointed first instructor of the program

1898
- Spanish-American War
- Eugene V. Debs helped found the Social Democratic Party

1899
- Boer War began between Britain and Africa (1899-1902)
- Filipino uprising against the United States (1899-1902)
- Cumming v. Richmond County Board of Education sanctioned segregated education
- TSNO first basketball teams organized
- First summer term at Central held

1900
- Boxer Rebellion in China
- United States announced Open Door Policy for trade with China
- American League of Baseball organized

1901
- President McKinley assassinated, Vice President Theodore Roosevelt assumed office
- William Miller Jenkins became governor of Oklahoma Territory, soon removed due to scandal
- Thompson Benton Ferguson became governor of Oklahoma Territory
- Frederick Howard Umholtz became President of TNSO
- TNSO athletes attended first track meet held at Guthrie

1902
- Voting rights for women in Australia
- Coal strike in the United States
- Alumni Association formed by graduates of the TNSO

1903
- Anti-Jewish Pogroms in Russia
- United States acquired rights to the Panama Canal
- First flight by the Wright brothers
- *The Vista* began publication at TNSO
- Legislature passes bill for a second building, the South Building, at the Normal School
- The first Central football game took place at Stillwater

Members of the all-male Odd Fellows Lodge located on Broadway in Edmond during the early 1910s. *Courtesy Archives and Special Collections, UCO Library.*

The Edmond Ladies Aid Society organized in 1889 and became the first women's group in Edmond, Oklahoma Territory. The members raised money for the first schoolhouse. *Courtesy Archives and Special Collections, UCO Library.*

Carriages close to campus in 1899 with Old North in the background. *Courtesy Archives and Special Collections, UCO Library.*

An early 1900s view of Edmond from the Territorial Normal School tower. *Courtesy Archives and Special Collections, UCO Library.*

CHAPTER TWO

Early Development
Central State Normal School (1904-1918)

The student enterprise ticket was launched in 1912 for $3.00. It admitted the ticket holder to four football games, three girls' basketball games, five baseball games and seven sessions of the lecture course.
Edna Jones

Good room and board can be obtained in private families at $3.00 to $3.50 a week. Unfurnished rooms can be rented at $2.00 to $4.50 per month, furnished rooms at $4.00 to $5.00 a month.
Annual Catalogue (1911-1912)

"If we rest, we rust"

During the early twentieth century, Edmond's sense of place was largely connected to the Normal School, especially athletics. Competitive sports at the institution served as an important tool for the burgeoning community. Between 1901 and 1904, the population of Edmond more than doubled to 2,600. Modern advances appeared on campus in the early 1900s as telephones replaced written communication and brick walks replaced the raised boardwalks. Edmond citizens and local newspapers understood that the local economy was connected to the success of the Normal School. Residents could often be seen on campus planting shrubs and flowers and maintaining the grounds.

In January, 1904, the name of the school changed from the Territorial Normal School of Oklahoma to Central State Normal School (CSN). Fourteen students attended commencement in 1904 in Old North Tower and then marched to the new South Building to receive their diplomas. "If we rest, we rust," was their class motto. Members of the Class of 1904 continued to keep in touch through the annual "round robin" letter and class reunions.

Curriculum and Enrollment

Since 1895, the curriculum consisted of a six-year course of study, meaning a four-year preparatory program followed by a two-year college program. By 1899, the curriculum offered a three-year elementary program followed by a four-year normal course. In 1914-1915 CSN again modified its curriculum to offer a six-year course of study that continued for 20 years. In addition to pedagogy and physical training, CSN required Latin, English, history, mathematics, natural and physical science, music, voice training, and drawing. The school year consisted of three regular terms of 12 weeks followed by an eight-week summer term.

Enrollment at Central grew steadily from its first class of 25 students in 1891 to 1,113 in 1908, with 934 in the normal department and 179 in the training school. The 934 students included high school and college students from 25 counties in Oklahoma, including 57 from eastern Oklahoma, and 14 states.

Statehood in 1907

When Oklahoma Territory joined Indian Territory to form the State of Oklahoma in 1907, delegates attending the constitutional convention strived to distribute institutions of higher education throughout the new state, especially in eastern Oklahoma. Considering that western Oklahoma already maintained institutions at Edmond, Alva, Norman, and Stillwater, the delegates decided to create three new normal schools—East Central at Ada, Southeastern at Durant, and Northeastern at Tahlequah, and two smaller agricultural institutions, Panhandle at Goodwell and Cameron at Lawton.

Instrumental Music Department

By Ruth Simpson, B.S. in Accounting, 2008

The music department was added because many viewed music education as not only a cultural enhancement but a necessary part of a well-rounded educational experience. According to the Normal School catalogue of 1901-1902, "It is from the soul that the true musician touches us; therefore, it is of the first importance that this quality we call musical soul shall be developed in all students."

Arthur Howard Greene became the Supervisor of Music in the early 1900s. A native of England, Greene was well-educated, earning his bachelors and masters in Music Education. Students admired Greene as was evident from the jokes his students included in the "Bronze Book Jokes" section of the 1920 *Bronze Book*:

> *Sophomore: "Why is Mr. Greene the fastest man in the world?"*
>
> *World-wise Junior: "Because time flies, but when Greene leads chorus, he beats time!"*

During his tenure, Greene also saw many changes to the department, including faculty, staff, and building additions. He retired at the end of the 1922-1923 school year, leaving behind a legacy of his passion of music for generations to come.

UCO hired its first orchestra director, Ida Waide Kitchen, in 1917. A preliminary concert band of a few members was organized in 1919. By the mid 1920s, when the department administration changed hands from Arthur Greene to Gladys Cox, the philharmonic orchestra had become well known around campus. The orchestra performed for various school functions, including the Senior Class play of 1927, "Expressing Willie," the dedication ceremony of the new Physical Education building in 1928, the play "Kempy" for the Criterion Club, and the play "The Merchant of Venice" for the Shakespeare Club.

The year 1927 was the first to have a real split between the band and the orchestra. The orchestra still included members of the band, but now band students had an option. In 1930, the first marching band was organized, under the direction of Norman Gregory. By late September, 1931, the marching band had received new uniforms modeled after the original school colors.

Throughout the 1930s, the band's popularity increased both around the school, playing for every athletic event on campus, and in the community of Edmond. In 1933, the first title of Band Queen was awarded to Melba Cooper and the first Drum Major was Clifford Cantlon. In 1936, Maurine Rice became the first female drum major. From that time, the number of drum majors and majorettes fluctuated between three and five each year.

By 1940, the marching band was well established and very popular, cheering on the Bronchos to victory in athletics. In addition, the orchestra was very busy,

Orchestra of

Central State Normal School's curriculum included music class for the model school located in Old North, 1912. *Courtesy Archives and Special Collections, UCO Library.*

performing for drama plays, as well as in the daily chapel programs. When the nation entered World War II, changes took place all over campus as the focus shifted to the war effort. As a result, many of the clubs and extracurricular departments, including the music department, were suspended by the school until the war ended. After World War II, the music department continued to grow with the addition of a new music building in 1952.

The music department has continued to flourish throughout the past century. Many clubs have formed to support music awareness and student participation, including the Phi Mu Alpha Sinfonia and the Sigma Alpha Iota, honorary music fraternities, added in the 1960s. The music program continues to shape the very character of the school, encouraging the campus community to broaden minds through music.

Thomas Butcher served as Central's sixth president. From 1906 to 1908, Butcher traveled around the region promoting the school and encouraging people to attend. *Courtesy Archives and Special Collections, UCO Library.*

Thomas W. Butcher (1906-1908)

Unfortunately, the troubling practice of dismissing college presidents and sometimes faculty with a change in governor continued during the early statehood years. When President Theodore Roosevelt appointed Governor Frank Franz, a former Rough Rider with Roosevelt during the Spanish-American War, Umholtz lost his job. Thomas W. Butcher (1906-1908), a Republican with a master's degree from Harvard, received the appointment as president of CSN. When the Democrats won control of the first state government in 1908, Butcher lost his job.

LEFT: Three years after the founding of the Territorial Normal School, in the fall 1894, under the leadership of President E.R. Williams, instrumental music was offered for the first time as an extracurricular activity. One year later, the State Regents added the music department. The main focus was piano, but other instruments were available for use and training. *Courtesy Archives and Special Collections, UCO Library.*

Recently retired as president of the Kansas State Teachers Association, Butcher had decades of teaching experience. Interestingly, Central had a long tradition of hiring instructors from Kansas. Five of the seven department heads were from Kansas. With his credentials, Butcher bolstered Central's reputation with his "intellectual veracity" as he traveled throughout the region promoting the school. The faculty at CSN considered Butcher "the most valuable find in the whole Territorial school system."

Historians have told a story regarding Butcher's dismissal which has since become legend. A member of the Board of Regents asked Butcher to come to Guthrie but assured him that he should not worry. Butcher waited in the lobby of a Guthrie hotel where he could be reached if policymakers needed him. While he was waiting and talking to friends, a newsboy scurried into the hotel lobby announcing the latest headlines: "Board of Regents Get Butcher's Head."

Politics was inextricably linked to the development of higher education in Oklahoma. During the crucial early years of CSN's existence, at a time when stable, consistent leadership would have been ideal, the school instead had six presidents in 17 years. In 1908, with the departure of Butcher and a Democrat as governor, rumors circulated that the new board would dismiss Republicans from the Central faculty. At statehood, two Democrats were on the Central faculty, and Edmond was predominantly Republican. In almost a clean sweep, 19 of the 26 faculty members who had served under Butcher lost their jobs as the board replaced them with Democrats.

In 1908, Edmond boasted a population of 1,833 and was strategically located between Guthrie and Oklahoma City. Meanwhile, Governor Haskell was working on moving the capital to Oklahoma City to pry it from the Republican stronghold in Guthrie. In Edmond, city growth continued with new homes between Broadway and Boulevard, and a new water system with a water tower in 1909, followed by new electrical and sewage systems in 1910.

Perhaps the most exciting innovation to change the way Edmond citizens thought about travel occurred when the Interurban connected Edmond to Oklahoma City and Guthrie in 1911. Anton H. Classen, John Shartel, and John Mitch helped secure the trolley line and celebrated the important event with speeches at Mitch Park. During these years, CSN hosted the Oklahoma County Fair on campus. The fair attracted hundreds of people to campus and included agricultural exhibits, entertainment, and a parade.

The Interurban as it would have looked in 1911 with porters standing at each door. The Interurban served as an important form of travel for students attending Central State Normal School and they received special rates. *Courtesy Archives and Special Collections, UCO Library.*

The Interurban with a large crowd gathered in front, 1914. The Interurban connected Edmond to Oklahoma City and later Guthrie as well as Norman, El Reno, Yukon, Britton, Moore, and points in between. *Courtesy Archives and Special Collections, UCO Library.*

The Interurban

By Amanda Cagle, M.A. in History/Museum Studies, 2007

"Well, by thunder! They've sure got them cars toted by lightnin'," exclaimed David Payne, an aging pioneer from Oklahoma City, as the sounds of the first Interurban trolleys started down the line on May 29, 1911. Gathering in Mitch Park, Oklahoma City leaders Anton H. Classen, John Shartel, John Mitch, and a crowd of nearly 2,500 cheered the maiden tour of the trolleys. Though there were a few lines running within the Oklahoma City area since 1903, this new connection of rails ran from Oklahoma City to the surrounding, and rapidly expanding, towns, added lines to Edmond and Norman.

By the peak of the trolley's popularity, in the mid 1920s, the tracks reached Guthrie. Interurban trolleys were more than vehicles of early mass transit for central Oklahoma, they were the artery through which the life blood of Edmond flowed. With regular availability of transportation and the initial low cost of tickets, the residents of Oklahoma City and neighboring areas began pouring into Edmond for the businesses, jobs, new homes, and more importantly, the Central State Normal School, with the chance for a better tomorrow it offered.

The "street railway line" was the brainchild of John W. Shartel, who arrived in Oklahoma in 1889. In true pioneer style, he tried his hand at several careers including real estate development and a law practice before devoting his full attention to the Metropolitan Railway Company. By 1904, Shartel and Classen joined together and created the newly-renamed Oklahoma Railway Company, these men had backgrounds in land development and urban expansion. Thus, the move to create uncomplicated, reliable, inexpensive transportation to the areas they were developing was logical and advantageous.

However, additional profits were made from the trolleys doubling as freight carriers for farmers and ranchers trying to get their goods into the crowded Oklahoma City market areas.

The appeal of the trolleys, as an early advertisement articulated, was the "frequent service, cheap rates, fast, clean, comfortable cars" and a certain "modern" flair. As a point of pride for the region, and particularly Edmond residents, these stylish little cable cars gave them more mobility and freedom than ever before, at a time when few people owned cars and the roads they depended on were unpaved and unreliable. The rail system was fundamentally responsible for getting numerous dirt roads paved, the installation of gas and sewer lines in newer residential areas, and the creation of hundreds of jobs throughout central Oklahoma. These rail cars truly urbanized central Oklahoma.

The trolleys ran every hour from 7:00 a.m. to 11:00 p.m., with an average trip between Central State Normal School and Oklahoma City taking about one hour. Later, the time was improved, taking only 20 minutes to make the same trip.

Funding to bring the Oklahoma Railway Company into Edmond required the community to raise the $15,000 needed to lengthen the rails and acquire additional trolleys. Funds were raised with individual citizens donating $15 each, soon totaling $6,000, and "voluntary lot assessment to raise the other $9,000 needed." Critics called the tracks that ran along the median of the main thoroughfare, "the ruination of the beautiful Boulevard."

The last trolley made its farewell journey on November 9, 1946, at a time when cars and bus transportation became more cost effective and efficient. Still, nothing could replace the memories of the old bell and the clanking of the "electric flyer" that David Payne had marveled at 35 years earlier.

James A. McLauchlin (1908-1911)

James A. McLauchlin, superintendent of the Magnum schools, became Central's seventh president in 1908. He received his M.A. degree from Davidson College and a Doctor of Literature from King's College, both located in North Carolina. McLauchlin worked as instructor of mathematics for one year at Southwestern Normal School at Weatherford before becoming president at Central.

From 1908 to 1911, James A. McLauchlin served as Central's seventh president. McLauchlin implemented strict rules concerning student decorum on campus. *Courtesy Archives and Special Collections, UCO Library.*

As president, McLauchlin added regulations to the *Annual Catalogue* concerning proper student decorum that included the prohibition of tobacco, curfew, and required participation in worship services. For instance, students were required to be quiet and orderly on the campus grounds and in boarding houses. Tobacco was a pervading issue throughout the first half of the twentieth century at Central, and the succession of presidents dealt with it in different ways.

For his part, McLauchlin stated, "The use of tobacco on the Normal premises is not allowed, and the State's anti-cigarette law will be rigorously enforced." Students also were expected to be in their rooms and studying one hour after sunset from Monday through Thursday evenings. Finally, students and faculty were expected to attend daily morning worship in the auditorium.

The strong emphasis on Christian leadership continued under McLauchlin. At the time, the state superintendent was a minister and at least four of Oklahoma's college presidents also were ministers. At Central, the handful of ministers on the faculty alternated leading devotional services.

After the wholesale political firing, all but two new faculty members were Democrats and held degrees from such esteemed institutions as Chicago, Columbia, and Yale. Many of them had attended and taught in normal schools. For example, Luther Jewett Abbott, a historian, was a graduate of Nebraska and Columbia. Isaac Henry Hughes held an M.A. from Yale and taught Latin. Hired as vice president and director of the training school, Stephen M. Barret had published a biography of Geronimo that became a standard work. During this time, it also was important that the faculty were Christians, namely Presbyterians, and active in church work. In fact, two ministers taught science courses.

A mother and daughter received two of the 12 full professorships at Central. Sallie Garrett Abernethey became head of the department of English. Receiving both her B.A. and M.A. from Pontotoc Female College in Mississippi, she taught at the Oklahoma Industrial School for Girls at Chickasha, where her husband had been president. Her daughter, Lula Abernethey Barr, with a B.S. from Mississippi Normal School, taught psychology and mathematics. Sallie Abernethey remained at Central two years and was succeeded in 1910 by Lucie Haskell, daughter of Governor Haskell. Lucie Haskell resigned at the end of 1911, and F. C. Oakes, formerly head of modern languages, became head of the English Department.

Old North with students gathered in the clock tower, 1910s. *Courtesy Archives and Special Collections, UCO Library.*

Students working in the Chemical Laboratory, 1908. *Courtesy Archives and Special Collections, UCO Library.*

Clock and Chimes

After 19 years, Old North received its clock and chimes on June 20, 1912. Many supporters of the "Clock-for-tower" fund made this dream a reality, including the Alumni Association, PEO Ladies of Edmond, Edmond Improvement League, State Board of Education, State Board of Public Affairs, faculty, and students. In fact, three students in the science department installed the clock and chimes.

The newly constructed central heating plant for both Old North and the South Building was a welcome addition in the winter of 1904-1905 when the temperature fell to a record-low 16 degrees below zero in February. Potbelly stoves continued to heat the smaller frame buildings on campus. Other buildings erected during this period included the library at Evans Hall in July, 1916, and the president's home in 1918.

Student Activities

Student life on campus was filled with debate clubs, drama clubs, YMCA, and YWCA. In addition to Pioneer and the Lyceum societies, many of CSN's new clubs centered on literature and debate. Debate clubs were divided according to gender, with Arena, Senate, and Forum for men, and Triumvirate for women. Interestingly, literary societies included men and women members.

In 1906 and 1907, Central students Edward Klein and Lura Leonard, respectively, won the annual oratorical contest between the normal schools. CSN continued a tradition of producing educated citizens, primarily teachers, with solid training in debate.

Other clubs attracted a smaller membership. For example, faculty sponsor Maude Drake and six students organized the first women's club at Central, the Shakespeare Club, a social club designed to promote the works of William Shakespeare. In 1914, the club created a rose garden in the northwest corner of what it now the Y-Chapel of Song. A second women's club, Tsa Mo Ga, studied American Indian history and culture and "played Indian" by donning what they thought to be American Indian attire.

The men's debate club posed with their official pennant in 1915. *Courtesy Archives and Special Collections, UCO Library.*

The Triumvirate Club served as the debate club for women on campus, 1914. *Courtesy Archives and Special Collections, UCO Library.*

CSN graduates established successful careers in teaching and other professions. Each year, many students took the exam for teacher certification. From the Class of 1908, Ed McCarrell became a teacher and then principal in Oklahoma City; Rolla M. Shreves later graduated from Harvard in history and economics; Grover C. Walmsley served as state lawyer in Anadarko; and George Wilson served briefly as president of the Oklahoma A&M.

With more than 50 graduates, the Class of 1909 was the largest graduating class to date. Graduates called out the class yell in unison, "Bowser! Towser! Rock and Rhine! Seniors! Seniors! 1909!" The senior class published the school's first yearbook, *Bowser Towser*, named after the class yell, and dedicated it to Richard Thatcher, the first president of Central.

The *Bowser Towser* was a publication filled with class history, favorite professors—F.C. Oakes was the Class Father—poems, and biographical sketches. Walter Isle, for instance, demonstrated the mobility and the versatility of CSN graduates. Born in Brunswick, Missouri, in 1889, and making the trip to Oklahoma in "boomer" style, he entered the public school of Edmond, from which he graduated in 1903, and then attended the Normal School. Isle represented CSN at the state oratorical contest in 1908, having won first place as orator in the school. Isle served as class president from 1907 to 1909 and graduated as valedictorian.

Like Isle, many students moved to Oklahoma Territory from elsewhere in the late 1890s and early 1900s, namely Kansas, Missouri, and Illinois. Examples included Frank Buttram, Edward Everett Dale, and Mary Hiatt. In 1902, Buttram enrolled in the Class of 1909, coming from the Chickasaw Nation where he received his early education and taught 15 months. Buttram was a member of the CSN male quartet, and had a great love of music.

Dale spent his early years in Fort Worth, Texas, and came to Oklahoma in 1889, where he taught eight terms of school. Dale enrolled at CSN as a sophomore and joined the class of 1909. Dale continued his studies under Frederick Jackson Turner, and became a well-known western historian at the University of Oklahoma.

Hiatt arrived in Oklahoma at the age of one and moved to Edmond at the age of six, spending her early days in the first public school building erected in Edmond. She entered the model school in 1898 and graduated from the eighth grade and entered the Normal department in 1903. The graduation of 1910 was a historic occasion when E. M. and Orville C. St. John were the first father and son to graduate in the same class at Central.

Governor Lee Cruce

When Lee Cruce became governor in 1911, many Oklahomans believed that politics would be banished from the state schools and the major turnover of faculty that occurred from 1907 to 1911 under Governor Haskell would dissipate. Cruce was happy to comply with keeping politics out of the schools—after he established his own system and reorganized the faculty.

Early in his term, Governor Cruce addressed the problem of competition among the state's 17 institutions of higher education. Cruce wanted to streamline the educational structure and reduce the duplication among education boards and departments of education. Many legislators during the session of January, 1911, agreed with Governor Cruce that the state had too many state-supported schools.

One legislator initiated a bill to eliminate 14 of the 17 state schools. The normal schools were called upon to justify their existence. State superintendents from other states such as Kansas and Illinois testified and defended the normal schools. Although threatened with possible elimination, in the end the normal schools survived.

As a reform measure, the legislature created the State Board of Education for the Normal Schools. The new board requested reports from the colleges and capped the salary schedule for the normal school presidents at $2,600. In April, the board investigated the normal schools in a series of campus visits and found them "mostly wanting." The board discovered divisiveness among faculty and staff, low performance standards, poorly qualified teachers, questionable practices of some presidents, and the common practice of maintaining large preparatory departments as a strategy to report large enrollment.

Following the reports and subsequent campus visits, the board dismissed five of six normal school presidents, including McLaughlin at Central and both presidents of the University of Oklahoma and the Agricultural and Mechanical College. The board replaced McLaughlin with Charles Evans, a friend of Cruce from his hometown of Ardmore, as president of Central. Evans had been considered for the post as president of the University of Oklahoma, but he did not possess a doctorate, and the board was concerned about negative repercussions from the university faculty had Evans received the position.

Charles Evans (1911-1916)

Although he held several honorary doctorates, Evans completed his master's degree in the summer of 1911 at the time he became the eighth president of Central. Evans had experience as superintendent of schools in Kentucky and then Ardmore. As Ardmore superintendent, Evans had devised and implemented plans for socialization activities for students, and he continued to emphasize extracurricular activities at Central. In addition, Evans was influenced by the City Beautiful movement as it extended to normal schools throughout the nation—beautiful school rooms and beautiful school grounds.

From 1911 to 1916, Charles Evans served as the eighth president of Central. Evans promoted the involvement of students in more social activities and worked to beautify Central's campus. *Courtesy Archives and Special Collections, UCO Library.*

Evans's first faculty contained a mix of five Republicans, all department heads, and eight Democrats. Evans retained 17 of the 30 faculty members, including F.C. Oakes in English, John Davis in physics and chemistry, and Lucy Jeston Hampton in history. Several instructors who had been dismissed in 1908 returned under Evans, including C.H. Roberts and B.F. Nihart.

In comparing the administrations of McLauchlin and Evans, certain observations can be made. When McLauchlin became president in 1908, faculty turnover had been extremely high, with 25 dismissed and five retained.

In 1911, under Evans, faculty turnover was lower, with 13 dismissed and 17 retained. Furthermore, the Evans administration placed less emphasis on political affiliation. There were no known Republicans under McLauchlin. Faculty movement under McLauchlin and Evans remained volatile and deliberately tied to politics. Although such overt

political concerns dissipated among the normal schools as the twentieth century advanced, it remained a pressing concern. As Oakes lamented in his history of Central, "Every change of Central's president since 1911 has been followed by a 'shake-up' of the faculty of Central. And the School has usually lost prestige in proportion to the ratio of such changes."

President Evans was a promoter who was not afraid to ask teachers to come to Central. He was a strong public speaker who promoted Central throughout the state and encouraged his faculty to do likewise. "Never before, nor since," Oakes wrote, "have so many members of a Central

BELOW: Chemistry Professor John Davis, 1914, served as the first instructor of photography on campus. The university has many of his glass plate negatives depicting campus and Edmond life in the early 1900s. *Courtesy Archives and Special Collections, UCO Library.*

faculty been made to stand before strange audiences and recommend Central." Evans encouraged students to promote the school throughout the state as well.

Under Evans, Central was the first state educational institution to place a $500 advertisement in *The Daily Oklahoman*. Evans also advertised in the *Oklahoma School Herald* to encourage teachers to attend Central during summer session. Under the heading "We have fun in Central," Evans included images of students at the swimming pool and engaged in other recreational activities. He also used *The Vista* as a promotional tool, placing copies of the student newspaper in the offices of county superintendents.

Evans achieved positive enrollment results from his promotions. Summer school in 1912 experienced a 42 percent increase. The following summer, Evans leased a revival tent to accommodate the swelling student body. Classrooms were packed beyond capacity and students in lecture classes of 300 or more took notes outside on the grass. Central's summer enrollment in 1915 was 2,831 students, second only to Cedar Rapids, Iowa, which had 160 more students. The next summer, Central claimed the largest summer normal session in the United States.

Central experienced a period of expansion and transition under Evans, as it moved into a more mature phase as a normal school. Central's campus was made up of two buildings, the North Building, which housed the training school, the department of education, and manual training, and the South Building, which housed the departments of English, science, and the library.

Using rather spontaneous, energetic teaching methods, President Evans championed extracurricular activities and interaction with the students. Quite often he would enter a classroom already engaged in lecture, interrupt the instructor, and take the class with him on a stroll of campus to learn about the significance of campus beautification. The campus was a sight to behold with more than 300 trees ranging from elm to cedar to poplar. A privet hedge bordered the campus and flower beds blanketed the grounds.

Students gathered on the lawn in front of Old North for story hour in 1915. "How to tell a story" became an important part of the teacher's curriculum. *Courtesy Archives and Special Collections, UCO Library.*

Athletics

Athletics at Central took center stage on campus, perhaps second only to debate contests, and included the Edmond community in civic pride, competition, and celebrations. Baseball, tennis, and track continued to be the leading spring sports at CSN during the early twentieth century and Central athletes competed well. In baseball, Central defeated A&M in 1907 and OU in 1913. J. E. Armstrong and Claude Nihart won the Intercollegiate Tennis Championship two years in a row in 1904 and 1905. At the annual track meet in Oklahoma City in 1907, CSN took first in shot put and the 220 dash. By 1910, the college had four tennis courts and a swimming pool.

The football program began in earnest in 1904, when Professor Boyd A. Hill, who had attended the United States Military Academy at West Point, became football coach and director of physical culture. Hill assembled the football team in October and suffered a crushing defeat of 23-0 in their first regular game against Guthrie High School in November.

After ironing out some of the kinks in the program, the team achieved a 7-0 victory over Epworth University, now Oklahoma City University, in Oklahoma City. In this game, Ed G. Klein carried the ball for Central's first touchdown. At a reunion of the team in 1933, Klein presented the ball to the college for the athletic trophy case. Today the famous ball is housed in Central's Laboratory of History Museum in Evans Hall. The school played its first regular schedule of five games in 1904, winning two and losing three.

Coached by Fenis Bentley, the football team's 1905 season included a win and a tie against A&M and a loss to the University of Oklahoma. By 1906, the team had a decisive win over A&M, 23-2, at Stillwater. In an exciting twist at the end of the regular season in 1910, a group of Central faculty, including Professors Thomas R. Corr, J. C. Adamson, F. C. Oakes, S. J. Payne, and Vern O. Wilson, challenged the football team to a game. Played before a record crowd of cheering faculty and students, the faculty team won a narrow victory, 6-5.

Central State Normal School's football field in 1908. When the Charles Wantland era began in 1912, Central developed quickly into a football power among the state colleges. *Courtesy Archives and Special Collections, UCO Library.*

The 1908 Intercollegiate Champion football team posed for their official portrait in front of Old North. 1908 was the same year that the Oklahoma Collegiate Conference had been formed, and consisted of state universities and colleges, including the University of Oklahoma, Oklahoma A&M, and Central just to name a few. *Courtesy Archives and Special Collections, UCO Library.*

LEFT: In 1912 Central State Normal School hired Charles Wantland as the football and basketball coach. Wantland would later become the first Dean of Men at Central in 1924. *Courtesy Archives and Special Collections, UCO Library.*

1st Basket Ball Team of C.S.N. Edmond, Okla.

Charles Wantland

CSN hired former OU standout, Charles Wantland, to coach football and basketball in 1912. As a student at OU, he had lettered in four sports. Under Coach Wantland, Central's football and basketball programs demonstrated marked improvement. In football, in 1914, Central won the normal schools championship, and five members of the squad were on the All-State Normal School team. CSN's standout athletes included W. Max Chambers, basketball captain and future president of Central, who lettered in four sports. In a basketball game with OU in 1916, Pat Johnson scored 33 points—more than the entire OU team output.

Considered a downtown landmark and one of the best basketball courts in the state, Central Hall housed athletics since 1915. Seeing a need for an athletic facility, but recognizing that the legislature would not appropriate the funds fast enough, Central decided to build the facility on its own by using the labor of faculty and students. Central bought the property located in the heart of Edmond just west of City Hall and hired an architect. Four hundred students participated in Central Hall's construction with a total cost of $4,000.

Central State Normal School's first women's basketball team was formed in 1908. "Bowzer! Towzer! Razzle! Dazzle! Zip! Boom! Bah! Edmond Basketball—Rah! Rah! Rah!" was a cheer used by the basketball team in Central's early years. *Courtesy Archives and Special Collections, UCO Library.*

Physical education at Central was an integral part of the curriculum for women during the early twentieth century. Carrie Belle Wantland, the sister of Coach Wantland, served as the athletic director for women. The Central women's basketball team, led by standouts Letha Meyers and Hala Beauchamp, defeated Epworth 19-8 in 1912. In 1913, Elsa Fisher came to Central from the Harvard School of Physical Training. Central's women's basketball team won the state championship that year. Fisher remained only one year. In 1914, Professor Williams and Emma Estill coached the women's basketball team on their new indoor court in Central Hall. In addition to basketball, women's physical education included volleyball, softball, gymnastics, dancing, tennis, and May Day festivals.

Evans Hall

By Kim Penrod, B.A. in History/Museum Studies, 2005;
M.A. in History/Museum Studies, 2007

Built in 1915, Evans Hall is the second oldest existing building and the third constructed as part of the Territorial Normal School of Oklahoma. Evans Hall faced west towards the new and growing community of Edmond, and provided much-needed library and classroom space for the campus.

The new structure was named after Charles Evans, the eighth president (1911-1916) of the university. Evans served when the school was a normal school conferring teacher certification to the graduates. The students, faculty, and Edmond leaders believed the time for increased infrastructure had arrived. During the summer of 1915, a large tent erected on campus used for supplementary classrooms dramatically illustrated to the community the urgent need for expansion.

Solomon Andrew Layton (1864-1945), one of Oklahoma's most prolific and preeminent architects, designed Evans Hall. Oklahoma landmarks designed by Layton include the State Capitol, the former Oklahoma Historical Society building, the Oklahoma County courthouse, and the original stadium at OU's Owens Field, as well as numerous county courthouses and buildings on nearly every state college campus.

Layton also designed the original Administration Building on Central's campus. Built in 1904, the structure was later condemned and destroyed to make way for the south wing of UCO's current Lillard Administration Building.

Standing three stories tall and containing 21,000 square feet, Evans Hall is an excellent example of Layton's architectural designs. Construction material for this building was poured using reinforced concrete allowing greater structural strength than required by architectural standards of its day. Evans Hall has classical symmetry and eclectic design with large arched windows, strong classical cornice molding, and arched Romanesque entrances on three sides of the building. The building remains as elegant today as the day it opened in 1915.

Over the years, Evans Hall has served as home for the first library, faculty offices, classrooms, Archives and Special Collections, and the University Alumni Association. In May, 1988, Evans Hall closed for renovations and structural repairs forcing the storage of the museum collections while classes moved to other

Charles Evans and Evans Hall

Central was the first state normal school to receive a library building. Through the efforts of President Evans and the influence of Judge J. T. Dickerson, a member of the legislature, Central received appropriations of $105,000 for this purpose. In 1916, the library building was dedicated and named Evans Hall in honor of President Evans. The preeminent Oklahoma architect Solomon Andrew Layton, who designed the new capitol building, drafted the plans for Evans Hall with distinctive arch-shaped windows. President Evans resigned in 1916 after Governor Williams rescinded a salary increase of $1,500 approved by the State Board of Education. Evans went to Tulsa University at a much higher salary. Instructors, including Oakes, were critical of Evans' emphasis on extracurricular activities and campus beautification over academic rigor.

buildings. President Lillard took a personal interest in saving Evans Hall from destruction when he came to the university in 1975. His enthusiasm for the renovations soon spread to the faculty and students of the university. An open house celebration on December 7, 1989, welcomed everyone to view the completed work of architect Robert C. Thomas and once again opened Evans Hall to faculty and students.

Today, Evans Hall is home to the College of Art, Media, and Design classrooms and offices on the first floor. The second floor is an open area utilized by the University Alumni Association, administration, and faculty for various meetings and special activities, with offices for the UCO Foundation at the south end of the building. The third floor balcony is home to the Laboratory of History Museum, highlighting artifacts of the school's early years. The Archives and Special Collections now occupy a portion of the second floor in the Max Chambers Library and the Alumni Association offices are in the new Alumni House.

A winter panoramic view of the three main buildings on Central's campus during the 1910s: Old North, Evans Hall and the Administration Building. *Courtesy Archives and Special Collections, UCO Library.*

Enrollment

During the early twentieth century, state teaching regulations helped maintain Central's high enrollment, making it the largest institution of higher education in the state. In 1912, the new state board required every teacher in Oklahoma to have at least 12 weeks of professional training in the normal school. The required professional training increased to 36 weeks by 1916. These state board regulations guaranteed secure enrollment at the normal schools.

This enrollment balloon would not last. The legislature passed a law allowing high schools to offer a normal training course, and as a result, Central lost at least 500 students to high schools in Central's district. At the same time, the University of Oklahoma's enrollment outpaced Central's for the first time in its history by approximately 200 students.

Emma Estill-Harbour retired in 1946 after serving Central for 34 years as a history professor. She chaired the social science department for 29 years. *Courtesy Archives and Special Collections, UCO Library.*

Central at 25

The institutional history of Central's first 25 years can be characterized as a transformative era marked by unprecedented growth, and as Oakes has stated, "having attempted the most with the least." Central had, and continues to have, the reputation of a friendly, economical institution.

Campus life was filled with student clubs, from the Pioneer and Lyceum to the new Efficiency and Farm Club of 1916. In addition, Central sponsored three student publications, the *Bronze Book*, *The Vista*, and the *English Department News*. In perusing the early *Bronze Books*, favorite professors emerge as class mother or father, including F. C. Oakes, Lucy Jeston Hampton, Emma Estill, and B.F. Nihart.

The faculty became more consistent during this time and students profited from their close mentoring and permanence on campus. For instance, the *Bronze Book* staff of 1915 dedicated the volume to the 12 women faculty at CSN. In September, 1916, *The Vista* emerged as a campus newspaper, when Central graduate Elmer Petree offered to sell his printing equipment to the college for $100. With the new equipment and a $1,200 loan from an Edmond bank to purchase a Miehle press, Central printed *The Vista* on

Professor F. C. Oakes teaching his students how to use a newspaper print machine during the 1910s. *Courtesy Archives and Special Collections, UCO Library.*

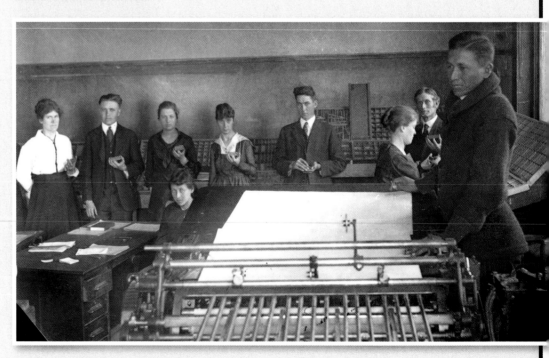

campus for the first time. Petree established the first printing office on campus and published *English Department News* and *Ripsaw*, the president's weekly bulletin.

In 1915, history professor Lucy Jeston Hampton organized the Central State Historical Society, the first departmental club on campus. The society's first project was to place a historical marker at the site of the Methodist Church at 19 North Broadway, where the first Territorial Normal School began class work on November 9, 1891. Buried in the foundation of the marker was a copper box filled with various records of the history of CSN and Edmond.

The Vista

By Richard Mize, M.A. in History, 2005

In November, 1903, student editors and writers at the Oklahoma Territorial Normal School produced the first monthly issue of the student newspaper, *The Vista*. It included fiction, poetry, literary criticism, news, commentary, and advertising. *The Vista's* mission was to "help to bind the students into one body in loyalty to the college ... promote its various interests, and ... give some medium of expression for a larger spirit of culture and some influence for a broader activity among our students."

Launched by English Professor Charles Read Baskerville, *The Vista* remained a largely literary journal for its first decade. In 1914, *The Vista* became a weekly news publication. The shift from scholarly aspirations to news and information was complete by mid-century, when the staff declared, "*The Vista* is sloganless but the staff generally agrees with Byron's words, 'Without or with offense to friends or foes, we sketch your world exactly as it goes.'"

Then as now, *The Vista* provides a laboratory for students of journalism and the printing. Student journalists at *The Vista*, like their peers at other college newspapers, have occasionally crossed pens with the college administration and state government. In the late 1960s, the paper opposed the governor's veto of a name change to Central State University. Editors also gave voice to the peace movement during the Vietnam War.

In the late 1970s and early 1980s, *The Vista's* editorial viewpoints were often at odds with authorities. One point of contention included opposition to a local bank permitted to erect a clock on campus that displayed advertising and news.

Issues of the newspaper, distributed free on campus, have been stolen or destroyed more than once by students angered by *The Vista's* positions. One editor leading a crusade against a religious organization he considered a cult was rewarded with sugar in his gas tank. The voice of the newspaper, reflecting students, is quieter now.

The Vista now publishes news, sports, opinion, and advertising biweekly. The newspaper has a regular-semester circulation of 4,000 on Tuesdays and Thursdays and a weekly summer circulation of 2,500. It usually comprises eight to twelve broadsheet pages. In 2000, *The Vista* launched a site on the World Wide Web, www.thevistaonline.com. It is a member of the Oklahoma Press Association, Columbia Scholastic Press Association, Associated Collegiate Press, and The Associated Press.

Staff members are paid hourly or by column inch of copy and per photograph published. Students taking a news reporting class submit stories for credit. *The Vista* is funded by advertising and student fees. *The Vista* is the oldest continuously published student newspaper in Oklahoma.

History Professor Lucy Jeston Hampton lecturing to students gathered in Evans Hall, 1913. *Courtesy Archives and Special Collections, UCO Library.*

Lucy Jeston Hampton

By Kim Penrod, B.A. in History/Museum Studies, 2005; M.A. in History/Museum Studies, 2007

Born in Grayson County, Virginia, in 1888, Lucy Jeston Hampton took pride in her distinguished family roots. Hampton's immediate family moved west in the late 1880s eventually arriving in present day Washita County, Oklahoma.

Hampton graduated from Southwestern State Normal College in 1909. She served for one year as principal of the high school in Clinton, where she received the Teacher of the Year Award. In 1910, she contracted to teach history at the Central State Normal School for an annual salary of $1,400.

During her early career at Central, Hampton took graduate courses at George Washington University, Columbia University, Stanford University, and the University of Chicago.

Returning to Oklahoma, Hampton quickly began to make her mark on the Central State Normal School and its students. In 1915, she founded the Laboratory of Original Evidence, the college's historical society, and was instrumental in erecting a red granite marker to commemorate the site where the Normal School first held classes.

The Laboratory of History Museum exists today with the collection of artifacts Hampton collected throughout her career. Many of these items provide a starting point for research projects for students in the university's Museum Studies program, while offering a glimpse into the rich history of the community of Edmond and the University of Central Oklahoma.

While in Washington, D.C., Hampton became enamored with the works of President Woodrow Wilson. Hampton continued her personal research of Wilson's works and exposed her students to his words. Former student and history professor, Herman Fulgraff,

Lucy Jeston Hampton, history professor and founder of the Laboratory of History Museum on Central's campus, early 1900s. *Courtesy Archives and Special Collections, UCO Library.*

remembered Hampton's classes with regard to President Wilson and her requirement that students commit to memory large amounts of information about Wilson's life and work. Fulgraff said about Hampton, "She was an interesting lady, she taught very good courses, and she was not nearly as demanding as her reputation on campus. Her demands were just very, very basic. She would enforce those requirements, you didn't want to chew gum in class, you didn't want to yawn in class, you wanted to be attentive."

During the 1920s and 1930s, Hampton was a prominent speaker on international government. She lectured regionally to more than 500 educational and civic groups. Having strong ideas on the role of women in government, she urged, "If women will immediately school themselves in knowledge of democratic law and why it has gone unenforced since 1931, they can render a magnificent service to all mankind."

Hampton attended the League of Nations assembly in Geneva in 1923. She cited the importance of women's roles in international treaties, such as Brest-Litovsk in 1918, and the Congress of Paris in 1919. Ironically, Hampton declined to run for governor of Oklahoma when urged to do so in 1933.

Hampton received national recognition in 1937 when her biography appeared in *Who's Who in American Women*. The honor came only one year after her selection as one of "Oklahoma's Ten Outstanding Women" by *The Daily Oklahoman*. Retiring in 1958, Hampton's career spanned 48 years of devotion to the university. In 1982, 17 years after her death, Lucy Jeston Hampton was inducted to the Edmond Hall of Fame.

Grant B. Grumbine (1916–17)

Central's early years were marked by presidents who did not hold lengthy terms. During the mid-1910s, two presidents took the helm at Central for only a year or two. The Board of Education selected Grant B. Grumbine, president of Northwestern State Normal School at Alva, to follow Evans. Under Grumbine, Northwestern State Normal's enrollment had outpaced Central. Grumbine held two degrees from Central College, Missouri. During his brief stint at Central, Grumbine advertised and promoted the school. He expanded the print shop at Central and transformed *The Vista* from a monthly to a weekly four-page newspaper. Grumbine reinstituted the *Annual Catalogue*, a publication that had been suspended under Evans.

In 1916 the Board of Education appointed Grant Grumbine as the ninth president of Central. Grumbine increased Central's visibility in a variety of ways. *Courtesy Archives and Special Collections, UCO Library.*

Grumbine lasted only one year at Central because, according to Oakes, he was "a blunt, honest, frank-speaking man who was unwilling to buy sufficient influence to keep his post." Though at Central briefly, Grumbine's accomplishments were many. The two Triangular debate teams defeated all other state normal schools. In addition, Central's student representative won the state reading contest. In athletics, the football team continued to perform well.

World War I

In January, 1917, *The Vista* first indicated the administration's position regarding the threat of war. A lecturer was scheduled to speak to CSN students as part of a lecture series. A front page story explained that the speaker would not appear at the specific request of President

Grumbine. The man had delivered a speech in Oklahoma City the night before that Grumbine found unpatriotic. The headline read "Please Do Not Come." The writer of the news story said Grumbine "declined to listen to a heated attack on those Americans whom the people of the United States, under the constitution, have elected to guide our destinies in this GREAT HOUR." Grumbine was further quoted as saying now is the time to "lift the spirit of PATRIOTISM high and get ready to defend with dignity and maximum effectiveness those principles without which the enjoyment of the greater life within us could find no TRUE expression in America."

Just days after the United States entered the war, *The Vista* again quoted President Grumbine from an assembly speech, "This day marked the beginning of a great wave of patriotism that shall show to Oklahoma and the rest of the world that SCHOOL TEACHERS are not made of flabby stuff, that they are ready to offer ALL to service, to the higher SERVICE OF THEIR COUNTRY." As a reflection of anti-German sentiment at home, the Board of Education dropped German from the curriculum and the state superintendent suggested that all German books in the library be removed and burned. Central's books survived such a fate.

By the next week, the entire paper had taken on a new look with a large American flag on the masthead and the headline boldly stated, "America and Central First." Two weeks after the declaration of war, ten Central students had "heeded their country's call." Pictures of men who joined the service were made by the campus photographer and printed in *The Vista*, a practice that would continue throughout the war.

There was an obvious scarcity of male students when classes began in September, 1917. An article in *The Vista* described it this way, "Never in the history of Central State Normal was there a more dramatic hour than when the opportunity came for the boys to answer their country's call. There was no noisy demonstration, no waving of banners, no false sentimentality—often mistaken for patriotism—but with a terrific calm that was ominous of the fearful crisis, those gallant young fellows without one moment's hesitation stepped forward and answered 'We are ready.'"

During a time of international entanglement and war, 40 faculty members, including Emma Estill-Harbour, Charles Wantland, Carrie Wantland Meyers, and F.C. Oakes, continued to keep class in session in CSN's three campus buildings, Old North, South Hall, and Evans Hall.

J.W. Graves served as the tenth president of Central from 1917 to 1919. Graves strongly encouraged all students to become involved in athletics and physical fitness. *Courtesy Archives and Special Collections, UCO Library.*

J. W. Graves (1917-1919)

J. W. Graves succeeded Grumbine as Central's tenth president. Formerly president of the School of Mines at Wilburton, Graves had served as president of Northwestern Normal School for one year before coming to CSN. He held a B.A. from Buchanan College, Missouri, and a Bachelor of Laws from Columbia. Thirteen faculty members retired at the end of Grumbine's presidency. During Graves's first year, the Board of Education hired eight new faculty including former Central President E. D. Murdaugh and Cora Stroud to the training department.

In 1918, Old North's attic was converted into barracks and housed members of the Students' Army Training Corps Unit. *Courtesy Archives and Special Collections, UCO Library.*

Students' Army Training Corps Unit soldiers in their make-shift tent mess hall located on Central's campus, 1918. *Courtesy Archives and Special Collections, UCO Library.*

As events in World War I intensified, President Graves sought preparedness on campus. As a committed outdoorsman and a former coach, Graves was perhaps more interested in athletics and physical fitness than academics. By February, 1918, 109 Central men had enlisted, represented by 109 stars on Central's service flag on campus.

In the spring of 1918, the War Department selected Central to house a Students' Army Training Corp Unit (SATC). In preparation, the top floor of Old North Tower became a barracks, a mess hall was built east of Old North Tower, and a tent-city appeared on the athletic grounds. About 150 men trained on campus. During the summer, Graves and eleven students traveled to Fort Sheridan, Illinois, to learn how to prepare civilians physically for the military. President Graves returned to campus inspired to implement local readiness.

On campus, Coach Wantland initiated a program for the college men, drilling them using the Infantry Manual of the United States Army. Most male students on campus enrolled in the Training Corps and by spring, 1918, 126 Central men had entered military service. *The Vista* printed an honor roll of "Central's Boys in Service" which included photographs and their location. Soldiers from Central received the paper free of charge, defrayed by student donations.

The first Central student casualty was Louis H. Isle, a football player from Edmond, who had enlisted in aviation, but his health failed and he died in Missouri. Isle's death began the Central tradition of placing a golden star on Central's service flag in his memory. His funeral in Edmond brought the community to a halt as schools and businesses closed.

Graves also approved military drill for women. Under the direction of Carrie Wantland Meyers, "Company B" prepared women to teach military fundamentals in school if the war continued. Before the end of the 1917-1918 academic year, nearly 100 women students had been trained in Army marching exercises.

Students participated in other ways to express their support for the war effort. Many student groups organized Liberty Bond campaigns and promoted sales through cartoons, editorials, and stories in *The Vista*. Articles encouraged students to "do their bit" and enroll in first-aid classes. As a result, nearly 600 women students became members of the Red Cross. Student organizations raised $1,500 for the War Relief Fund, while the library collected books and magazines for the training corps. Everyone did their part.

As Central transitioned to a post-war climate, football resumed its prominent place in Oklahoma culture. The football team had to rebuild its program because all but one letterman had gone to war. During the 1917 season, Central played seven games and lost three to OU, A&M, and East Central.

Fans continued to support athletic events on campus during the 1910s. *Courtesy Archives and Special Collections, UCO Library.*

Members of the women's "Company B" Students' Army Training Corps Unit practicing with rifles on the lawn of Old North during the late 1910s. *Courtesy Archives and Special Collections, UCO Library.*

BELOW: Central State Normal School's Band during the 1910s. *Courtesy Archives and Special Collections, UCO Library.*

The last class to graduate from Central Normal School presented the arches at the northwest entrance of the campus as a class gift to the school. Following their graduation, CSN's name changed to Central State Teacher's College, marking a new era in the history of Central.

The 1908 interior of Central's library, located in the Old Administration building. *Courtesy Archives and Special Collections, UCO Library.*

Chapter Two Timeline

1904

• Russo-Japanese War began (1904-1905)

• TNSO became Central State Normal School (CSNS)

• Completion of Administration Building or Old South at CSNS

• The first B.A. degree at Central was offered but then discontinued and would
  not be available again until 1921

• Central's first official football team was organized

1905

• German miners strike in Ruhr

• Industrial Workers of the World founded

1906

• Theodore Roosevelt won the Nobel Peace Prize

• Upton Sinclair's *The Jungle* exposed conditions in the meatpacking industry

• Frank Frantz became Governor of Oklahoma Territory

• Thomas W. Butcher became President of CSNS

1907

• Oklahoma obtained statehood

• Charles N. Haskell became Governor of Oklahoma

1908

• William H. Taft elected President of the United States

• Muller v. Oregon upheld an Oregon state law limiting maximum hours for
  working women

• Henry Ford introduced the Model T, the first mass produced automobile

• James A. McLaughlin became the President of CSNS

1909

• Mexican Revolution (1909-1911)

• National Association for the Advancement of Colored People (NAACP) founded

• The *Bowser Towser*, the school's first yearbook, was published by the senior
  class

1910

• Oklahoma had more Socialist Party members than any other state in the union

1911

• Lee Cruce became Governor of Oklahoma

• Charles Evans appointed President of CSNS

1912

• Balkan Wars began (1912-1913)

• African National Congress founded in South Africa

• *Titanic* sank

• Woodrow Wilson elected President of the United States

• Margaret Sanger spoke out in support of birth control for women

• On June 20 the clock and chimes in the Old North tower dedicated

1914

• World War I began

• Federal Trade Commission established

1915

• German U-boat sank the *Lusitania*

• Albert Einstein's General Theory of Relativity

• Robert L. Williams became Governor of Oklahoma

• Central State Historical Society organized by Lucy Jeston Hampton

1916

• Sigmund Freud's *Introduction to Psychoanalysis*

• Jeannette Rankin, of Montana, first woman elected to the U.S. House of
  Representatives

• Grant B. Grumbine became President of CSNS

• Completion of Evans Hall at CSNS to house the library

• Central claimed the largest summer normal school enrollment in the United
  States

• Central printed a copy of *The Vista* for the first time on campus

1917

• Bolshevik Revolution began in Russia

• Zimmerman Note sent to Mexico by Germany

• Selective Service Act passed

• Conviction of members of Industrial Workers of the World in California, Illinois,
  and Oklahoma

• James W. Graves became the President of CSNS

1918

• Worldwide influenza epidemic began

• Students' Army Training Corps began at CSNS

• President's home erected

CHAPTER THREE

The 1920s and the Great Depression

Central State Teachers College (1919-1938)

When I started there were three buildings, Old North, Evans Hall, and the Administration Building, which is no longer there. The year I started school, they were building Mitchell Hall and then they added Wantland Hall. We had a number of little houses down the hill that were music buildings. There was a football field where the University Center and home economics building are now.
Kathryn Kunc

Miss Plunkett was the kind of teacher who would walk up and down the front row and pinch people and gouge them and whack on them. Nobody went to sleep in her classes. And I would like to say that for the most part, nobody went to sleep in mine either. Now, I didn't poke and pinch and do those things, but I loved to teach.
Virginia Peters

The 1920s

In 1919, the Oklahoma legislature passed bills creating separate boards of regents for all schools under jurisdiction of the State Board of Education except the normal schools. The normal schools became four-year institutions guided by a teacher-training curriculum. Significantly, Central Normal School changed its name to Central State Teachers College (CSTC) and became a four-year college with B.A. and B.S. degree-granting privileges. Students received the four-year degree and teaching certificates at graduation.

Even with rising enrollment and the return of soldiers from World War I, CSTC did not have dormitories in the 1920s. Students continued to secure room and board in private homes near campus for $6.50 a week. The cost

The 1920 graduating class on the campus lawn. Because of the shift to the bachelor's degree, the Class of 1920 was the last class to graduate with life certificates with two years of college work. *Courtesy Archives and Special Collections, UCO Library.*

Lilly Davis, Professor John Davis's wife in 1919 with Edmond citizens and World War I soldiers. *Courtesy Archives and Special Collections, UCO Library.*

for students remained low with an incidental fee of two dollars per term. In September, 1920, Central changed to the semester plan, plus a half-semester summer term. CSTC and four other colleges in Oklahoma participated as members of the North Central Association of Colleges and Universities.

After World War I, students tried to return to a feeling of normalcy, but not before reflecting on what the war meant to them. Students dedicated the *Bronze Book* of 1919 "to the soldiers and sailors who so willingly offered their lives on the altar of democracy—that the peoples of the earth might have peace." *The Vista* returned to covering campus events and did not return to national and international events until the Great Depression.

The nation turned inward and focused on domestic concerns. Postwar sentiments, including the rise of Christian fundamentalism and conservatism, made their way to Edmond and CSTC. The "wild living" of cities with dancing, drinking, and jazz was thoroughly rejected in Edmond. As Stan Hoig explained, "While other parts of the nation were indulging in the excesses of speak-easies, bathtub gin, and gangsterism, Edmond was exercising the restraints of fervent piety."

During the 1923 summer term, for example, more than 200 students received college credit for attending a Sunday school class conducted by a professor. Nearly half the assembly speakers that year were ministers. Under the heading "Moral and Religious Influence," the quarterly bulletin of CSTC in 1926-1927 stated, "For the most part, only those people move to Edmond whose aim is the very highest for their children, and the students who come are usually those who are seeking the choicest there is in life for them. Edmond has no pool halls. There is no foreign element, no negro element, no strictly labor element, and no slum element—just all good, honest, high-minded people of sterling worth." A local newspaper editor encouraged the "right" kind of people to move to Edmond and celebrated the five Protestant churches, but did not mention the town's

oldest church, St. John's Catholic Church.

With the community impulse to regulate morality, groups such as the Ku Klux Klan staged public displays of coercion and racial violence as a means of social control. In the town of Arcadia, just east of Edmond, a shootout at the home of an African American farmer in August, 1920, resulted in the death of the farmer, a government agent, and a deputy. Authorities apprehended the farmer's nineteen-year-old son and later a mob of ten men lynched him three miles outside of town.

In July, 1922, hooded Klansmen and Modern Woodsmen marched from Stephenson Park, then known as South Park, up Broadway to Central and back. The parade participants carried an American flag, a lighted cross, and a multitude of signs reading, "Bootleggers Beware!," "America for Americans," "Married Men and Married Women Joy Ride with Your Own Husbands and Wives," "Keep the Home Life Sacred," and "Put the Bible in the Public Schools." Although many of the marchers were from Guthrie and Oklahoma City, the KKK had members and sympathizers in the Edmond area.

Edmond had made modest civic improvements during the 1920s. By 1920, the city installed street lights, three lamps on a post, on Broadway between Main and Second streets. In July, 1921, the Chamber of Commerce completed a large campground at the east end of Second Street for tourists passing through town with their automobiles.

The park provided shade, ovens, wood benches, and water fountains.

During the same summer, Edmond received the Better Cities Contest top award, and celebrated with a mile-long parade featuring floats, decorated cars, and folk dancing in the streets. By 1924, Professor F.O. Seymour of CSTC opened Edmond's first concrete swimming pool south of Stephenson Park. The pool was a welcome presence in town and a major improvement over the red dirt pool on Central's campus constructed in 1915.

Enrollment

During the 1920s, students traveled significant distances to attend Central, hailing from 66 counties in Oklahoma and at least 22 states. Competition for enrollment remained fierce, as junior colleges in smaller towns provided opportunities for higher education for students who could not afford to attend larger colleges or could not leave their family responsibilities. Many of the junior college students transferred to Central to complete their degrees.

Enrollment continued to increase from 517 students in September, 1919, to 586 in September, 1920. The first regular degree class of nine students graduated from CSTC in 1921. Central also continued to issue life certificates in record numbers, leading one school representative to boast that CSTC had certified one-fifth of the teachers in Oklahoma.

The legislature did not necessarily want CSTC in Edmond to expand, considering that the University of Oklahoma was 32 miles away in Norman and the A&M College was 50 miles away in Stillwater. By the early 1920s, OU's aggressive regional recruitment of high school graduates included Oklahoma City, Norman, Ardmore, Guthrie, Ponca City, Enid, Kingfisher, and El Reno, thereby cutting into Central's district. Oklahoma A&M, as well as Oklahoma City University, Oklahoma College for Women, Phillips University, and the University Preparatory College at Tonkawa, also vied for many of the students in Central's district, again creating an extremely competitive environment. In contrast, East Central and Southeastern did not have such competition in their districts.

Dr. Thomas H. Wyche and his summer class enjoy "story telling hour" outside under the shade trees in 1920. *Courtesy Archives and Special Collections, UCO Library.*

During the late 1920s, Central maintained healthy enrollment while competing vigorously with the other five teachers colleges. New state teaching certification requirements helped to drive up the enrollment figures at all institutions. The state superintendent called for an end to the county certificate system in favor of the State Board of Education issuing all teaching certificates. In order to meet the new certification requirements, county certified teachers attended summer term at the teachers colleges.

In 1921, Central's total enrollment was 2,578 and by 1926-1927 enrollment grew to 4,081. All teachers colleges grew during this period, but Southeastern stunned the others as it climbed from an enrollment of 2,962 in 1921-1922 to 4,974 in 1926-1927, surpassing Central. No longer could Central claim to be the largest of the six teachers colleges in Oklahoma, a cloak Central had worn proudly for more than 25 years.

While Southeastern was Central's closest competitor in terms of numbers, Northeastern and East Central were not far behind. Central's budget remained the largest among the six teachers colleges in 1927, receiving $162,220 from the legislature, with $125,020 earmarked for salaries. East Central received the second largest appropriation of $153,992, with $124,292 for salaries.

John G. Mitchell (1919-1931)

The election of Democrat J.B.A. Robertson as governor in 1918 meant political shakeups at the state's colleges. Governor Robertson's administration dismissed five of the six presidents of the normal schools, only retaining the president of Southwestern. John Mitchell, superintendent of Pryor schools, replaced J. W. Graves as president of Central.

Mitchell's presence as president of CSTC for 12 years demonstrated stability—a quality that was lacking in previous administrations. He attended Cumberland University followed by George Peabody College, both in Tennessee. At the time of his selection as president, Mitchell was completing his M.A. at OU. He was a Southerner like four of his predecessors, Williams, Murdaugh, McLaughlin, and Evans.

President Mitchell was more pragmatic than scholarly.

His colleagues considered him a gentleman of "unblemished character" and "untiring energy." Like McLauchlin, Mitchell emphasized student conduct. He was particularly preoccupied with deterring women from smoking. The catalogue of 1920 offers a glimpse of the times, "Edmond has no pool halls or smoke [smoking clubs] houses." Although Central presidents and perhaps the faculty smoked or used tobacco products, they prohibited such conduct among their students.

Mitchell surrounded himself at Central with friends, family, and students from Pryor. Mitchell hired six teachers from his school district in Pryor and referred to them as "my friends" throughout his tenure. They exemplified the model teachers he wanted at Central. To his credit, some of the Pryor teachers made important and lasting contributions at Central.

John G. Mitchell, the eleventh president of Central, held his position from 1919 to 1931. Under his leadership, high standards of student conduct were a priority as well as increased enrollment on campus. In 1926, Central named the new theatre building in honor of President Mitchell. *Courtesy Archives and Special Collections, UCO Library.*

Edgar Wax, his high school principal and teacher of mathematics, and Grady C. Watkins, Associate Professor of English at Central, were Mitchell's only two "friends" that William H. Murray did not sweep out in the spring of 1931. Mitchell also hired his relatives to work at Central. Two of Mitchell's nephews, for example, worked as assistant registrar and clerk. In the 1924-1925 school year, Fred McCarrel succeeded L. B. Ray as director of the Training School, a position Ray had held since 1918. Mitchell also hired W. T. Doyel as Registrar, a newly-created position. Doyel went through all the previous student records and created a card index system for instant reference.

In addition, Mitchell recruited students from Pryor to attend Central. These students served as class officers, became active in campus activities, and received high grades. In fact, Mitchell wanted all students to receive high grades.

Instructors were questioned regarding their evaluation process if they did not comply. Mitchell also continued President McLaughlin's plan of "relieving" students from their examinations if they received a score of 80 in recitation. Some professors liked this no-examination policy because it meant less work.

During the 1920s, many Oklahoma educators and policymakers advocated advanced degrees for college presidents and faculty. Feeling the pressure of this new trend, many people in higher education looked for "easy" graduate programs offering correspondence or summer programs. While other college presidents in Oklahoma received advanced degrees from Columbia or Peabody, Mitchell considered himself a business executive rather than an educated man and preferred to remain at Central and encourage his faculty to pursue graduate training. As an incentive to faculty, Mitchell was the first president at Central to establish sabbatical leave with half pay. Lucy Jeston Hampton, for example, received a master's degree from Columbia during this period.

The modern educational philosophy of the 1920s also meant an emphasis on extracurricular activities. Young assistant professors from the Teachers College at Columbia University canvassed the country advocating more outdoor activities and more recreation. Columbia also wanted to revise the teacher-training curriculum to reflect the new philosophy. "Weighty personages were imported from Teachers College," Oakes wrote, "to bring the backward western course of study up to New York City's 'modern' status."

In this effort to be modern, science was privileged over the humanities and the B.S. was privileged over the B.A. Such reform benefited Charles Wantland's athletic program with a succession of football victories under President Mitchell. In fact, Mitchell and Wantland even experimented with having the athletes work as janitors to maintain the campus grounds and buildings.

Coach Wantland and Athletics in the 1920s

Coach Wantland quickly rose through the ranks at Central to become director of athletics and college life in general. By 1924, he served as Central's first dean of men. As Oakes explained, "It was not long before all his requests for more money, more equipment, more jobs for athletes, and more money for medical service to the teams, was granted gratefully, often before the requests had been made formally. Thousands of people had come to know Mr. Wantland who had never heard Mr. Mitchell's name." In many ways, athletic events helped promote a feeling of school spirit and unity on campus. Students and faculty

An early 1930s view of the tennis courts where Thatcher Hall now stands.
Courtesy Archives and Special Collections, UCO Library.

The Spurs served as "yell leaders" during athletic events in 1938. *Courtesy Archives and Special Collections, UCO Library.*

attended pep meetings, assemblies, bonfires, and parades to engage in campus life and support school athletics. Wantland championed the popular notion of developing character in students through extracurricular activities.

Wantland established a program of eight sports, including the introduction of wrestling. Orin Roy Stuteville, outstanding heavyweight wrestler, coached the first wrestling team at Central in 1920. He later became a member of the Olympic wrestling team in 1924. On Wantland Day, October 27, 1950, Stuteville established an annual $300 scholarship for Central athletes. Another Central wrestler, Ray Clemons, made the 1936 Olympic wrestling team. Many of the football players also were on the wrestling team.

During his long tenure as athletic director and football coach at Central State, Wantland achieved a record of 96 wins, 39 losses, and 17 ties. This included the conference championship for football in 1923, 1924, and 1929. In 1923, Central beat A&M 14-6 at Lewis Field and downed Iowa State at Ames 14-13 in a tremendous upset. The 1924 team defeated OU 2-0, Baylor, the Southwest Conference champion, 14-6, and Tulsa 21-0.

In the early 1920s, Charles and Carrie Belle Wantland, siblings and the directors of physical training, formally recognized the accomplishments of student athletes. Everett Hafer received the first Wantland Medal, awarded each year to the most accomplished

In 1937, the Central Broncho football team became the Collegiate Conference champions. Coaches (left to right): front row, Gene Smith; middle row, Dale Hamilton and Head Coach, Claude Reed, far right. *Courtesy Archives and Special Collections, UCO Library.*

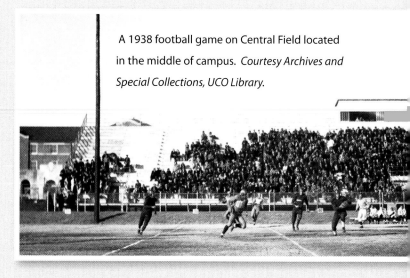

A 1938 football game on Central Field located in the middle of campus. *Courtesy Archives and Special Collections, UCO Library.*

The 1937, the best all-around athletes, playing three or more sports, were Francis Jacobson and Otis Delaporte. They are seated with their plaques in front of the old administration building. *Courtesy Archives and Special Collections, UCO Library.*

undergraduate athlete. Hafer Park in Edmond bears the name of this outstanding CTSC student athlete.

In 1922, Coach Wantland and President Mitchell organized the Letterman's Club, consisting of all male athletes who had earned one or more letters in any sport. His wife, Agnes Wantland, suggested the name "Bronchos," for Central's football team. The Letterman's Club made her an honorary member in this all-male club.

The physical training program for women also made advances during the early 1920s under Carrie Belle Wantland. Women athletes created their own Letterman's Club for Women. Established in 1923 by Zona Smith, the Women's Athletic Association had 150 members. New sports at Central included hockey, golf, and track. Emma Plunkett, a graduate of Peabody College and Oklahoma A&M, joined the women's physical education staff in 1928 and remained a solid fixture on campus for decades.

Central's baseball and basketball teams continued to compete well during the 1920s. In track, Central won the OU Invitational Track Meet over all the other normal schools. Track stars such as Elmer McLane, two-mile champion, helped build a competitive track program at Central. In 1923, Central's first cross country team defeated OU, 19-17. In 1924 Earl Carruth of Central ran the 220-yard dash in record time. Frank Shaw placed fifth in the United States National Decathlon. John E. Williamson won fame as a track man and four-year letterman, joining the school's coaching staff in 1927.

The new gymnasium, Wantland Hall, a tribute to the success of Wantland's athletic program, officially opened in February, 1928. At $100,000, the structure was the costliest to date and included a modern swimming pool.

The 1934 track team in front of the campus tennis courts with their coaches, Raymond Swartz and Douglas Woods. The 1934 track team was one of many Collegiate Champions throughout the 1930s. *Courtesy Archives and Special Collections, UCO Library.*

Why Broncho?

By Felicia Harrison, B.A. in History/Museum Studies, 2008

In 1922, Agnes Wantland, wife of football coach Charles Wantland, suggested the Broncho nickname in a contest for naming the football team. Thereafter, Broncho became the nickname for all athletic teams. As a result of selecting the winning name, Mrs. Wantland became the first woman to be an honorary member of the Letterman's Club.

Students often ask about the unusual spelling of "broncho," although according to the New World Dictionary, broncho is accepted for the more commonly spelled "bronco." Both have the same meaning—a wild or only partially tamed horse or pony of the Western Plains.

Supporting the Broncho football team in 1998 was Candace Dawn Carollo, feature twirler for the UCO Marching Band until fall, 2001. She performed for the football half-time shows and homecoming parades. One of the fondest memories of her twirling career at UCO was when Carollo first led the UCO homecoming parade through downtown Edmond.

Eric Oesch, a journalism/public relations major and 1983 graduate, enjoyed his time as Buddy Broncho. Although Eric was never an athlete, he loved sports and thought a great way to become involved in an extracurricular activity was to "try out" to be Buddy Broncho, the school mascot. One day, Eric went to the dean of men's office to inquire about how one could "try out" for the mascot position. Much to his surprise, the ladies in the office were thrilled to see him and practically gave him the mascot costume within minutes of the inquiry. They said, "You want to be Buddy Broncho? When can you start?" A tuition waiver, part of the compensation for being Buddy Broncho, more than compensated for the heat inside the costume.

Candace Carollo, the UCO Featured Twirler from 1998 to 2001, poses with Buddy Broncho at a football game. In 2002, she graduated with a B.A. in history and serves as administrative assistant in the Department of History and Geography. *Courtesy Candace Carollo.*

Barbara Farbin steps off stage after receiving a gift from Santa during Central's annual "Christmas Party for Children" while student Eric Oesch as Buddy Broncho applauds. *Courtesy Archives and Special Collections, UCO Library.*

The Shakespeare Club's Peace Profit float in the 1936 homecoming parade. The Shakespeare Club was one of many clubs that began in the 1920s and 1930s. *Courtesy Archives and Special Collections, UCO Library.*

Student Activities

Student activities on campus remained the backbone of the liberal arts education at Central. "All the benefits to be derived from a college education are not obtained in the classroom," the *Bronze Book* of 1925 reminded students. The debate clubs continued their longstanding tradition of competing with one another on campus and vying for top honors at the state level.

In February, 1921, the Central chorus of 125 students, the largest student organization on campus, performed at the State Teachers meeting. While athletics continued to dominate campus activities and coverage in the *Bronze Book* during the 1920s and early 1930s, new student clubs such as the science club, the home economics club, the Latin club, Les Metieres art club, and the Blue Curtain Players flourished on campus.

The first homecoming issue of *The Vista* appeared on November 15, 1924. *The Vista* included many stories about Central alumni. Mell Nash was perhaps one of the most notable graduates during the 1920s. At the age of 30, Nash became State Superintendent of Schools. *The Vista* covered the story with the front page headline stating, "One of Central's Biggest Men." Central administrators invited Nash to speak at the dedication of the new auditorium, Mitchell Hall, in 1926. Business students took shorthand of his speech and *The Vista* printed it.

Mitchell Hall

In 1925, both the school and the town benefited when the legislature appropriated $130,000 for Mitchell Hall. In order for construction to begin, Central purchased land adjacent to the campus for the new building and relocated the existing businesses, J. T. Stripling's Normal Hill Grocery and Luther F. Rice's Campus Corner, across the street. Funds for an auditorium demonstrated a significant move on the part of the legislature to allow the teachers colleges to expand.

President Mitchell, cognizant of the importance of advertising and improving relations between Central and the public, initiated specific programs to accomplish that goal. Central hosted guest lectures by politicians, including Governor Robertson and former President William Howard Taft, as well as ministers and nationally-known entertainers. Mitchell also invited Leon Phillips and Robert S. Kerr as assembly speakers at Central before they became governors of Oklahoma. Mitchell encouraged faculty to make public speaking engagements, to assist county superintendents in organizing teachers association meetings and literary and track meets, and to volunteer as judges for county contests.

Another of Mitchell's advertising plans was to employ 30 to 50 of the smaller school superintendents in Central's district to teach at CTSC during the summer terms. In 1928, for example, Central hired 56 extra teachers for the summer term. It was hoped that the superintendents would encourage their high school students to attend Central. This was a common practice among the teaching colleges and the University of Oklahoma during this period.

The exterior of Mitchell Hall, named after President John G. Mitchell, as it looked in the 1960s. Constructed in 1926, Mitchell Hall served as a gathering place for students attending campus plays, musicals, and lectures. *Courtesy Archives and Special Collections, UCO Library.*

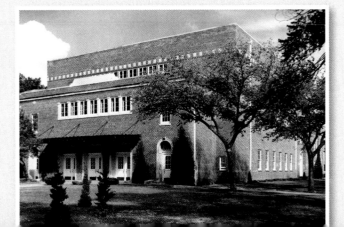

Students of physical education professor Emma Plunkett during a circus program on campus, 1932. Men and women students, staff and faculty participated in the circuses. *Courtesy Archives and Special Collections, UCO Library.*

Emma Plunkett

By Michelle Byrd, B.A. in General Studies, 2004

Emma Plunkett was born August 7, 1901, in Greenville, North Carolina, and grew up in a very eclectic household in Augusta, Georgia. Her parents instilled in her the ideals of standing up for what she believed in and of discipline. After she earned her B.S. from Peabody College, Plunkett moved to Oklahoma. In 1928, she became the only female instructor of physical education and the Director of Women's Health and Physical Education at Central State Teachers College. She took an active role in strengthening the Women's Athletic Association, and convinced administrators to allow women to receive school sweaters for showing excellence in their sports, including field hockey, volleyball, basketball, softball, tennis, badminton, swimming, archery, and table tennis.

Plunkett believed a student, whether male or female, should be well rounded in all areas of life. Her courses were unique because her students participated in dance, theater productions, gardening, and various other activities she believed would educate the whole person. In 1929, she organized the first CSTC circus, and it continued until 1941.

Plunkett was instrumental in bringing to the campus such speakers as Robert Frost and Amelia Earhart. She was influential in convincing administrators to beautify the campus—she even won approval to bring magnolias from Georgia to plant in front of Wantland Hall, home of physical education faculty offices and classrooms.

Plunkett coached women's competitive athletics for 27 years at Central. In later years, she focused more on administrative work. She spent many hours on presidential committees on health and physical education. Although she retired in 1966, her time at Central did not end. By the time she handed over Central to several former students, who had become her colleagues, she had created a legacy. She often returned to guest lecture in classes of former students, including Virginia Peters. In 1997, when Plunkett died at age 95, she and her sister, Josephine, bequeathed $1 million to UCO.

Great Depression

During the Great Depression, Edmond did not suffer from a population decline as much as other parts of the state did. In fact, the population of Edmond increased from 3,576 in 1930 to 4,002 in 1940. Central played an important role in keeping the local economy afloat during difficult times, but the development of the Edmond Oil Field west of town also resulted in growth.

As a weekend excursion, Edmond residents would pack picnic lunches and drive west of town to observe the oil fields. As more Americans traveled highways in their automobiles, civic leaders understood that the future of Edmond depended on US-66 and US-77 highways passing through town.

The Great Depression played a role in the enrollment increase at Oklahoma colleges. Many young people decided to enroll in college courses while continuing to look for work. During the mid-1930s, Central's enrollment continued to outpace sister institutions. New requirements for elementary teachers in 1934 helped bolster enrollment at Central, especially during the summer sessions. For example, Central's enrollment climbed from 3,020 in 1934-1935 to 4,262 in 1935-1936, a 39 percent increase. OU noted a modest three percent increase to 7,956, while Oklahoma A & M had 5,628 students, a seven percent increase. Similarly, East Central and Southwestern had slight increases.

William H. "Alfalfa Bill" Murray was elected governor in 1930. During the campaign, Central State's President Mitchell called Murray his third choice in the Democratic primary. When Murray took office in 1931, he dismissed President Mitchell and replaced him with Malcolm A. Beeson.

Malcolm A. Beeson (1931-1935)

In the early 1930s, Central trailed Southeastern and East Central in enrollment. During Malcolm A. Beeson's four years as Central's twelfth president, Central was first in enrollment among teachers colleges. This trend continued during the next decade, except for the 1938-1939 school year.

Born in Alabama, Beeson studied agronomy at Auburn Polytechnic and the University of Alabama

and completed some course work at Johns Hopkins University. His doctoral degree had been "conferred" by a smaller Mississippi college. In 1901, Beeson organized the Meridian Male College in Mississippi, and served as president until 1914. In 1910, the Meridian Female College granted Beeson the degree of honorary doctor of science. Before serving as president of Central, Beeson had been dean of the department of agronomy at Oklahoma A&M.

Beeson was an innovative president. He hired a former banker to direct purchasing and disbursement of funds rather than handle the finances himself. He established several Greek letter and honor societies. Beeson also instituted an annual speech tournament in 1932, under the direction of the English Department, bringing high school students from Oklahoma and surrounding states to the event.

Beeson tried to establish a graduate program, but it quickly collapsed. When Beeson became president, Wantland resigned as director of athletics. Beeson appointed Claude Reeds of the University of Oklahoma as the new athletic director. Beeson selected Peter W. Swartz to coach wrestling and Pat Taylor to coach baseball.

As the twelfth president of Central from 1931 to 1935, Malcolm A. Beeson established several honor societies and promoted student involvement in campus activities. *Courtesy Archives and Special Collections, UCO Library.*

Beeson quickly became a popular president among students and faculty. He tended to side with students in their minor grievances with faculty. Student activities continued to thrive under Beeson's leadership. The college supported women's and men's glee clubs, women's and men's quartet, orchestra, and band. The student council, the League of Young Democrats, and the Blue Captain Players, a dramatic club organized by the new registrar, formed in the early 1930s. Other student groups maintained their popularity, including German and French clubs, Senate,

Arena, Criterion, Shakespeare, Pioneer, Lyceum, and Quill.

Far different than most of his predecessors, Beeson made few changes to the faculty. Central maintained 55 faculty members including the training department. New instructors included Guy C. Chambers, head of the department of modern languages, and Charles N. Ott, head of the department of chemistry. Fred H. Ives returned to campus as head of the department of agriculture and John Gecks was the band instructor. During the summer term of 1932, Beeson employed 45 additional teachers, including eight leading superintendents in Oklahoma school systems.

For the year 1931-1932, Central enjoyed a nine percent increase in enrollment to 4,679, including 459 students in correspondence and 436 in extension. The University of Oklahoma's increase was slightly less than eight percent, but held at 10,742. Central maintained a slight lead over its nearest competitors among the teachers colleges, East Central and Southeastern.

Campus Activities

Athletic achievements, especially in football, wrestling, and track, helped maintain the campus community through the Great Depression. In football, Central reclaimed the collegiate championship in 1931-1932, after losing it to East Central the previous year. At homecoming in 1933, the 1904 football team, Central's first regular team, attended as honored guests. Those in attendance included O. E. Hopkins, Arthur Imel, Ralph Gilmore, Ed G. Klein, Peter W. Swartz, Ed McCarrel, and W. R. Seig.

At the banquet, Klein, the first player to make a touchdown for Central during the first season, presented the football used in that game to the college for the Broncho trophy case. Central won the conference football championship from 1936 to 1938, as well as the basketball championship from 1935 to 1938. Wrestling, track, and tennis teams also took top honors.

Student clubs and other activities also helped soothe the campus spirit during the Depression. Debate at Central continued to remain strong. In fact, Central won the majority of state debate contests. The Alumni Association offered a $25 prize for the writer of a school song. The Arena Ambassadors, the popular campus orchestra, provided music for all school parties.

Edna Jones, penmanship instructor and alumni secretary, organized the Second Generation Club in 1938. Beginning with 85 charter members, the club attracted the sons and daughters of former Central students with the charge, "Once a Centralite, always a Centralite." The first president was Maxine Hubbard, whose mother, Sadie Laughton, attended Central in 1892.

The writers' club, organized by Mollie Ruth Bottoms, an English instructor, published several volumes of student and faculty work. In April, 1939, the writers' club and Central hosted the renowned poet Robert Frost. The club continued to be popular during the 1940s.

During the Depression, a subscription to *The Vista* remained 50 cents per year until 1935 when the price for an annual subscription increased to 75 cents. Members of the Alumni Association received *The Vista* by mail. During this period, the newspaper did not utilize advertising as a source of revenue and the school absorbed the costs of publication.

Reversing a 22-year power struggle with the president's office, *The Vista* returned as a forum for the students in 1937. National advertisements reappeared in *The Vista* in 1938, something not seen since 1916. By the late 1930s, the price of an annual subscription was $1.00.

The coronation of the "Homecoming Queen" on Central Field during the 1938 homecoming football game. *Courtesy Archives and Special Collections, UCO Library.*

Thompson's—More than a Bookstore

By Julie Bennett-Jones, B.A in History, 2005; M.A. in History, 2007

Although not affiliated with UCO, Thompson's Bookstore is an unofficial UCO landmark. Located across the street from the university, at 101 North University Drive, Thompson's has served thousands of UCO students since 1930.

The legacy began with William "Bill" Peyton Thompson, the first family member to attend what is now UCO in 1914 and 1915, receiving his teaching certificate. His wife, Alice Buck Thompson, also attended from 1930 to 1934, obtaining her bachelor's degree in math and science.

In 1930, Bill and Alice established Thompson's Bookstore. In time, other family members also graduated from UCO. Lowell, Alice and Bill's son, graduated in 1950. He later served as president and member of the board of the UCO Alumni Association.

Mike Thompson, grandson of Bill and Alice, played on the varsity basketball team for UCO before graduating in 1975. Later he served on the board of the Alumni Association and the Athletic Association. Mike's wife, Gayle, also has roots at UCO as a 1974 graduate. Nick and Jeff,

sons of Mike and Gayle, also attended UCO. Nick transferred to Oklahoma State University for an architecture degree. Jeff played varsity baseball and majored in finance at UCO.

The Thompson family connection permeates the history of UCO. A member of the family has attended the University under nearly all of its name changes. For a time, the family lived where the campus police station is located.

"My parents walked to the bookstore and my children rode their bicycles a million miles on the brick sidewalks of the campus," the late William "Bill" Buck Thompson wrote in a letter to UCO in 1999. Thompson said, "I can't imagine life growing up without Central."

UCO acknowledged the longtime commitment of the Thompson family by naming them the Family of the Year in 2002.

The location of Thompson's Bookstore in the 1930s was 117 North College, now called University Street. Four generations of the Thompson family are UCO alumni. *Courtesy Archives and Special Collections, UCO Library.*

An interior view of Thompson's Bookstore, 1961. Thompson's continues to serve thousands of students each semester at the University of Central Oklahoma. *Courtesy Archives and Special Collections, UCO Library.*

The 1931 Central State Teachers College marching band practicing with Old North in the background. Band Director, J. J. Gecks is standing at left. *Courtesy Archives and Special Collections, UCO Library.*

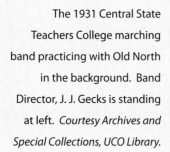

Cliff Otto served as the acting president at Central for only two months from July 9 to September 7, 1935, after Governor E. W. Marland dismissed President Beeson. *Courtesy Archives and Special Collections, UCO Library.*

Cliff Otto (July 9–September 7, 1935)

When Governor E.W. Marland assumed office in 1935, he appointed a new State Board of Education. The board, along with the state superintendent of public instruction, John Vaughn, visited the six teacher training colleges and compiled reports. Based on their assessments, and following a long tradition of patronage based on political party, Marland dismissed five college presidents, including Beeson at Central. One board member, Grace Norris Davis suggested Professor Cliff Otto as "Acting President" of Central. Davis and Otto had been classmates at Southwestern.

Otto served as acting president of Central for two months in 1935. He had been head of the department of science for 15 years. He had experience with the community as president of the Kiwanis Club, Master of the Masonic Lodge, and participated in Chamber of Commerce events. Otto had been chairman of the Faculty Athletics Board and was well regarded by the faculty.

Many hoped Otto would become the permanent president. He was active during his two months as acting president. During this time he had to engage in discussions with the State Budget Officer. Under the officer's recommendation, Central's appropriation for teachers' salaries had been reduced during the previous four years, from $170,680 to $116,545. In 1935, the Budget Officer proposed to further limit salaries to $113,000. Otto asked for at least $120,000, which he knew to be inadequate, but better than the lower figure. After lengthy discussions, the Budget Officer reluctantly complied with Otto's request, allowing Central $120,000 for the maintenance of the faculty for each of the 1935-1936 and 1936-1937 school years.

John Ohlyer Moseley (1935-39)

Two days before freshman orientation and registration, Otto telephoned from Oklahoma City to announce to the faculty that a little known professor from the University of Oklahoma, John Ohlyer Moseley, had been selected president of Central. In addition, all faculty were retained except one from Otto's department. Otto emerged unscathed from his temporary position as president and served as dean of the faculty and head of the department of science.

Three members of Marland's State Board of Education were from Ponca City, the governor's hometown, including the noted writer John Joseph Mathews from Pawhuska.

Representing Oklahoma, Mathews and Moseley had studied together as Rhodes Scholars at Oxford University. Mathews recommended his friend, then associate professor of Latin at the University of Oklahoma, to become president of Central.

Moseley was a well-educated man with a B.A. from Southeastern Normal School and an M.A. from OU. Trained as a teacher, he served as head of the department of Latin and English and coached sports at Durant High School. In addition to his studies at Oxford, he had advanced studies at Columbia and Stanford. He received the honorary degree of Doctor of Laws from Austin College.

John Ohlyer Moseley served as the thirteenth president of Central from 1935 to 1939. Moseley promoted Central by encouraging faculty members to prepare lectures and present them to the community. *Courtesy Archives and Special Collections, UCO Library.*

Moseley made bold changes in curriculum and social behavior at Central. He reinstituted examinations for all students as a prerequisite for college standing. He asked faculty members to prepare lectures for campus audiences, as well as the general public, in an effort to encourage scholarship and promote Central throughout the state.

ABOVE: President Moseley (center) with fathers and daughters in front of Murdaugh Hall on Central's annual Dad's Day in 1938. *Courtesy Archives and Special Collections, UCO Library.*

Thatcher Hall, one of two residential dorms built by the WPA in the mid-1930s, provided housing for 150 men. *Courtesy Archives and Special Collections, UCO Library.*

Smoking on campus grounds returned under Moseley, defying the longstanding ban in effect from 1908 to 1935. At the same time, Moseley expanded the health program to include a full-time physician, nurse service, and an infirmary for faculty, staff, and students. Many people found his policies to reflect a more modern administrative style.

Construction projects on campus reaped the benefits of New Deal programs instituted by President Franklin D. Roosevelt and Congress. In 1935, Central received funds through the Works Progress Administration (WPA) for construction of two residential halls, Thatcher Hall for 150 men, and Murdaugh Hall for 300 women, at a cost of $600,000. In 1938, Central received federal funds to build modern steam tunnels from all major buildings to the heating plant. Other WPA projects on campus included construction of underground, concrete tunnels for all utilities, concrete sidewalks to replace brick ones, tennis courts, and a sewing room for costumes at Mitchell Hall. The music department received additional quarters. The entire campus received a makeover with landscape improvements and new trees.

As a WPA project, concrete walls were added to the existing steel bleachers to construct a stadium for Central Field. *Courtesy Archives and Special Collections, UCO Library.*

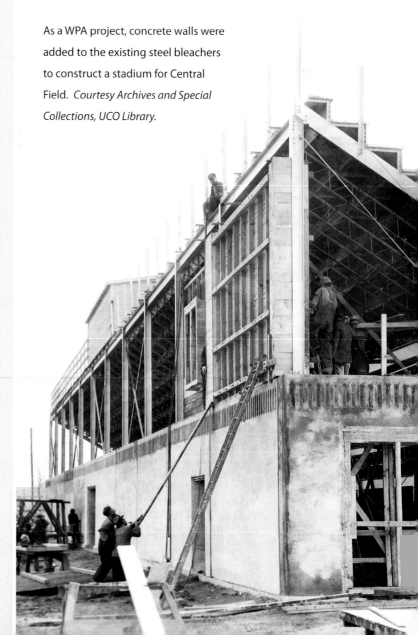

Central State Teachers College had experienced the highs and lows of the 1920s and 1930s. Still reeling from the international effects of World War I, students and faculty demonstrated marked resilience as Central became a four-year degree-granting institution. Enrollment soared to new heights as students arrived on campus from hometowns throughout Oklahoma and at least 20 other states. The campus expanded with the construction of Wantland Hall and Mitchell Hall. Two new dormitories met the demand for new students wanting to live on campus.

Residents of Murdaugh Hall enjoyed gathering in the lounge area in 1937. *Courtesy Archives and Special Collections, UCO Library.*

Murdaugh Hall was one of two residential dorms built in 1937 by the WPA. Murdaugh provided housing for 300 female students. *Courtesy Archives and Special Collections, UCO Library.*

Chapter Three Timeline

1919

· Eighteenth Amendment for Prohibition passed

· Race Riots broke out in Chicago

· James B.A. Robertson became governor of Oklahoma

· CSNS became Central State Teachers College (CSTC)

· John G. Mitchell named the 11th President of Central

1920

· Warren G. Harding elected President of the United States

· Nineteenth Amendment for women's right to vote passed in United States

· National urban population surpassed rural population for the first time

· Last Central class to graduate with a life certificate with only two years of college work

· Central's first wrestling team established

1921

· Women gained voting rights in Sweden

· Margaret Gorman named the first Miss America

· Tulsa Race Riot

1922

· Mussolini formed a fascist government in Italy

· Irish independence

· Rebecca Felton of Georgia, first woman appointed to U.S. Senate temporarily, served for only two days

· Mrs. C. W. Wantland, wife of athletic director, named the "broncho" as the mascot for CSTC

· The Lass O and Spur pep clubs established at Central

1923

· Worldwide inflation except in Britain and Czechoslovakia

· Central's first cross country team established

1924

· Lenin, leader of Russia died; succeeded by Stalin

· President Harding died; Vice President Calvin Coolidge assumed office

· Charles Wantland became Central's first dean of men

1925

· Scopes Trial in Tennessee pitted religious fundamentalism against modernity

1926

· National Broadcasting Company (NBC) established the first national radio network

· Gertrude Ederle became first woman to swim the English Channel

· Completion of Mitchell Hall at CSTC

1927

· Charles Lindbergh made the first solo flight across the Atlantic Ocean

· Babe Ruth set home run record

· Warner Brothers produced *The Jazz Singer*, the first feature length motion picture with sound

· Henry S. Johnston became governor of Oklahoma

1928

· Great Britain granted full voting rights to women

· Herbert C. Hoover became President of the United States

· Central's new gymnasium, Wantland Hall opened

The Royce Café was a popular eatery for both Edmond residents and Central students during the 1930s.
Courtesy Archives and Special Collections, UCO Library.

ABOVE: Acee Blue Eagle, the acclaimed Pawnee-Creek artist, created WPA murals depicting American Indian dance and culture on the interior walls of Mitchell Hall. Unfortunately, the murals were covered with blue paint in the 1950s during the renovation of Mitchell Hall. *Courtesy Archives and Special Collections, UCO Library.*

LEFT: An example of one of Acee Blue Eagle's murals that lined the walls of Mitchell Hall in the 1930s. *Courtesy Archives and Special Collections, UCO Library.*

LEFT: Acee Blue Eagle, internationally recognized Pawnee-Creek Artist, painted murals on campus as part of the WPA. *Courtesy Archives and Special Collections, UCO Library.*

1929
- World economic crisis begins
- Stock market crashed and the Great Depression began
- Governor Johnston impeached and removed from office
- William Judson Holloway became governor of Oklahoma

1930
- Otto W. Jeffries named the first Dean of Central College

1931
- Scottsboro case
- William "Alfalfa Bill" Murray became governor of Oklahoma
- Malcolm A. Beeson becomes President of CSTC

1932
- Franklin D. Roosevelt elected as President of the United States
- Central football team won the collegiate championship

1933
- Hitler elected Chancellor of Germany
- Holocaust began in Germany
- Frances Perkins appointed first woman member of a presidential cabinet by President Roosevelt as secretary of labor
- FDR's New Deal passed
- Twenty-first Amendment repealed Prohibition

1934
- Long March, relocation of Chinese communists
- Indian Reorganization Act repealed Dawes Severalty Act
- Completion of Acee Blue Eagle's Murals in Mitchell Hall at CSTC as a part of WPA projects on campus

1935
- Italy invaded Ethiopia
- Dust Bowl began
- Ernest Marland became governor of Oklahoma
- Professor Cliff Otto served as president of CSTC for two months
- John O. Mosely became president of CSTC
- Dr. Emma Estill-Harbour named to the Oklahoma Hall of Fame
- President Mosely lifted the 1908 on-campus smoking ban

1936
- Spanish Civil War began
- Amelia Earhart spoke at CSTC
- Central placed on semester system rather than term

1937
- Japan invaded China
- Completion of dormitories, Murdaugh and Thatcher Halls, at CTSC
- Central's stadium erected

1938
- First federal minimum wage established

CHAPTER FOUR

The War Years

Central State College

Many of us tried to get through school as quickly as possible so that we could work in the war effort.
I did get through very quickly within three years. Then I started teaching school because I still was not 21.
Mary Helen Lillard

We had plenty of exercise because the art department was on the fourth floor of Old North.
We had an outside entrance with metal stairs—klunk, klunk, klunk. We didn't need to run, but Emma Plunkett thought we did.
We had tennis at 7:00 a.m. five days a week. Uniforms had to be starched and ironed and subject to inspection.
I was heartbroken because I made As in my classes and a B in tennis—but I lived.
Kathryn Kerr Kunc

There was a family atmosphere because the classes were small and we knew the faculty members.
Often, we had the same instructors for several classes. Oklahoma history with Dr. Joe Jackson was a special treat.
He dressed up like Alfalfa Bill Murray and other characters of Oklahoma history. He would often ask students about their hometowns.
He would point to me and say, "Virginia Lee Peters, Drumright, Oklahoma, do you know about Drumright back in the oil boom days?"
And he'd start a big rambling thing like that and so I think there really was a very close feeling between faculty and students.
That family atmosphere was part of it.
Virginia Peters

There was a reason that A.G. Hitchcock was called "Mr. Central State College."
For a time, you couldn't get a degree without A.G. Hickock approving it. You would go in to see him
and he would take a memo pad and write on the memo pad the things you had to have for a degree.
You protected that with your life. If you did what he put on that pad, you would graduate. If you lost it, you couldn't prove it.
And the word was out – when he gives you that, put it where you'll keep it.
Joe Jackson

During the late 1930s, the six presidents of the teachers colleges in Oklahoma petitioned the State Board of Education to broaden the original mission of the schools as teacher training institutions to offer training in other disciplines. The legislature agreed and in 1939 the teachers colleges became state colleges.

Central had granted teacher-training degrees for 48 years, but the revised mission provided new opportunities for students who had interests other than teaching. Central became a four-year liberal arts college and the name was changed to Central State College.

R. R. Robinson (1939-1948)

When President John O. Moseley resigned as president of Central State College to become dean of students at the University of Tennessee-Knoxville, Roscoe R. Robinson, president of the University Preparatory School at Tonkawa, became the new president of Central. Assuming the post in his mid fifties, Robinson was "mature, solid, and substantial," according to Oakes. Robinson received his B.A. at Lebanon University in 1911, M.A. at the University of Oklahoma in 1918, Ph.D. at Peabody College for Teachers in 1928, and later Doctor of Laws from Oklahoma City University.

Robinson had extensive teaching experience in Oklahoma. He was principal of Perry High School (1911-13), superintendent of Perry City Schools (1913-17), professor of education at East Central State Teachers College (1918-21), head of the department of Education and director of the Training School at East Central (1921-25), dean of the faculty at East Central (1926-28), and president of the University Preparatory School, Tonkawa (1928-39).

With such training and experience, Robinson was well equipped to assume the top post at Central. Following a tradition of Christian leadership among Central presidents, Robinson also participated in church work and civic organizations. The Rotary Club, for example, welcomed Robinson to Edmond with a banquet attended by Central faculty and Edmond citizens.

adults, a positive change for Central State College. Robinson sought a balance between study and extracurricular activities. However, extracurricular activities continued to receive greater attention than scholarship. For example, the *Bronze Book* of 1939 contained a list of 20 outstanding students under the heading, "Who's Who in Central State College." The criteria for making the list included extracurricular activities, scholastic standing, and personality. The majority of the students listed, however, were those heavily involved in extracurricular activities. The same pattern continued in 1940 and 1941.

Student organizations blossomed under Robinson. During his first year at Central, 409 students participated in 11 student study clubs and societies such as Arena, Criterion, and Shakespeare. Central also sponsored music groups, Greek fraternities and sororities, and athletics.

Roscoe R. Robinson served as the fourteenth president from 1939 to 1948. During his tenure he traveled throughout the state encouraging people to attend Central State College. *Courtesy Archives and Special Collections, UCO Library.*

Robinson continued the tradition of advertising Central's ability to provide quality education throughout the state. Early in his presidency, he appointed a woman journalist, Louise Moberly, as editor of *The Vista*. With Moberly at the helm, the four-page weekly newspaper became a member of the Oklahoma Senior College Press association and won numerous state awards.

Oakes had offered a positive assessment of Robinson and considered him among the best of Central's presidents. "President Robinson," Oakes wrote, "was approachable, kindly, and helpful. He tarried about the College as much as possible; he made a faculty meeting interesting; he was considerate at all times; yet firm and effective. In his dealings with students, Mr. Robinson would err, if at all, on the side of leniency." He approached college students as

Students constructed the traditional bonfire tower for Central's homecoming in 1939. *Courtesy Archives and Special Collections, UCO Library.*

There were many ways to recognize and encourage proper conduct and study, as noted in the *Quarterly Bulletin* in July, 1939. Central awarded numerous awards to students, including the Gregory Medal for excellence in debate; the "Excellence in Latin" Medal; the Senior athletic medal, for athletic achievement and maintaining a "C" average in at least 12 hours of course work; the Wantland Athletic Award for men; the Freshman Athletic Award for men; the Senior Athletic Award for women; and the Freshman Athletic Trophy for women. In addition, the American Association of University Women sponsored two medals, one for the best all-around senior woman in the college, and the other for the best all-around senior woman in the high school and training department.

Formal parties flourished during the Robinson era. Each spring President Robinson hosted a reception for the senior class in his home. An elegant, elaborate affair, faculty also attended and assisted the president and his wife in congratulating the students. In 1938-1939, Central students participated in more than 40 formal parties. By the early 1940s, the number of formal parties had more than doubled.

It was a difficult time for anyone to serve as president of a college in Oklahoma. Governor Leon C. "Red" Phillips and the legislature had cut all college appropriations by 30 percent. Such cuts resulted in reduced instructor salaries and other problems. Central's budget paled in comparison to money appropriated for OU. During Robinson's first year, the total disbursement to Central was $171,865 for 2,581 students, or $66 per student. In contrast, OU received $2,306,822 for 10,007 students, or $230 per student.

World War II

Another obstacle at the outset of Robinson's presidency was the outbreak of World War II. In 1939, a Civilian Aeronautics Authority (CAA) Unit was established on campus under the direction of Professor Cliff Otto, with 18 men and two women taking courses in ground instruction and instrument study. The students also participated in flying instruction at Wiley Post Airport in Oklahoma City. During the eight-week flight training program, naval cadets lived in barracks to the east of the gymnasium and dined in Murdaugh Hall.

The threat of America entering the world war affected students personally with the introduction of the Selective Service Act in the fall of 1940. Students learned when and where to register. Some joined the military, assuming that the United States would not be able to stay out of the fighting that encompassed Europe and the Pacific. Central's enrollment continued to decline due to the rumors of American involvement.

Golden Jubilee (1940-41)

Central celebrated its 50th Anniversary, or Golden Jubilee, from Homecoming in 1940 to Homecoming in 1941. The *Bronze Book* of 1940 was a special volume bound in gold. Robinson printed 5,000 copies of a special issue of *The Vista*. The issue is a rich mine of information about the school. Central planned a three-day Homecoming Festival for the occasion, beginning Saturday, November 9, 1940. The event was one of the most significant in Central's history. The entertainment consisted of a homecoming parade, free barbeque, football game, president's reception, alumni banquet, alumni dance, Sunday morning union church service, a Sunday afternoon concert by the A Cappella Choir of 100 voices, and an Armistice Day program on Monday. Edmond businessmen sponsored the homecoming barbeque and served food to approximately 6,000 people. Three sides of beef, 300 pounds of onion, 500 pounds of potato chips, 6,000 donuts, and 6,000 apples fed the crowd. Volunteers brewed coffee in a 50-pound steel stock tank.

In the evening, several hundred people attended a formal alumni banquet and dance, one of the most elaborate in the history of Central. Taking center stage at the event was a five-tier birthday cake topped with a replica of Old North. On each tier were ten candles representing the decades of the school. The candles of the first decade were lighted by Reverend Calvin Young, who entered Central on the opening day. The second decade candles were lit by C.M. Howell, Class of 1910, third decade by Charlotte Grass, Class of 1920, fourth decade by Precious Miller Goode, Class of 1930, and the fifth decade of candles by Earlene Specht, Class of 1940.

After Nila Scott, president of the Second Generation Club lit the lone candle on Old North, guests lit individual

Following homecoming, other special events during the year included the Founders' Day Banquet with speaker Clyde Howell of the Class of 1910, the alumni luncheon at the Mayo Hotel in Tulsa during the annual state teachers meeting, Old Timers Day in April, 1941, with historian Edward Everett Dale as speaker from the Class of 1909, and homecoming in October, 1941, with the traditional events such as a parade, game, banquet, and dance. The Alumni Association modernized the football programs with a colorful cover and national advertising. Central won the state championship in football and tennis in 1941.

candles on their tables and held them as they said, "We do give thanks for the abundance that has been Central's and pledge ourselves to the cause of the institution." First Ladies, Myrtle Phillips, wife of Governor Leon Phillips, and Margaret Robinson, Central's first lady, cut the cake. Second Generation club members served the cake and distributed bronze and blue boutonnieres, grown for the occasion by Leslie Moore and his wife, both Central graduates. The next day the music department performed a concert followed by a union church service in the evening.

On Oklahoma Day, November 16, Jessie D. Newby and her education class planted 12 red bud trees on campus to the south of the president's home. In a christening ceremony, the class named the trees for outstanding Oklahomans, including Will Rogers, Wiley Post, and Jennie Harris Oliver.

Following a long tradition of formal functions on campus, formal dances continued during homecoming festivities. In January, 1941, the spring semester began with a formal dance in Murdaugh Hall as students were greeted by President Robinson, his wife, and faculty members. Flowers, ferns, and lights transformed the ballroom into a "spring flower garden," while more than 200 couples danced to the tunes of the Jack Sanders Orchestra from Oklahoma City.

Oklahoma State Regents for Higher Education

In partnership with Governor Phillips, the legislature recommended a constitutional amendment to create the Oklahoma State Regents for Higher Education (OSRHE). In March, 1941, state voters approved the amendment and OSRHE was formed as the umbrella organization for all state institutions of higher learning in Oklahoma. The nine-member board was appointed by the governor and confirmed by the State Senate for nine-year terms. Phillips promised that no colleges would be abolished.

Planned sweeping changes of Oklahoma's higher education system were placed on hold, however, when Japan attacked Pearl Harbor on December 7, 1941, and the United States entered World War II. At their regular meeting on October 26, 1942, regents asked colleges and universities to support the war effort. In addition, regents announced their intention to move cautiously in making recommendations for the improvement of the Oklahoma system of higher education "to avoid disruptions caused by hasty decisions and overnight changes."

The War's Effect on Central

Enrollment at Central declined during World War II. Edmond citizens began planting victory gardens to support the war effort and provide produce for their family meals. Following the bombing of Pearl Harbor and the declaration of war, The Vista reported the news and interpreted it according to what it meant to the campus community. The headline read, "All-out War Policy Advanced by Leaders on Central Campus," with responses from different campus leaders regarding the declaration of war.

President Robinson encouraged students to remain calm. After the initial shock of war, life at Central continued on its normal course for several months. Debates, campus elections, and Christmas parties proceeded on schedule. By February, 1942, student groups sold defense stamps and bonds on campus.

The introduction of rationing and other wartime realities soon altered the normal course of student life at Central. As a temporary wartime measure, the yearbook was not printed, prompting some people to call the war years "the forgotten years." The administration canceled band trips and other special travel. As more college men were drafted, the men's athletic program was suspended.

Women students continued to organize dances on campus, though without men, as reflected in Murdaugh Hall's "Manless Dance" nights in 1942. As a more somber mood hovered on campus, the regular jokes column in The Vista and annual Halloween pranks no longer seemed appropriate.

Class schedule changes in 1942 reflected wartime concerns. To accommodate a new course on the science of aviation in state high schools, Central offered an aviation course for high school teachers. Central also offered first-aid courses and a course in patriotic American literature.

In the summer of 1942, Central accelerated the undergraduate program so a regular four-year course of study could be completed in three years by extending the summer term and condensing the regular semesters to 16 weeks. That summer Central also offered new courses such as civilian protection, welding, a training course for auxiliary officers for civilian defense, and a new history course on the Far East.

The Forgotten Years

By Lisa Pham, B.S. in Biology, 2009

Between 1941 and 1945, a part of history was forged by the "sons and daughters" of Central State College that forever changed the campus, the nation, and the world. CSC, along with America, was hauntingly altered when Japan struck Pearl Harbor on December 7, 1941. The unprecedented attack carried out on American soil was an extremely petrifying and alarming experience.

Mary Helen Lillard, CSC student during World War II, and wife of UCO President Bill Lillard, remembered being very frightened, "We didn't know whether the Japanese would gain control of Pearl Harbor, then proceed to the mainland of the United States," Lillard recalled, "or whether Germany would attack America's eastern seaboard."

However, fears did not affect the immediate desire that arose to join the war effort in any possible way. For example, eager men who were too young to serve borrowed identification cards of older men in order to join the military.

The perennial "Dad" of the class of 1942, Dr. Fred McCarrel, described in his poem, "Precaution," the "stern duty" that called upon not just the American troops, but also the American people, to make a "contribution against a ruthless, zealous foe," Japan. One effort was to allow CSC to be transformed into a military training ground for those on their way to serve overseas. Students living in the two dormitories, Thatcher and Murdaugh, were moved to house trainees. Barracks were constructed to accommodate the great number where six to seven servicemen already occupied a single dorm room.

The women of CSC made great contributions such as giving up their rationing stamps when they enrolled. There were stamps for all sorts of things like food, nylon hosiery, and gas, because the war drained the country of supplies. Paper was even a commodity that was in short supply. Between 1942 and 1947, CSC's *Bronze Book* was not published. Only one woman on campus drove a car, and buying tires was nearly impossible.

Emma Plunkett, the well-known physical education instructor, who labeled her students as "war babies," gave up driving her car, and instead rode a bicycle to classes as one of her countless ways of supporting the war. Asked to surrender much of life's necessities and time, students and faculty members eagerly complied.

The air was filled with an overwhelming nationalism and those who could not physically fight in the war worked relentlessly in alternative avenues to aid the nation in wartime. Many students rapidly completed their studies at school in order to work for the war effort. At the time, *The Vista*, issued special editions in dedication to the servicemen. Each issue reported news of students being held as a prisoner of war, of other soldiers recovering in a hospital from wounds suffered in battle, and tragically, of those killed in battle.

Each publication contained a compassionate column from Roscoe R. Robinson, CSC president from 1939 to

A 1941 basketball game in Wantland Hall. Central's football team played limited schedules in the early 1940s before it was suspended. Former CSC football, basketball, and track star Dale Hamilton became football coach in 1941 and led the Bronchos to conference championships his first year with a 6-2 record, and 7-0 in 1942. Coach Hamilton reported for active duty in the Naval Reserve as a physical education instructor in April, 1943. Play did not resume until after World War II.

Mary Helen Lillard (front row on left) accompanied by other Central women on the window veranda in Murdaugh Hall. *Courtesy Archives and Special Collections, UCO Library.*

1948, expressing the community's gratitude, support, and indebtedness to the serving men and women. History professor Lucy Jeston Hampton kept a meticulous record of every man and woman who left CSC for the war, and to this day, the records fill two file cabinets in the university archives.

Because of the suspension of the printing of the CSC yearbook and limitations on the publication of *The Vista*, some refer to life on the CSC campus during World War II as "the forgotten years."

"Centralites at the Front"

Men students at Central joined the Army, Navy, and Air Corps. In October, 1942, *The Vista* launched a new regular front-page column called "Centralites at the Front," providing news about Central's servicemen. Initially, the column did little more than report names and addresses of servicemen, but later it covered honors, promotions, and, unfortunately, deaths.

The Vista also produced seven special issues dedicated to servicemen. The first special issue was on the first anniversary of Pearl Harbor. It honored 470 men and five women, including eleven faculty, serving in the miltary. The staff reported nine Centralites as killed or missing in action, including Lieutenant Marshall Anderson who received the Distinguished Service Cross two days before being killed in air combat in the Philippines.

Servicemen on Campus

Central State College hosted several different military training stations on campus during the war years. The first group of servicemen to arrive at CSC was met without comment, and perhaps even disdain. Parents of women students were concerned about having servicemen on campus and what it might mean for social relations. Some students were inconvenienced when they were forced to move from their dorm rooms to make space for the servicemen.

An editorial in *The Vista* pleaded with the campus community to "make do" as part of their patriotic duty. The editorial said, "Yes, we had rather forgotten that our country was in war, but Central students should be proud that they have been called upon to help in the great cause of winning the war."

In December, 1942, the campus hosted classes for the Army Air Force Technical Training Command (AAFTTC) for Administrative, Supply, Engineering, and Operations clerks. Eighteen hundred men were trained in groups of 600. Students vacated Murdaugh and Thatcher residence halls to accommodate the soldiers. Perhaps some of the parents' fears were well founded, for these men were older than the coeds and came to Oklahoma from New York, New Jersey, Pennsylvania, and elsewhere.

The headline "Centralites at the Front" made its way onto the front pages of *The Vista* during World War II, and eventually reported everything from honors, to promotions, and even deaths. *Courtesy Archives and Special Collections, UCO Library.*

Special Edition for Service Men

THE VISTA

For Victory...
Buy
UNITED STATES DEFENSE
BONDS ★ STAMPS

Z 586   PUBLISHED WEEKLY THROUGHOUT THE SCHOOL YEAR AT CENTRAL STATE COLLEGE, EDMOND, OKLAHOMA

VOLUME NUMBER XXXXI   THURSDAY, APRIL 1, 1943

Fighting Centralites Serve Country on Mar

'College Front' Morale Kept High at Central State

WAR WORK STRESSED IN CURRICULUM; STUDENTS CONTINUE REGULAR STUDIES

One of the most important "home fronts" today is the "college front," a phase of American war activity that is being supported and continued by the nation's colleges, including Central State College.

War Work Stressed

A wide variety of war work is being done at Central, most of it directly supplying badly-needed soldiers, sailors, defense workers, professional men and women and fliers where they are most needed.

Such work, mentioned above, is being carried on in addition to the regular college work which continues uninterrupted. Liberal arts and sciences and the training of teachers remains the primary object of the college.

At present Central is training

LIEUT. GAGE SERVES UNCLE SAM IN SIGNAL CORPS OF U S ARMY

Thomas B. Gage is a first lieutenant of the 45th division signal corps of the U S Army. He entered the service as a national guardsman in September of 1940.

Lieut. Gage received his B S degree at Central in '40. While at CSC, he was a laboratory assistant in the chemistry department.

19 Women From Central Join Service

WAAC CLAIMS 13; THREE JOIN WAVE

Nineteen former Central State

Lee Roy Ziegelgruber, above, is an aviation cadet at the Army Air Force School at Victoria, Tex. He was accepted for this service in August, 1942.

Cadet Ziegelgruber was a student at Central for two years. He

A TRIBUTE

Again Central State College pays humble tribute to those who are engaged in active service for this country of ours—to those who are doing what we can't do.

For those who have already paid the supreme sacrifice, that this nation might live, we reverently bow our heads, and to their parents, relatives and friends we extend sympathy.

Here's to every fighting son and daughter of Central, wherever you serve—we're proud to call you ours!

The Editor

Ten Former CSC Men See Second World War Action

NINE COMMISSIONED OFFICERS IN LIST

Ten former Central State College

600 Men, V CSC in Arn

COLONEL, LIEU IN SCHOOL'S SE

An army of nea time service of approxi and marines is the co the armed forces of th

Naval Aviation Cadets on the steps of Thatcher Hall, their residence quarters in 1944. During World War II Central hosted Army and Navy pilots for a government flight training course. *Courtesy Archives and Special Collections, UCO Library.*

Central later received a Certificate of Service Award in recognition of meritorious service rendered the AAFTC during the war.

A Navy Air Corps Primary and Secondary Ground School also was housed on campus and trained more than 1,000 pilots during the war. *The Vista* welcomed the *Cler Okie*, the Army school newspaper. Experiencing rationing firsthand, *The Vista*, a weekly newspaper, reduced publication to twice a month.

The campus family embraced visiting servicemen. During the Christmas season, Central hosted a formal dinner and dance in honor of the Naval cadets. Many Edmond townspeople invited them to holiday dinners in their homes. Families or friends who wished to visit the cadets for the holidays could stay in Murdaugh, the women's dormitory, for a small fee.

Central Goes to War

By 1943, CSC's course schedule reflected changes brought on by wartime. Evening courses in accounting and other subjects addressed a need for students who worked during the day. Correspondence study allowed servicemen to continue course work. Courses were added in engineering, drawing, and blueprint reading to supply workers for technical war posts through its industrial training program.

In March, 1943, CSC offered full-time Navy flight training. Navy cadet pilots took courses including navigation, meteorology, aerodynamics, engines, theory of flight, and civil air regulations. The federal government heavily recruited CSC graduates, especially women, for wartime employment. Women at Central also participated in wartime programs including the Women's Accepted Volunteer Emergency Service (WAVES), Women's Army Auxiliary Corps (WAAC), U.S. Coast Guard Women's Reserve, engineering cadet training, and radio technician training.

Even with changes brought on by war, Central continued its original mission of training teachers and educating other students in a host of other programs. Because of a teacher shortage, the State Board of Education authorized the war emergency elementary teaching certificate. Central offered two workshops during the summer term for teachers who wished to qualify.

Students on campus participated in home-front activities in a variety of ways. Students organized a Fats Salvage Drive to collect used fats and oils for making glycerine. The YWCA made cartoon booklets to send to soldiers overseas. Some clubs decided to temporarily suspend activities during wartime. The Arena Club, the oldest debate club on campus, ceased activities because all its members had gone to war.

By the mid-1940s, campus morale improved. Student groups planted trees and shrubs on campus to honor Central's men and women in the service. *The Vista* reported society stories and dances, and the popular gossip column returned. A welcome sight, Central men occupied Thatcher Hall for the first time in two years. Called "The Foxhole University," Central was one of 15 colleges in the Southwest to offer work through the United States Armed Forces Institute.

Formal occasions continued on the Central campus, with the Robinsons hosting the annual president's reception for new students in the recently redecorated Murdaugh Hall in September, 1943. Members of the faculty escorted students from the door to the receiving line that included the Robinsons, Dean Chambers and his wife, and other administrators. The faculty also served punch in the west reception room.

On campus, students organized 75-minute dances each week, even if there was a shortage of men. By December 9, 1944, 841 men and women from Central had joined the military. Naval Flight Training moved into Thatcher Hall, moving the few men on campus into housing in Edmond. Women's sports gained popularity due to no football, track, or men's basketball during the war. In fact, the presence of men on campus was so scarce, that Central presented an all-woman cast of "The Wonder Hat" in February, 1944.

Central's involvement in the war was staggering. More than 1,000 Central students, staff, and faculty members served in the war, with 580 in the Army and 298 in the Navy. Forty-four women served in the WAACs and 11 in the WAVES. *The Vista* reported 42 Centralites killed, 18 missing, and 12 prisoners of war.

Postwar Changes

When the war ended, many veterans took advantage of the G.I. Bill and returned to college campuses. The enrollment swell strained campus facilities and produced unique challenges and unprecedented growth and expansion. Higher education was reinvented following World War II. No longer would students aspire to receive their college degree and return to their hometowns. They wanted to be educated to take advantage of new postwar employment opportunities in defense, industry, and business, especially in the rising Sunbelt states.

The campus reflected the postwar changes occurring across the nation. Enrollment at Central soared to new heights with the largest freshman class to date. Some 600 freshmen enrolled at CSC, equaling the size of the sophomore, junior, and senior classes combined, for a total enrollment of 1,200 students. Veterans made up one third of the student body. Veterans who were not high school graduates took general education development tests as part of their college entrance requirements. Eight CSC faculty members who served during the war returned to campus.

To accommodate the tremendous growth in enrollment following World War II, and with funding from the Federal Housing Agency, Central provided housing units for veterans and their families. Each unit contained a kitchen, breakfast nook, living room, bedroom, and bathroom. Vacant lots near campus were transformed into homes within six months. The veterans' village, named "Centralville," housed forty families with children.

Children of "Centralville," living with their families in married student housing, playing together on campus, 1951. *Courtesy Archives and Special Collections, UCO Library.*

Centralville

By Stephanie Fields, B.A. in History/Museum Studies, 2007

At the end of World War II, many returning veterans headed to college campuses. The G.I. Bill gave former servicemen a $90 monthly allotment while they attended school. In addition, their tuition, fees, and books were provided. In order to receive the assistance, however, ex-servicemen had to enroll in 12 hours during the regular academic semesters, six hours in the summer, and two hours in August. Disabled veterans could obtain additional benefits. CSC welcomed approximately 400 veterans in 1946. The school hired new faculty members, broadened classroom facilities, and prepared to take on as many as 2,500 to 3,000 new students.

Many of the veterans came with families, and Central had to find a way to board them. There had been no previous married student housing so

Homecoming and Football Resume

Homecoming resumed in 1946. Seven football players returned in time for the Bronchos to take second place in its conference by the end of the 1946 season. Basketball returned after a three-year hiatus with an 11-5 season. CSC won the state championship in tennis and baseball and captured second place in track.

One of Central's longstanding traditions, the Golden Jubilee, marking fifty years since graduation, began in 1947 with two members of the first graduating class of 1897, Ida Belt and John Adams. They automatically became charter members of the Half-Century Club.

the families were housed at first on the third floor of Thatcher Hall, then the men's dormitory. Soon, officials built 40 family units on property owned by the school northeast of the campus. Dedicated to G.I.s and their families, the complex was named "Centralville."

The first 20 units built were two-story apartments. The floor plan had a living room and a kitchen/dining room combination on the first floor. The upstairs had two bedrooms and one bath. The second 20 apartments were single story and had a different layout. Even though the units were partially furnished, each family was permitted to decorate as they pleased.

Residents added to the community. The Centralville Wives' Club bought playground equipment and fenced in an area for their children to play. Gardens were planted in nearby vacant lots to provide food. Families held many events in the complex, including Halloween and Christmas celebrations, Easter egg hunts, and birthday parties for the children.

Living in the low-rent apartments gave hundreds of students the opportunity to obtain their education. Only veterans attending CSC were allowed to live in the new housing, and families with children were given preference. Joe C. Jackson, former dean of college and professor of history and political science, and his wife, Enid, were among the residents of Centralville.

The Vista printed several articles focused on veterans and their families. A weekly column reported on new babies born to the tenants of Centralville. Other articles focused on informing veterans about campus issues and answering questions about benefits.

By the 1960s, Centralville was in a state of decay, having served families for nearly 20 years. A new generation of war-boom babies was sweeping the campus and more modern accommodations were needed. In 1964, Centralville was demolished and the new Broncho Apartments was built for married couples and families.

Family housing units for veterans returning from World War II secured through the Federal Housing Agency. Called "Centralville," the village housed 40 families with children. *Courtesy Archives and Special Collections, UCO Library.*

Campus Legends

By Krysta Reith, B.A. in General Studies, 2005

Every college campus is full of urban legends, myths, and ghost stories, and the UCO is no exception. With UCO being one of the oldest schools in Oklahoma, it has its our fair share of spooky stories and tall tales. The stories range from a famous building on campus actually being haunted to the infamous "Lover's Rocks" in Fink Park. These tales live on when students gather to share ghost stories about the untold legends of UCO.

Alumni from the first half of the twentieth century fondly remember their time at Central, and often mention a special place, "Lover's Rocks." Some say the location was just south of campus in what is now Fink Park, while other stories pinpoint the rocks just east of campus.

According to tradition, on Sundays, many male students called upon female companions for a trip to "Lover's Rocks." Couples often carved their initials in the soft, red rocks. The area was said to be about the size of a normal house, flat on top with two crevices perfect for sitting. So the question remains, who moved "Lover's Rocks" and why? Is the continual expansion of UCO the reason for moving "Lover's Rocks" or is there a deeper meaning?

Mitchell Hall has been visited by many famous people, from pilot Amelia Earhart to poet Robert Frost to the famous Oklahoma Indian artist Acee Blue Eagle. The most celebrated guest, however, is not really a guest, but a permanent occupant—Thornton.

Thornton is the Mitchell Hall ghost. Legend has it, he was a janitor who fell from the balcony—others say he was killed in an electrical accident. Whatever the cause of death, Mitchell Hall has a houseguest. Thornton is said to move objects, call for help, and drop pebbles on students. One former UCO student recalled an encounter where he saw Thornton from an upstairs window. He went on to describe Thornton as a "middle-aged man, wearing a heavy coat, like a trench coat, and having medium-length hair."

Many drama and music students place blame on Thornton for things that go wrong during a production. Even though there are no official records of the Mitchell Hall ghost, it still does not explain all the strange occurrences.

Tall tales of any university make life more interesting. Many of these stories may be fabricated, but they add excitement and apprehension to college life. When swapping stories late at night with college roommates, do not forget to include Thornton the Mitchell Hall ghost, or even what became of "Lover's Rocks." These mysteries may one day be solved, but until then they serve as just two of the fascinating legends of UCO.

The most famous ghost story told by UCO students surrounds the haunting of Mitchell Hall. *Courtesy Archives and Special Collections, UCO Library.*

Chapter Four Timeline

1939

• Finnish-Russian War began

• World War II began with German invasion of Poland

• Leon C. Phillips became governor of Oklahoma

• CSTC became Central State College (CSC)

• Roscoe R. Robinson became President of CSC

1940

• Trotsky assassinated in Mexico

• First peacetime military draft in America

• Frank Sinatra scored his first number one hit

• Central begins year long Golden Jubilee celebration for their semi-centennial

1941

• Pearl Harbor

• Oklahoma State Regents for Higher Education (OSRHE) created

• Groundbreaking for "Y" Chapel of Song

• Central won state championship in both football and tennis

1942

• United States entered WWII

• Wartime schedule cut semester to 16 weeks at CSC

• Students move out of Thatcher and Murdaugh Halls so soldiers can move in

• Central opened Army Air Force Training Detachment for clerks

1943

• Zoot-suit Riots in Los Angeles

• Robert S. Kerr became governor of Oklahoma

1945

• International Monetary Fund and World Bank created

• President Roosevelt died; Vice President Harry S. Truman assumed office

• United States dropped atomic bombs on Hiroshima and Nagasaki

• Beginning of the Cold War between Russia and the United States (1945-1989)

1946

• British Prime Minister, Winston Churchill, delivered Iron Curtain speech

• Dr. Benjamin Spock published *The Common Sense Book of Baby and Child Care*

• Two G.I .Bills passed by Congress provided for education of veterans

BELOW: The wait-staff of the Wide-a-Wake Café in front of the building during the 1940s. The café served as a popular hang out for Central students as well as Edmond residents. It was also a popular stop on "Route 66." *Courtesy Archives and Special Collections, UCO Library.*

BELOW: Freshmen orientation at Central during the 1940s. *Courtesy Archives and Special Collections, UCO Library.*

Mary Helen Lillard (passenger side) and a carload of women during the war years. *Courtesy Archives and Special Collections, UCO Library.*

CHAPTER FIVE

The 1950s

Central State College

I lived in Thatcher Hall with Wayne Goodman, my teammate on the football squad.
Our room overlooked what was then the football field, located where Broncho Lake is now.
Gary Lower

Everybody ate all of their meals in Murdaugh Hall. Thatcher Hall didn't have a cafeteria.
So the boys and the girls all ate together. It was in the basement of Murdaugh Hall. It was a really nice atmosphere.
Elaine Lower

Dorms had house mothers who lived in the building. We respected them like our own mothers or grandmothers,
so there was not too much "ornery" stuff, loud noises, and foul language.
Dale Reeder

We had chapel every Wednesday morning at 11:00 a.m. in Mitchell Hall.
Loree Rice

Veterans Return to Campus

The Oklahoma City metro was bustling as part of the postwar growth in Sunbelt cities. With the G.I. Bill and the baby boom, veterans and families flocked to the suburbs, including Edmond, and put greater demands on higher education. Students even came to CSC who did not necessarily want to become teachers. Following a national trend, normal schools such as Central State joined the reconceptualization and growth of normal schools into colleges. In keeping with the times, the *College Bulletin* outlined the unveiling of modern departments: Business Education, Modern Languages, Education, Art, Agriculture, Mathematics, Science, Physical Education for Men, Physical Education for Women, Industrial Arts, Social Sciences, and English.

Students in line for lunch in the Murdaugh Hall cafeteria during the 1950s.
Both Thatcher Hall men and Murdaugh Hall women ate in the cafeteria.
Courtesy Archives and Special Collections, UCO Library.

W. Max Chambers (1949–1960)

On Friday, October 1, 1948, at 6:00 a.m., President Robinson died suddenly of a heart attack. Once news of his untimely death traveled to campus, classes dismissed from Friday through Monday. The funeral was held on the following Monday afternoon in Mitchell Hall. Regents selected Dean George P. Huckaby, a member of the Class of 1929, as acting president. He served in that position for nearly a year.

W. Max Chambers, the fifteenth Central president, served from 1949 to 1960. The present-day library is named in honor of President Chambers. *Courtesy Archives and Special Collections, UCO Library.*

With the arrival of W. Max Chambers as the fifteenth president in 1949, Huckaby resumed his work as dean. A Central graduate from the Class of 1914, Chambers was an outstanding athlete who had lettered in football, baseball, track, and basketball. He was superintendent of the Okmulgee public schools for 18 years before returning to Central as president. President Chambers received his B.A. and M.S. degrees from the University of Oklahoma and his Ed.D. from Colorado State College. His formal inauguration took place at Mitchell Hall on November 13, 1949, with former Central president Charles Evans and Governor Roy J. Turner in attendance. Oklahoma City's WKY-TV filmed the ceremony—the first televised event in Edmond history.

President Chambers is credited with positive changes on campus, but most importantly, he put an end to mandatory political contributions from faculty. Joe Jackson recalls meeting with Chambers in the president's office when a large man entered the room and did not remove his hat. The man said, "I'm from the Democratic Party. We're here to make our annual collection. I will leave these cards with you. You collect the money from your faculty and I'll come by and pick it up."

Chambers shocked the fund raiser when he picked up the huge stack of contribution cards and threw them in a nearby wastebasket. Jackson recalled, "The man turned white and said, 'I wish you hadn't done that!'" Chambers said, "Well, I did it, and as long as I'm president, there will be no forced solicitation of the faculty." Although politicians threatened to fire President Chambers each year of his tenure at Central, they were unsuccessful.

Journalism professor Reba Collins and art professor Kathryn Kunc stopping to talk on campus. *Courtesy Archives and Special Collections, UCO Library.*

Conrad Galey (above and far left), Comanche and a graduate of 1956, majored in marketing at Central State. After graduation, Galey moved to Montana, taught school and received the MBA. During his time in Montana, Northern Cheyenne people introduced him to the Northern Style Grass Dance, and Galey became a champion dancer on the powwow circuit. When he returned to Oklahoma, Galey introduced the Northern style of singing and dancing to the Southern Plains. Galey established a successful Jostens distributorship selling class rings. *Courtesy Conrad Galey.*

Raising Standards and Enrollment

In 1950, CSC received formal acceptance into the North Central Association of Secondary Schools and Colleges. As part of this system, credits earned at Central transferred to other colleges in the association. Prompted by criticism from the North Central Association, Central sought to improve faculty credentials by encouraging professors to return to graduate school. In addition, President Chambers was mindful of the need to hire professors with advanced degrees. By the late 1950s the situation showed marked improvement, with one-third of the faculty possessing doctorates.

Central conformed to new state regulations relative to certification and no longer offered life certificates—a five-year standard certificate was granted instead. Faculty members began cooperative study under the auspices of the North Central Association Study program. Beginning in the 1950s, Central offered a new program leading to a Bachelor of Science degree in nursing education.

In 1951, CSC received approval to offer a limited amount of graduate work that could transfer to the University of Oklahoma or Oklahoma A&M toward a master's degree. During the summer term, more than 100 students enrolled in Central's first graduate courses.

Debate Team

The debate team's activities resumed after World War II. Professor Joe Jackson was hired as debate coach. Cleeta John Rogers and C.H. Spearman, Jr. were standouts. Both later served long terms as members of the Oklahoma Legislature. In 1949, Spearman won both the local and state American Legion Oratorical contests. In 1951, Rogers and Spearman won the senior men's national championship, followed by Royce Hansen who captured the title the following year. Lenore Owens and Joyce Kennedy won the women's national championship. An impressive record helped secure the debate team's reputation as a nationally competitive team.

Kappa Alpha Psi fraternity members and pledges proudly inspect their scholastic trophy presented by Interfraternity Council in 1968. *Courtesy Archives and Special Collections, UCO Library.*

Origins of Greek Life

By Annette Moore Ryan, B.S. in Business, 1964, CSC

The nostalgia of the 1950s hit the CSC campus with a dramatic impact when some of the social clubs became affiliated with National Panhellenic Conference Sororities and Interfraternity Conference Fraternities (NPC). Delta Sigma Epsilon Sorority installed Alpha Omega chapter with ten charter members on April 22, 1950. The National Delta Sigma Epsilon Sorority merged with Delta Zeta in 1956 and became the Epsilon Upsilon Chapter at CSC.

In May, 1950, Beta Mu chapter of Sigma Sigma Sigma Sorority received their Charter and became the second NPC Sorority. Epsilon Sigma chapter of Sigma Kappa Sorority followed in 1959, with the merger of Pi Kappa Sigma and Sigma Kappa. The early Shakespeare Club of 1908 became the Epsilon Nu Chapter of Alpha Gamma Delta Sorority in October, 1960. In 1912, the Criterion Club organized to study literature. Members of the Criterion Club voted to go Greek and became Alpha Omicron Pi Sorority in 1959. Alpha Kappa Alpha joined the Greek Women in 1968 when they formed the Beta Beta Chapter. Alpha Kappa Alpha is one of the nine African American organizations of the National Pan-Hellenic Council.

First on the entry list of National Fraternities, Eta Chapter of Phi Lambda Chi Fraternity came to CSC in 1955, but this chapter later seceded from their National Fraternity to become the local social fraternity of Phi Lambda Nu. Epsilon Sigma Chapter of Tau Kappa Epsilon followed on February 23, 1957. On May 5, 1962, the Phi Lambna Nu social fraternity formed the Zeta Nu Chapter of Alpha Tau Omega Fraternity. Beta Zeta Chapter of Sigma Tau Gamma Fraternity received their charter May 20, 1959.

The Epsilon Gamma Chapter of Kappa Alpha Psi brotherhood of the National Pan-Hellenic Council of African American Greek organizations came to the campus in 1962. The Senate Social Club voted in the spring of 1963 to become affiliated with Acacia Fraternity. Zeta Sigma Chapter of Alpha Phi Alpha Fraternity came to the CSC campus in 1969. In December, 1969, the Kappa Sigma National Fraternity established the Kappa Pi Chapter on campus.

The men and women members of Greek organizations led the way for social and scholastic interaction on the Edmond campus. Introduction of the National Greek System brought motivation for more achievement and excellence among the students. Participation in a structured group environment brought members' social, scholastic, and leadership skills to full fruition.

Much of the social life on campus in the 1950s and 1960s revolved around the sororities and fraternities. A Panhellenic "Ribbon Dance" became a yearly tradition and occurred after Sorority Rush in the fall to introduce new pledges to Greek members. The pledges proudly wore their ribbons at the dance, and the life of a new pledge formally began. Sometimes permanent sorority and fraternity relationships began at the Ribbon Dance. Fraternities serenaded sororities at their houses and official sweetheart pairings were celebrated by the sorority members.

Social etiquette was prevalent. "Tea Tables" and "Reception Lines" were evident during most events. Panhellenic teas and a spring Panhellenic dance occurred annually. Gloves and pearls were still definitely part of the attire of sorority members at formal receptions. The fraternity men wore suits and ties for these occasions. Fraternities also sponsored an annual spring formal dance.

In the early fall semester, freshmen and upperclassmen attended a President's Reception. The students dressed in their best attire and stood in line to shake the president's hand. They would next proceed to the very elegant and formal refreshment table. A state fair-like atmosphere existed on campus yearly as Greek members celebrated homecoming. Members built floats for the homecoming parade, entertained alumni, cheered the football team to victory, and attended an all-college dance in the evening. Sorority candidates vied for homecoming queen and campaigned in the Student Union weeks before election day.

Members of the Greek organizations were encouraged to be active in student government which led to debates and campaigns to win a position on the Student Government Board.

Teas, receptions, and polite conversational skills were a traditional part of Greek organizations until the late 1960s when the nostalgic gave way to the complex stages of rebellion and political leanings. Students began to protest rules and regulations creating upheaval for the Greek faculty sponsors and Alumni Advisory Boards. A "new age" slipped onto the campus, but the students of the Greek system held on to their traditional ideals and hopes for a brighter future.

Greeks began to negotiate for chapter houses in 1959. All Greek members originally lived in Murdaugh or Thatcher halls and had their meetings at a designated place on campus. In the 1960s hopes for a "Greek Row" on east Chowning Street existed. Two sororities, Delta Zeta and Sigma Kappa, and the Kappa Sigma fraternity purchased land and built houses on east Chowning Street. Alpha Gamma Delta built

a new home on Jackson Street. Other Greeks leased or bought large residential homes close to the campus. Sigma Sigma Sigma Sorority leased a home at 200 East Campbell in 1959. President Garland Godfrey and his family lived on the bottom floor of the Tri Sigma house during the renovation of the president's home in the summer of 1960.

Greek life demanded time and great effort from members in order for chapters to survive. There were struggles to maintain membership, fill a house, and meet scholarship criteria of the campus Panhellenic and Interfraternity councils. Some of the chapters experienced hardships and did not survive. However, time has proven the value of Central's Greek organizations. Philanthropy endeavors sponsored by the fraternities and sororities have touched lives all across America. Area service organizations and institutions receive the benefits of Greeks who support local community projects. Alumni members return to the campus often and most remain active in alumni chapters.

University deans, faculty sponsors, and housemothers contributed greatly to the growth of Central's Greek system. Dedicated alumni served on chapter advisory boards as liaisons between national councils and campus administration in the maintenance of high social standards.

Students enjoyed the Greek Sorority/Fraternity Ribbon Dance in the first Student Union, 1958, located in the center of campus. Currently, the space houses the Art Building, showcasing the Melton Gallery, a campus treasure. *Courtesy Archives and Special Collections, UCO Library.*

Celebration of Central's 60th year began with two big days—Charles Wantland Day and Homecoming Day. On October 27, 1950, more than 300 former Central athletes from all over the country gathered on campus to honor Coach Wantland, athletic director and football coach of Central from 1912 to 1930. Wantland had worked with four Central presidents, Charles Evans, Grant B. Grumbine, James W. Graves, and John G. Mitchell, who attended as honored guests. Dr. Orin Stuterville of Evanston, Illinois, gave $300 to establish a Wantland Scholarship for Central athletes.

Homecoming Day, October 28, 1950, was filled with the typical festivities of a parade, football game, buffet supper, and dance. It also offered the new Alumni Friendship Tent. Under the tent, alumni board members served doughnuts and coffee throughout the day. Three alumni from the 1900 class—Lyda Hart Hall, B. S. Haug, and Angie Lynch Butcher—were present for their golden anniversary celebration. At the buffet supper a six-tiered birthday cake was cut by Central's first lady, Myrna Chambers, a Central graduate of the Class of 1934.

The cake presented at the Diamond Jubilee celebration in 1950 honored Central's sixtieth anniversary. *Courtesy Archives and Special Collections, UCO Library.*

Dean Joe C. Jackson

By Kathi Nehls, B.A. in History, 2005

For more than seventy years, Joe C. Jackson spent time in Oklahoma classrooms and even at ninety-three years of age, Dr. Jackson continued to teach occasional classes at his church. Born in Berwin, Oklahoma, now the town of Gene Autry, Jackson was the first member of his community to graduate from high school. He later worked his way through the University of Oklahoma where he majored in English, History, and Political Science and received his B.A. in 1934. Before assuming his first teaching position at Sulphur High School, Jackson married his high school sweetheart Enid; it was a union that would last sixty-eight plus years. Jackson taught for several years at Sulfur and after completing his Master's degree at OU in 1940 accepted a position as principal of Bristow High School. In addition to his administrative responsibilities, he coached the debate team and taught classes at the local junior college.

During his eleven years at the Creek County High School, he coached several championship debate teams and drew the attention of Central's president R.R. Robinson. In 1948, while working on his doctorate at OU, Robinson offered Jackson a teaching position if he would coach the University's debate team. Jackson recalled it was his ability as a coach that got him the position at Central. "He would not have hired me as a professor of history and government. Coaching debate is what got me the job." Among his first recruits were C. H. Spearman and Cleeta John Rogers and within three years Central had a championship team. Under Jackson's tutelage, the team went on to compete in national tournaments at West Point where they faced Ivy League schools, never finishing lower than quarterfinals. As successful as Jackson was with the debate teams, it was coaching of a different kind that occupied most of his twenty-eight years at Central.

Dr. Joe Jackson served as the Dean of the College from 1951 until 1969 when he became the Vice President for Academic Affairs. He helped to change the name of Central State College to Central State University from the late 1960s until it finally passed in 1971. *Courtesy Archives and Special Collections, UCO Library.*

Called to the phone one afternoon in 1950, Jackson heard a voice on the other end of the line say, "I'd like to speak to the Dean of the College please." He replied, "Well sir, we don't have a Dean of the College right now. I suggest you call Dr. Chambers." Jackson remembered a laugh at the other end of line, "This is Max Chambers, the board elected you Dean of the College today." Chambers continued, "Let me know at the end of the day if you'll take it or not." Jackson recalled being scared to death by the offer, and walked into Dr. Chambers' office intent on declining the position. Chambers greeted Jackson with "Hello Mr. Dean." Jackson replied, "I'll take it." Between 1951 and 1976 when Jackson finally retired, he served as Dean of the College and later as the University's Vice President of Academic Affairs.

During his long tenure as Dean, Jackson considered the day in 1971, when Central State College became Central State University his single most important accomplishment. C.H. Spearman, Jackson's former debate student, by then

a state legislator, sponsored the bill to change the school's status. Jackson and Spearman looked on together while Governor David Hall signed the bill officially changing the college to a university. Jackson, in a 2004 interview said, "Now, here is where I am real proud of myself – right here. The day after we were made a university – by name- Dr. Godfrey called me in and said, 'Dean Jackson' – he always called me Dean Jackson for some reason or other – he said, 'Dean Jackson, I know and you know we're no different today than we were yesterday. We were not a university yesterday and we are not a university now. We're Central State College now, although our name is Central State University.' He said, 'I want you to do what's necessary to organize the faculty and make us a university.'" Jackson recalled hiring about fifty new faculty members, most of them holding doctorates, reorganizing departments into schools, and upgrading curriculum.

For more than a quarter of a century Jackson steered the academic course of the university and recalled that Central weathered the challenging years of the late 1950s and 1960s with relative calm. His efforts on behalf of higher education extended beyond his responsibilities at the University and included oversight of the development of Oklahoma's junior college system. For both his role at Central and his work throughout the state, Jackson was recognized in 1996 when he was inducted into the Oklahoma Educator's Hall of Fame. Jackson's part in the development of post-graduate education at Central was also memorialized on April 24, 2002, when in recognition of his efforts in building the university's graduate program and his many years of service as the school's chief academic officer, President Roger Webb dedicated the Joe C. Jackson College of Graduate Studies and Research.

When asked how he wished to be remembered by future Bronchos, Jackson thought for a moment and said, "Well, I would correct some mistakes that I made and do some things a little different than I did, but I would still be a teacher – still be a teacher. The most important people in Oklahoma are the people that are teaching these kids – college, university, kindergarten whatever it is – the most important people in the world. . . And that is what I have attempted to do over the years. I wouldn't change a thing."

The Korean War

During the Korean War, enrollment at CSC declined by 25 percent as many male students interrupted their studies to enlist. "The urge to beat the draft board to the draw," Chambers stated, "has resulted in a considerable exodus of young men to the recruiting offices of the Navy and Air Force. Other young men are taking advantage of offers to work in war industries. Young women have found their wedding dates stepped up to coincide with troop training assignments. Young men and women have left the college classrooms in unusual numbers due to the influence of national defense activity." Students were not the only ones who served. Football coach Dale Hamilton, captain in the 45th Division, requested a leave of absence to serve two years in Korea.

To sustain CSC during the Korean War, President Chambers contracted with the Defense Department to establish an Air Force clerk-typist school on campus. Thatcher Hall served as barracks for the trainees. Faculty members were assigned to teach the new curriculum. Class work for the first group of 25 began April 23, 1951. A new group arrived each week and stayed 12 weeks. The trainees marched from place to place on campus. A popular cadence as they marched went like this, "I've got a girl in Murdaugh Hall, all she will say is 'Hi you all.'"

Financing Higher Education

Financing higher education continued to be problematic in the 1950s. Investigating the old charge that Oklahoma had too many institutions of higher learning, State Regents discovered that Oklahoma was eighteenth in the nation in total number of institutions, twenty-fourth in total number of senior colleges in ratio to number of college-age residents, twenty-fifth in total number of senior and junior colleges in ratio to number of college-age residents, and twenty-seventh in the number of institutions in proportion to the total area.

In 1955, to address outdated facilities on college campuses throughout the state, the state legislature passed a capital improvement measure that provided more than $13 million to update higher education facilities. Student fees also increased to keep pace with rising educational costs.

By the late 1950s, hundreds of Central students took advantage of federal student loans. Under the National Defense Act, students could receive loans if they planned to teach or demonstrated skill in science, math, engineering, or foreign languages.

Building Projects

During the final five years of President Chambers' administration, a period of unprecedented growth began. Plans were made to build a new gymnasium, cafeteria, two

During the Korean War soldiers came to Central's campus to participate in the Air Force clerk-typist school. Similar to the situation following World War II, CSC's enrollment rebounded following the Korean War in 1953 as veterans returned to college campuses. *Courtesy Archives and Special Collections, UCO Library.*

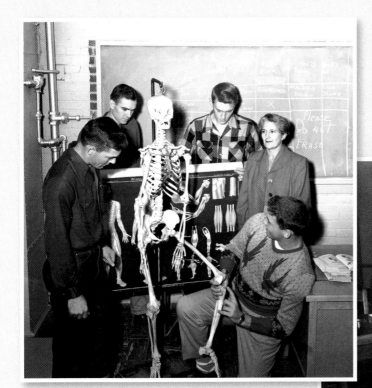

Emma Plunkett (left), professor of physical education, and Ethel Derrick (below), professor of biology, dedicated their careers to teaching students at Central. Derrick is pictured here with Bob Loomis. *Courtesy Archives and Special Collections, UCO Library.*

dormitories, home economics facility, another classroom building, and extensions to the industrial arts and science buildings. In order for the campus to accommodate student demand, the physical boundaries of the campus needed to expand. Chambers had outlined a plan for campus expansion, including plans for new buildings, but lacked sufficient funds.

Howell Hall

Housed in cramped quarters of the Administration Building for decades, the science faculty had been advocating a new science building since the 1930s. Howell Hall, the new science building constructed during the late 1940s, represented the first classroom building project since 1914. Ernest Howell had joined the faculty at Central in 1919 and taught all physics courses during the 1920s and 1930s. He headed the science department for more than two decades before he died unexpectedly in March, 1941. The new science building, located east of Wantland Hall, was named in his memory.

Plans called for two wings of Howell Hall—the West Wing to house biology and chemistry, and the East Wing to house physics. Delays in obtaining building materials caused biology and chemistry classes in fall 1947 to meet in the older Administration Building quarters. A year later,

biology and chemistry classes moved into Howell Hall, and construction began on the East Wing. The new facility for physics and photography contained laboratories with modern equipment. The basement housed aviation and geology. By the early 1950s, biology, chemistry, physics, photography, agriculture, and home economics were all taught in the science building.

Y-Chapel of Song

The project of building a small chapel on the CSC campus began under the leadership of Dr. Jessie D. Newby, Latin professor, and the YWCA in April, 1941, with their initial gift of more than $1,500. The project was put on hold during World War II. But eight years later, with $28,000 in private contributions from fundraisers, construction on the chapel began.

The construction of Y-Chapel was completed in June, 1949. On November 23 of that year, faculty, students, and alumni placed a time capsule marking Central's first 50 years in a concrete crypt in the southwest corner of the chapel, with instructions that read, "To be opened by the president of Central State College when its Centennial Anniversary is celebrated in 1991."

The first wedding in the new chapel occurred on January 26, 1950, when Wayne Nichols married Gae Marie England. Coincidentally, the bridesmaids wore bronze and blue satin dresses.

During the 1950s, CSC also sponsored a Religious Emphasis Week, with many of the guest lectures and faculty and student seminars taking place in the Y-Chapel.

Remodeling and Renovation

CSC remodeled and refurbished several buildings on campus and constructed four more. Major additions included a student union, library, and fine arts building. Dorms were filled to capacity. As part of the state legislature's capital improvement measure, CSC received $400,000 from a state building bond issue and began a program of modernization and repair.

Plans included remodeling the Administration Building and adding outside Venetian blinds. The remodeling of Mitchell Hall produced an unwanted result when Acee

Student Ray Gilliand creating the Knight window for the Y-Chapel in 1948. The stained glass windows in the Y-Chapel have helped to beautify the campus since the 1940s. *Courtesy Archives and Special Collections, UCO Library.*

Blue Eagle's WPA murals on the interior walls were covered with blue paint as part of the redecorating process. A new lighting and public address system and new bronze and blue stage curtains were installed in Mitchell Hall. Old North Tower and Murdaugh Hall also were remodeled.

Other renovations included the reflooring of Central Field Stadium. College Street was extended from Mitchell Hall to Old North Tower and widened ten feet by the city of Edmond to allow for parking spaces. The Student Center opened in an old building north of the stadium, and included a book exchange, a "juke box," and an area for ping pong and other games and cold drink and candy vending machines.

Student involvement was visible in every inch of the chapel, from the slabs of elm wood they carved for the ends of the pews, to the glazed and fired ceramic tile for the walls. Students designed and crafted the 15 stained-glass windows, each representing a song. *Courtesy Archives and Special Collections, UCO Library.*

In 1949, Central students and staff, as well as Edmond residents, placed a time capsule in concrete in the southwest corner of the Y-Chapel with plans to open it in 1991 during Central's centennial. *Courtesy Archives and Special Collections, UCO Library.*

LEFT: Winifred Stayton taught third grade and supervised student teachers in Room 204 of Old North Tower for thirty-one years. *Courtesy Archives and Special Collections, UCO Library.*

Campus Expansion Continues

During the 1950s, campus expansion continued with the school's first Student Union building, fine arts building, and an addition to the Industrial Arts building. Construction for the new student union, a $250,000 structure strategically placed in the center of campus, south of Murdaugh Hall and west of the stadium, began in 1951. Plans for the modern building included a ballroom, living room, rooms for student clubs and the Alumni Association, modern fountain, bowling alley, bookstore, post office, and barber and beauty shops.

Central broke from the tradition of naming buildings after past officials and named the new library—a $500,000 structure with central air conditioning and capacity for 100,000 books—for the current president Max Chambers in 1957.

The Health and Physical Education building, a combination activity, classroom and canteen building, was constructed. In addition, the Baptist Student Union replaced its old building with a new student center on the same site located at the south end of campus.

In 1953, Central State began building a new circle drive and a parking area west of Old North and Evans Hall. Many older Edmond residents lamented when the last of the trees planted on the campus in 1896 finally died. Dr. Mell A. Nash, chancellor of the State Board of Regents of Higher Education and Central alumnus, donated 30 elm trees to take the place of those lost.

By 1955, with enrollment topping 1,456, President Chambers continued his appeal to regents for funds to continue campus expansion, including providing more parking. The college already had purchased property north of Thatcher Hall for parking and the process of purchasing vacant land adjacent to the campus continued during the late 1950s.

Graduate College

CSC administrators and faculty held many formal and informal discussions concerning the development of a fifth year of study for teachers. During the early 1950s, there were 17,000 teachers in Oklahoma. In Central's district, two-thirds of teachers did not possess a Master's Degree. Because the state provided funding and support for public schools to encourage teachers to have the fifth year of training, CSC anticipated the need and provided summer programs for teachers seeking Master's Degrees.

During the early 1950s, OU faculty members taught summer graduate courses at Central. Students taking the graduate courses could then transfer to OU or OSU to complete the Master's Degree. President Chambers called it "the most definite step of progress our institution has made since 1919, when Central State was first made into a four-year college."

On April 27, 1953, the Oklahoma State Regents for Higher Education authorized CSC, along with the other five regional institutions, to offer the Master of Teaching degree, a fifth-year teacher training program leading to the Master's Degree in Education. The schools first had to gain approval and direction from the North Central Association. In September, 1953, Central submitted its request for a master's program during a self-survey to North Central. Norman Burns of North Central responded with hesitation, citing "competence of the faculty" as one of the major reasons. And yet, the letter continued, "The college should feel free to proceed with the instruction of the program if it wishes to do so." Central did proceed.

The first meeting of the Fifth Year Council, later called the Graduate Council, met February 18, 1954, with President Chambers presiding. Other members included Joe Jackson, E. C. Hall, and Guy Chambers. The first student, Goldi Oldham Jones, was admitted to the new Fifth Year Teacher Training Program, for the Master of Teaching Degree, April 1, 1954. Jones received her undergraduate degree from Central in 1938 and her life certificate for teaching in 1949.

The new program directly sparked enrollment, with 125 students enrolling in the new graduate program in the summer of 1954. The first class of 27 students graduated with the Master of Teaching Degree in the summer of 1955.

Students in the first Student Union in 1958. *Courtesy Archives and Special Collections, UCO Library.*

The first African American students at Central State College were graduate students (top row, from left) Addie Lee Jordan, Corean Armstrong, Lanita Burton, and Gertrude Dulan, (bottom row, from left) Mamie Ealey, and Elizabeth Hilton Threatt in 1954. *Courtesy Archives and Special Collections, UCO Library.*

African American Students and Higher Education

In the late 1940s and early 1950s, decisions by the United States Supreme Court, based upon cases involving Oklahoma students such as Ada Lois Sipuel, required graduate school programs to be opened to African American students. In 1954, the Supreme Court, in *Brown v. Board of Education of Topeka*, found that separate but equal educational facilities were inherently unequal and overturned the Plessy decision of 1896. The Brown decision desegregated public education in the primary and secondary schools and undergraduate education in Oklahoma.

The first African American students at CSC were graduate students pursuing their Master's Degree in teaching. In the fall of 1954, Addie Lee Jordan of Oklahoma City and five other women, Corean Armstrong, Lanita Burton, Gertrude Dulan, Mamie Ealey, and Elizabeth Hilton Threatt, became the first African American graduate students to attend Central.

Burton, Ora, *Luther*
Busch, Robert, Jr., *Oklahoma City*
Butler, Murray, *Oklahoma City*
Calaway, Bob, *Edmond*
Callicoat, Doyle, *Oklahoma City*

Murray Butler (center), Alberta Eddens, and Olivia Nash were the first African American undergraduate students at Central State College in 1955. *Courtesy Archives and Special Collections, UCO Library.*

Reba Collins

By Jennifer Collins, B.A. in History, 2005

My grandmother, Dr. Reba Collins, was born in August, 1925, in Shawnee, Oklahoma. Facing social expectations to stay at home and raise her three children, she chose to return to school as a middle-aged woman. During these tremendous challenges, she reached heights in her career she never had dreamed. On her journey from a high school dropout to a Professor Emeritus at UCO, she had a most interesting life.

Collins began classes at Central State College in 1955. Before she graduated with a journalism degree in 1957, she had been editor of *The Vista* and received the Outstanding Future Teacher Award from Delta Kappa Gamma. While working as an instructor at CSC, she attended graduate school at Oklahoma State University and received her M.A. and Ph.D. in journalism.

Her master's thesis at OSU traced the history of *The Vista* and her doctoral dissertation examined Will Rogers, the legendary writer and journalist. When she became head of Public Relations for CSC, she was one of only eight women in the United States to hold such a university position. At the same time, she lobbied the Oklahoma Legislature to change CSC from a college to a university.

In 1975, Collins became director of the Will Rogers Memorial in Claremore, Oklahoma. Drawing on her expertise, she wrote eight books on Will Rogers, received many awards, and served as an adviser for the "Will Rogers Follies." In 1990, Collins retired at the age of 65.

Even in retirement she worked tirelessly writing two columns for the *Edmond Sun* and *Bethany Tribune*, and book reviews for *The Daily Oklahoman*. She held the titles of Professor Emeritus at UCO and Director Emeritus of the Will Rogers Memorial. She received many accolades for her historical writing—Oklahoma Journalism Hall of Fame in1998, UCO Family of the Year Award in 2004, and Historic Preservation Award from the City of Edmond in 2004.

Growing up, I knew that my grandmother was an important person, but I never appreciated everything she was able to do until I entered UCO as a student in the spring of 2002. I cannot even dream of being able to influence people's lives as she did when she taught at UCO, but I can work hard for the things that I want by using her life as an example.

My grandmother was a woman of diverse accomplishment and great achievement. I am blessed to have had her in my life, just as UCO is blessed to be able to claim her.

Journalism Professors (left to right) Reba Collins, Ray Tassin, Henry Hunt and Stan Hoig at the old flat bed printing press in the CSC print shop in 1967. *Courtesy Archives and Special Collections, UCO Library.*

Athletics

The men's basketball team captured the conference title in 1954. In 1955, the football team had its best season since 1942, as tri-champions of the conference. A major factor in the team's success was tackle Harold Cook, senior social studies major from Oklahoma City, named to the NAIA All-American team. The women's basketball team, including Virginia Peters, shared the state championship with Oklahoma A&M and Phillips University in 1954. Women's field hockey and volleyball also took top honors in 1954 and 1955.

Two CSC alumni joined the athletic department. Al Blevins, an outstanding passing quarterback at Central during the late 1940s, and a letterman in basketball and baseball, replaced Jim Tyner as head basketball coach in

Swimmers gathered in front of the Mermaid mural located in Wantland Hall in 1953. *Courtesy Archives and Special Collections, UCO Library.*

Football coach Dale Hamilton huddled with his players, 1953. In 1958, Dale Hamilton stepped down as head football coach and assumed the post of athletic director. During his 12 years as head football coach in the late 1940s and 1950s, Hamilton posted a stunning 75-24-5 record, and was named to the NAIA Football Hall of Fame. *Courtesy Archives and Special Collections, UCO Library.*

In 1957, Homecoming Queen Elaine Lower was crowned with a football helmet. Elaine wore the football helmet for the rest of the game, cheering on the Bronchos. "You sat out there in all your finery and watched the rest of the football game and supported the team," she remarked in a 2004 oral history interview. The following year, a new tradition began as the homecoming queen received a tiara rather than the traditional football helmet. *Courtesy Archives and Special Collections, UCO Library.*

1957. Blevins also served as backfield coach for football and as an instructor in the physical education department. A year later, Blevins succeeded Hamilton as head football coach. John Smith replaced Blevins as head basketball coach and served as assistant football and tennis coach.

President Chambers Retires

After 11 years of service as president of Central, President Chambers retired in June, 1960. "Every aspect of the campus has been influenced by Dr. Chambers' progressive and protective touch," *The Vista* lauded, in an article announcing his retirement. It was true. With Chambers at the helm, CSC experienced significant growth in enrollment, faculty, and new construction. At age 67, perhaps President Chambers could have continued to lead CSC forward, but chose to take advantage of a new retirement policy instituted by state regents.

RIGHT: A reception for President Max Chambers was held in the President's house located on campus, 1952. *Courtesy Archives and Special Collections, UCO Library.*

1959 Homecoming Queen DeLois Neal parading in a convertible on Central Field during the homecoming football game. *Courtesy Archives and Special Collections, UCO Library.*

The 1958 Homecoming football game with Thatcher Hall in the background. *Courtesy Archives and Special Collections, UCO Library.*

The College of Liberal Arts Since the 1950s

By Melissa Brodt, B.A. in History, 2006

Since the 1950s the College of Liberal Arts (CLA) has witnessed significant changes in its organizational structure and academic programs. During the 1950s and 1960s the CLA was called the Division of Language Arts and Humanities. Before the construction of the present-day Liberal Arts building in 1969, the Division of Language Arts and Humanities classrooms were spread out across campus. The Social Studies Department held its classes primarily in Evans Hall, while the English and Languages Departments were housed in the Old South Administration building.

Dr. Guy C. Chambers served as chair of the Division of Language Arts and Humanities in the 1950s and 1960s. After his retirement, Dr. Frank Finney, a professor in the English Department, assumed the position.

In 1968, due to the efforts of the Edmond Urban Renewal Authority, a tract of land was purchased by Central to serve as the future site of the Liberal Arts and Humanities building. In July, 1969, faculty and students were able to move into the new building. Finally, all departments were under one roof.

The English department experienced a first for Central in 1969 when Dr. Frank Finney hired Paul Lehman as Central State's first African American faculty member.

On April 15, 1971, Governor David Hall signed a bill that changed the status of Central State from a college to a university. With that change came a reorganization of the schools within the university. The Division of Language Arts and Humanities became the School of Liberal Arts.

In 1971, the School of Liberal Arts named its first dean. During Dr. Frank Finney's 13 years as dean, he oversaw the development of stronger programs and curriculum in the School of Liberal Arts. He worked closely with the faculty to develop fair teaching loads. Upon the death of Dr. Finney in 1984, Dr. Frank Wert was named the new Dean of Liberal Arts. Under Dr. Wert's leadership, Liberal Arts underwent reorganization from school to college. Dr. Wert also instituted a policy for the promotion of faculty members.

Under Dean Wert, the College of Liberal Arts had 13 disciplines that included Foreign Language, Humanities, History, Music, Creative Studies, Visual Arts, Communication, English, and Sociology.

With the appointment of Dr. Clifton Warren as dean in 1986, more changes began to take place in the College of Liberal Arts. Dean Warren established a ten-year plan that set standards for each department within the College of Liberal Arts and aided in the development of the future needs of each discipline. After serving 14 years as the Dean of the College of Liberal Arts, Dr. Warren stepped down from his post and Dr. T.H. Baughman, a professor of history, assumed the position, continuing the tradition of academic rigor.

In 2001, the College of Arts, Media and Design was formed with Dr. Christopher L. Markwood as dean. Dr. Markwood previously had been the Assistant Dean of the College of Liberal Arts since 1996. The formation of the College of Arts, Media and Design took several programs away from the College of Liberal Arts and placed them in the newly-formed college. These four departments were the Department of Art, the Department of Design, the Department of Music, and the Department of Theatre, Dance and Media Arts. The new college was formed with the mission of providing for the development of excellence in the fine arts, arts education, and the performing arts.

After four years, Dr. Baughman left the position of dean to focus on teaching and research. He was replaced by Dr. Pamela Washington, a professor in the English Department and the Associate Dean of the Liberal Arts College. Under Dean Washington's leadership, the College of Liberal Arts continues to strengthen its programs and to encourage students to become active in opportunities that expand their scholarly goals.

Since the 1950s, the College of Liberal Arts has seen many changes, but the one thing that always remains steadfast is the college commitment to helping students learn.

Under the leadership of Dean Cliff Warren, the College of Liberal Arts established the *New Plains Review*, a journal that features student research, and the prestigious artist-in-residence program. *Courtesy Archives and Special Collections, UCO Library.*

Chapter Five Timeline

1947

• India gained independence

• Truman Doctrine and Marshall Plan

• Jackie Robinson became the first African American on a major league
  baseball team

• Roy J. Turner became governor of Oklahoma

• Central accepted into the North Central Association of Secondary
  Schools and Colleges

1948

• Establishment of the Jewish state, Israel

• Berlin blockade began (1948-1949)

• Gandhi assassinated in India

• George P. Huckaby became acting President of CSC after Robinson dies

• Sipuel v. Board of Regents of University of Oklahoma opened black
  admission to law schools nationwide

• The Board of Regents of Oklahoma Colleges (BOROC) created

• Construction of Y Chapel of Song

1949

• Chinese Revolution ended

• Greek Civil War ended

• North Atlantic Treaty Organization (NATO) created

• Max Chambers became President of CSC

• Completion of Howell Hall (Science Building) at CSC

1950

• Korean War started

• Senator Joseph McCarthy began anti-Communist crusade

• *McLauren v. Oklahoma State Regents* integrated Oklahoma graduate schools

• Cover-up of Acee Blue Eagle's Murals in Mitchell Hall at CSC

• CSC received formal acceptance into the North Central Association of
  Secondary Schools and College

• Celebration of Central's 60th anniversary

1951

• First television broadcast of *I Love Lucy!*

• Johnston Murray became governor of Oklahoma

• Central State College approved for limited graduate work

• Air Force clerk-typist school established on campus

1952

• Dwight D. Eisenhower elected President of the United States

• *The Today Show* aired on NBC

• Completion of the Art and Music Buildings at Central State College

1953

• Student Health Center opened at Central State College

• Merle Keyser completed a Mural of Mermaids in Wantland Hall

• Central authorized to offer the Master's of Teaching degree for the first time

1954

• Dien Bien Phu fell to Vietminh

• Army-McCarthy hearings ended

• *Brown v. Board of Education* ruled segregated schools unequal

Women students prepare for a 1955 dance in the Student Union. *Courtesy Archives and Special Collections, UCO Library.*

Students in the reception area of Murdaugh Hall preparing for a formal dance on campus. *Courtesy Archives and Special Collections, UCO Library.*

1955

• James Dean starred in *Rebel Without a Cause*

• Raymond D. Gary became Governor of Oklahoma

1956

• Hungarian Revolt

• Suez Crisis

• Riots in Poland

• Elvis Presley signed with RCA

1957

• Ghana became the first sub-Saharan African independent nation

• Space Race began when Soviets launched Sputnik

• Completion of Max Chambers Library at CSC, later the Communications Building

1958

• Completion of the Physical Education Building at CSC

1959

• Fidel Castro took over Cuba

• J. Howard Edmondson became governor of Oklahoma

A Central couple makes a purchase at the concession stand located in the Broncho Theater in 1958. *Courtesy Archives and Special Collections, UCO Library.*

ABOVE: The inside cover of the 1956 *Bronze Book*.

Central

CHAPTER SIX

The Building Years

Central State College

*In all of my speeches, I always argued that education is an investment, not an expenditure.
I would want my legacy to be that we upgraded the level of faculty, the level of students, and the level of the entire campus.*
President Garland Godfrey

*There was a closeness on campus. During the Godfrey years, there were times when Mrs. Godfrey would ask
six or eight women to her home for coffee or tea and doughnuts or sandwiches.
It was informal, yet lovely. She was a wonderful lady.*
Kathryn Kunc

*We were a very small faculty, you knew everybody, and soon I knew all the teachers.
When I'd go over to the old student union, there was one little cubby hole where they had a teacher's table,
and the teachers would invite me to have coffee with them. I was older, and I enjoyed visiting with them.
And teachers really cared.*
Reba Collins

Edmond

The unprecedented growth of Edmond in the 1960s, according to historian Stan Hoig, transformed the once "small provincial town into an urban community." In fact, Hoig has called Edmond's rapid growth during the 1960s the second "land rush," reminiscent of the land run days of 1889.

In 1940, Edmond was a small college town of some 4,000 residents. By the 1960s, Edmond had become a suburb of Oklahoma City boasting a population of nearly 9,000. Many Edmond residents worked at Tinker Air Force Base and traveled Interstate Highway 35 to commute to their jobs.

Bedroom communities such as Edmond cropped up throughout the United States as families strived to create safe havens to raise their children in the Cold War era. By 1963, Edmond had eight grade schools, a dozen churches, and public amenities such as a hospital, theater, swimming pool, and several parks, making it an attractive location for young families. Boulevard remained a two-lane road south of Fourth Street, and Broadway Avenue remained a two-lane road from the south edge of town to Britton Road.

Most businesses were found along the two blocks of Broadway north of Second Street. Hoig wrote, "Curbed streets were rare west of the railroad tracks; traffic lights were few and far between; the choice of eating

The Red Chimney Restaurant, located across the street from Mitchell Hall, was a popular student hangout in 1963. *Courtesy Archives and Special Collections, UCO Library.*

establishments was quite limited; frame houses still outnumbered brick ones; and most people attended church on Sunday."

City planners remained optimistic about growth, particularly the most rapid development in southeast Edmond. Once the new sewer disposal plant was ready, the western portion of Edmond opened to further development.

The rapid growth and development in Edmond mirrored unprecedented growth of the Central campus. During the 1960s, CSC transitioned from a teacher's college to a prosperous, diversified commuter college. Course offerings, including evening courses, accommodated the changing student body filled with students who worked at least part-time and often full-time. All Oklahoma colleges and universities grew in student body during this time, but Central demonstrated the most marked growth of all the higher educational institutions in Oklahoma, climbing from 4,300 students in 1960 to 10,600 students in 1970.

As the sixteenth president of Central State College from 1960 to 1975, Garland Godfrey oversaw the expansion of the campus through new buildings as well as increased student enrollment. *Courtesy Archives and Special Collections, UCO Library.*

Garland Godfrey (1960-75)

Garland Godfrey assumed the helm at Central State at a time of great change. With baby boomers flocking to college and university campuses in a national trend never seen before, administrators had to act quickly to respond to the demand. Buildings needed to be constructed to provide classroom space for the new students. More instructors were needed. For a small campus such as Central—29 acres—the response was clear. In order to meet this new demand, the campus must expand.

Born in 1909 five miles outside of Magazine, Arkansas, Godfrey was the fifth of eight children in a large farm family, and the only one who obtained a college education. He took his first teaching job in a rural school when he was 17 years old. "When I'd finished eleventh grade in high school," Godfrey recalled in an oral history interview in 2004, "I took the county examination and taught one summer term, two months in Shady Grove, Arkansas, then I went back and finished my high school, twelfth grade, then I taught the next two months in the summer, and six months in the winter before I entered college at Arkansas Tech in 1929."

During the early 1930s when he was in his early 20s, Godfrey received his B.A. in history and his M.A. in English from Oklahoma A&M. He met his wife, Jocille Morris Godfrey, in the First Baptist Church choir in Stillwater, where she was a senior in high school. For the next 25 years, Godfrey continued to teach and coach in rural schools, gaining experience as principal and then superintendent at Pryor for 17 years and Durant for 8 years.

While superintendent of schools at Pryor, Godfrey developed a friendship with Oliver Hodge, State Superintendent of Public Instruction and a member of the Board of Regents for Oklahoma Colleges. In fact, Godfrey had aspirations to serve as president of one of the regional colleges, but Hodge encouraged him to receive his doctorate first. Godfrey complied and received his doctorate in education from Oklahoma State University in 1957.

The Board of Regents selected Godfrey to replace retiring President Chambers in 1959. Chambers' retirement announcement and Godfrey's appointment came at the same board meeting in January, 1960. Therefore, plans could be made for an orderly change in the presidency, the first time in the history of the institution for this to occur.

The transition between the Chambers and Godfrey administrations was smooth. Godfrey served as president of Central for 15 years, the longest term to that point. After the lengthy history of short presidential terms in Central's early years, the Godfrey tenure followed by President Bill Lillard's 20 years of service, marked an era of continuity during a time of dramatic social change.

Students could view a movie for less than one dollar, including refreshment, during the 1950s and early 1960s at the Broncho Theater. *Courtesy Archives and Special Collections, UCO Library.*

The Broncho Drive-In served as a curb service café during the 1960s. *Courtesy Archives and Special Collections, UCO Library.*

As Godfrey took the helm, he faced great challenges: the need for more faculty and staff, higher salaries, additional classroom space, and student housing. Godfrey projected needs based on a student population of 7,500 in 25 years but the school surpassed that figure in the next decade.

When the Godfreys arrived on campus, they made temporary quarters in the women's dorm before moving into the 40-year old president's house. Their two daughters, Miriam and Anna Lee, had recently married. Their two sons, Joe Bill and John, both high school students, lived at home.

Godfrey evaluated the Central campus classroom buildings, from Old North to the buildings quickly constructed following World War II. He also noted two overcrowded dormitories built in the 1930s, a student union, auditorium, mini-gymnasium, called the "Snake Pit" by basketball fans, and a stadium "so small that fans overflowed onto the sidelines and into the mud and snow, even behind the goal posts."

Parking on campus was a great concern. Students and faculty parked on the oval in front of Old North and behind the stadium. Edmond residents complained that student cars blocked their driveways and took up space in front of their homes.

BELOW: During the 1960s, the football field stood in the middle of campus near the dorms. The 1962 football team went undefeated and went on to win the National Intercollegiate Championship. *Courtesy Archives and Special Collections, UCO Library.*

Athletics

In 1962, Central State's football team appeared to be on the verge of its first bowl bid after a successful season, but a final game loss to unrated Panhandle A&M College killed those hopes. In post-season play in 1962, the Broncho football team won the NAIA national championship by defeating Lenoir-Rhyne College in Sacramento's Camelia Bowl.

With a national championship football team under its belt, CSC began developing 20 acres, the former site of the Jamieson Dairy, into a modern sports center with a fieldhouse and football field. A $50,000 fund-raising drive was initiated to fund the project. The new Hamilton Field House opened in 1965.

ABOVE: Homecoming on October 13, 1962, at Central Field for the game against East Central. The Bronchos played before an overflow crowd of 8,000 who watched them win 40-20. *Courtesy Archives and Special Collections, UCO Library.*

LEFT: During the 1960s a circle drive stood in front of Old North and Evans Hall. *Courtesy Archives and Special Collections, UCO Library.*

BELOW: Central students parked in front of the Student Union in 1961. *Courtesy Archives and Special Collections, UCO Library.*

Coach Phil Ball on the sidelines with his team during a 1970 football game. The 1970 football team had an excellent season, and finished with 9 wins, and only 2 losses. *Courtesy Archives and Special Collections, UCO Library.*

Physical Education Professor Virginia Peters prepares to teach a fencing class. Peters was a constant at Central for more than 40 years. Peters started at Central in 1953 and went on to direct the women's athletics program. *Courtesy Archives and Special Collections, UCO Library.*

Growing Pains

Headlines in *The Daily Oklahoman* during the early 1960s trumpeted unprecedented growth at Central State, as thousands of baby boomers flocked to campus in record numbers. The campus expansion project spilled into nearby residential areas to meet the demand. During the summer of 1962, five new buildings were under construction on campus—two new dorms, East and West halls, two new classroom buildings, a new business building, and an addition to the mathematics building.

"We're just growing and growing," Duty E. Whorton, CSC physical plant manager, said as he pointed out several private residences just off campus the college had purchased. "We've bought several lots adjacent to the campus," he said, "and will probably acquire more as we go along."

Fortunately, Godfrey had experience with building projects as superintendent at Pryor and Durant. Frequently, Godfrey turned to self-liquidating bonds to construct additional buildings on campus. More money was spent on new construction under Godfrey's watch than had been spent in the entire previous history of the school.

At the same time, however, President Godfrey remained concerned that the massive building program still would not meet the needs of an ever-growing student population. "We're building now," he said, "but even when all of our new buildings are finished, they won't be big enough." For example, the Max Chambers Library, one of the newest buildings on campus, constructed in 1957, already was too small.

Built in 1963, the Business Building provided classroom space to the growing number of students who enrolled in marketing, management and other general business classes. *Courtesy Archives and Special Collections, UCO Library.*

Continuing with the building program charted by Chambers, Godfrey appointed Asbury Smith, chairman of the industrial arts department, as chairman of the campus planning committee. Godfrey sought input from faculty, staff, and students when drafting a building's plan and purpose. Whether it was the home economics building, the university center, the dorms, or the field house, Smith gathered a "campus-wide group" to discuss and develop the plans.

1962

- West and East Halls
- Central Cafeteria
- Married student apartments
- Administration Building (the Old South Building later known as Language and Humanities demolished)
- Howell Hall doubled in size

1965

- Hamilton Field House
- Chambers Library

1967

- College Center
- Conversion of old Chambers Library to Communication Building
- Conversion of old Student Union to Art Building

1969

- Home Economics Building
- Liberal Arts Building
- Remodeling of Mitchell Hall and Old North Tower

ABOVE: The Administration building, Old South, in the 1950s. In 1971, Central demolished Old South and replaced it with the Lillard Administration building. *Courtesy Archives and Special Collections, UCO Library.*

BELOW: Professors Asbury Smith, Floyd Frazier, Clarence Yoesting, and Roy Valla (left to right) stand together with shovels to initiate the groundbreaking of a new addition to Howell Hall in June, 1962. *Courtesy Archives and Special Collections, UCO Library.*

BELOW: The Art Building originally served as the Student Union. The new student union was built in 1967 in an effort to make way for future students at Central. *Courtesy Archives and Special Collections, UCO Library.*

East and West Halls

In 1962, two new dormitories opened, more than doubling campus housing. East Hall, the new men's dorm located on the corner of Roberts Street and Ayers Avenue, and West Hall, the new women's dorm located a block west on the corner of College Circle and Ayers, contained central heat and air and were considered "modernistic in design." Students dined in the new cafeteria that included a banquet room, which meant that more than one dinner-meeting could be held on campus at the same time.

Later, Centralville was razed and brick apartment complexes were constructed for married student housing. More wings were added to the dorms and one wing of the Administration Building was constructed.

College Center

In 1965, the Board of Regents for Higher Education approved $4.5 million for CSC to build a new Student Union and additions to student dormitories. Plans also were developed for a Greek Row and the new cafeteria. There was talk of changing the school from a college to a university, and State Representative C.H. Spearman, Jr., proposed just that in the Oklahoma legislature.

Bids for the Student Union were taken at the September 14, 1965, meeting of the Board of Regents. Financed through the sale of self-liquidating bonds at no cost to the taxpayer, the facility was paid for through receipts from sales and student fees. The $3.2 million University Center was dedicated in 1967. The old Union—the place where faculty members gathered daily for their morning coffee and conversation—was converted into space for the growing Art Department.

The aesthetic look and feel of the new university center's interior was largely the work of Jocille Godfrey. In fact, she, her husband, and the two architects went to Chicago to select the furniture for the new college center. The Godfreys designed the five dining rooms in the center based on the theme of the Five Tribes, as an integral part of Oklahoma history. Each room represented one of the nations.

Jocille Godfrey was known for her hands-on approach to decorating for special events and banquets. In preparation for a guest speaker, she would always place a bronze Broncho in front of the podium, pat it on the head, and dress it up.

Garland and Jocille Godfrey at a Physical Education Christmas Banquet, 1960s. *Courtesy Archives and Special Collections, UCO Library.*

English Professor Katherine Butler and Jocille Godfrey preparing Silver Tea Service for a party. *Courtesy Archives and Special Collections, UCO Library.*

Carrie Belle Wantland Meyer, Dorm Hostess at Thatcher Hall, serving Tea to guests during an annual campus "Parent's Day" event in 1960. *Courtesy Archives and Special Collections, UCO Library.*

Urban Renewal

The expansion of the CSC campus did not come without controversy. Urban renewal, a new federal program to reclaim older construction and use the land to champion growth and new city planning, was a nationwide issue during the mid-1960s. The City of Edmond studied the possibilities of urban renewal for the city. Locally, the issue of urban renewal also provided a forum for Edmond residents, city planners, and the college to discuss their relationship and hope for a shared vision of their community.

Often contentious, urban renewal discussions transformed and solidified the partnership between Edmond and Central State College. The City of Edmond hired consulting engineers Carter-Burgess of Fort Worth, Texas, to prepare a preliminary master plan for city improvements and city growth. The study concluded that not only would Central State benefit from urban renewal for land acquisition to allow the campus to grow, but Edmond would benefit from the program with municipal projects such as a new city hall, city schools, city sewer and water development, and improved streets.

In order to qualify for federal aid, the project needed approval of Edmond residents. Once approved, the federal government funded completion of a survey and planning phase. Locally, Edmond created a commission to acquire the land and relocate residents who had been displaced.

For more than 40 years, Alvin Alcorn's leadership focused on the growth of Central and its partnership with Edmond. His contributions to the expansion and vitality of the school and community are legendary.
Courtesy Archives and Special Collections, UCO Library.

Alvin Alcorn

By Brodie Pitts, B.A. in History, 2006

During the Depression years of the 1930s, Alvin Alcorn developed his attentive eye for detail and his conserving demeanor. Born during the summer of 1919 in Geary, Oklahoma, Alcorn's early life on the family farm nurtured his confidence and work ethic. He graduated from Geary High School before earning his B.S. at Southwestern State University. While seeking his master's in school administration at Oklahoma State University, he met and married his partner for life, Naomi Parker, in 1940.

During his 12 years employment at the State Board of Education, Alcorn learned the financial complexities and daily operations of Oklahoma schools, and made the political connections necessary to secure his entrance into administration of a state university.

Alcorn became Central's first comptroller in 1960. With a student body of 3,500, the university's economic affairs lacked the complexity of larger institutions. He garnered financial control of the university by establishing budgets for separate departments. He said his earliest challenge was teaching the professors to use purchase orders for their supplies.

Alcorn spearheaded Central's rapid financial and institutional growth throughout the 1960s and 1970s. He assisted President Garland Godfrey with campus growth and the urban renewal program of 1965. The campus increased to 200 acres and the school added over twenty new buildings.

Before Alcorn retired as executive vice-president in 1984, his peers honored him with the Educator of the Year Award, his most prized award. He continued participating in higher education as a member of the Foundation Board at UCO and the Board of Regents for Rose State College.

Inducted into the Edmond Chamber of Commerce's Hall of Fame, Alcorn also helped the city develop into the thriving community it is today. Alcorn was a major leader in assuring community prosperity. He was an initial supporter of United States Senator Robert S. Kerr's plan to impound the water collected by the Deep Fork River to create Arcadia Lake as a source of fresh water for Edmond.

Alcorn's vision of Edmond and Central's future grew hand in hand. He was a founding member of the Edmond Economic Development Authority and named as its first honorary trustee in December, 2004.

During urban renewal, some residents willingly left their homes and relocated to houses in other parts of Edmond, while others protested and lost the fight. *Courtesy Archives and Special Collections, UCO Library.*

In August, 1964, 200 residents attended a meeting in the Student Union on the question of urban renewal. In his remarks, President Godfrey made his case for the justification of expanding the campus to meet the challenge of soaring enrollment. He noted that by fall, Central State expected an enrollment of 6,500 students. In order to prepare for the continuing enrollment surge, Central State needed to acquire more land in developed areas adjacent to the school for classrooms and living space. President Godfrey and other administrators maintained that urban renewal was the only feasible way for Central State to expand in terms of acreage.

Home owners in the target neighborhoods around the campus were primarily retired or rented their homes. Home owners wanted assurance that they would receive a fair market price for their homes. President Godfrey and city officials pledged that fairness would be the hallmark of relocating residents whose land was needed for CSC expansion.

The urban renewal project allowed the campus to expand to 200 acres. In May, 1965, the city council approved a $2.5 million 124-acre urban renewal program for CSC. In June, 1965, the city authorized studies concerning future water distribution and sewage expansion needs. In the fall, enrollment hit 7,721 while the college began celebrating its 75th year, and voters approved the needed urban renewal program by a narrow margin of only 47 votes.

In April, 1967, Central received two federal grants totaling $4.5 million from the Housing and Urban Development Department and Office of Education. With the funds, Central acquired 118 acres of land to be added to the existing 76-acre campus. Construction planning began for the new liberal arts building and conversion and expansion of the student union for additional classrooms. Two months later, Edmond's Urban Renewal Authority purchased its first five homes in the project area. Quickly, other properties were purchased and houses torn down to make way for the expanding campus.

Many people believed that it was for the greater good that residents had to give up their property surrounding the campus in order for CSC to thrive. One observer who had grown up with the growth of the campus was Linda Jones. She had attended kindergarten at the training school, graduated from the college, and served as Director of Communications. She was somewhat saddened at the demolition of homes in the area, but knew in her heart that the campus had to be larger to accommodate the growing student population. Jones never doubted that the urban renewal project was the only option for CSC to grow.

By 1970, through purchasing neighboring property and urban renewal, Central State College expanded to nearly 200 acres. The result was a major change in the physical landscape of campus. Not only was the campus larger, but major construction projects were underway.

The asphalt that we walk on today was once a community of modest homes with hardwood floors and mature fruit trees in manicured yards. As we tell the story of Central's growth and celebrate it, we must also pause and reflect on those who left the security and familiarity of home for the greater community purpose of higher education.

Urban Renewal in the 1960s

By Molly McLeod Mirll, B.A. in History, 2005; M.A. in History, 2007

As plans were unveiled to expand the size of the CSC campus, a nationwide debate was in process on the issue of urban renewal. Rights of eminent domain clashed with rights of private ownership, resulting in local social unrest, and, quite often, heartbreak. President Godfrey's actions during the early years of the 1960s caused heated controversy in the community, but his prudent and adept decisions provided campus expansion.

As a practical way of acquiring additional acreage, Godfrey recommended the assertion of his institution's eminent domain rights, as stipulated under the Fifth Amendment to the United States Constitution. He turned to the school's comptroller, Alvin Alcorn, for help with handling the fiscal aspects of his plan. Using their appointed authority, Central's administrators successfully purchased surrounding homes—those located north of Ayers Street and on both sides of Roberts Street.

Godfrey's actions sparked local discontent, as many homeowners suffered personal distress and anguish over the thought of being relocated. Though one resident referred to the methodology as being communistic, Godfrey emphasized that administrators had every right to take homes without the owners' approval, but that he wanted to see them satisfied. The president instructed Alcorn to include an additional ten percent to the recommended purchase amounts.

Rapid changes occurred under Godfrey's leadership. Homes continued to be acquired, and construction plans included a new administration building, field house, and renovations to Old North Tower. By 1962, the fall semester's student-teacher ratios, surpassing suggested levels of seventeen to one, stood at twenty-seven pupils per instructor. Frustrations also arose over parking at the campus, as only 1,000 spaces existed to accommodate 3,141 registered vehicles.

By the fall of 1963, the school's officials realized a 478.4 percent growth rate had occurred over the past decade. In 1965, state allocations failed to provide adequately for his facility's needs; the monies covered an anticipated enrollment of 4,890, while 6,661 people registered for classes. Campus statistics revealed those in attendance heralded from 28 states and 20 foreign countries. The college's student-teacher ratio had climbed to thirty-to-one. While three other state institutions provided more than 200 square feet of instructional space per student, Central's remained at 54.

Resentment against the federally funded project to expand the campus festered throughout the winter of 1965 and into the following spring. In March, a group calling itself the Citizens League for Responsible Government circulated an anti-urban renewal petition. The explosive issue caused immense uproar among the small community's populace. Ultimately, the petition was declared invalid, but it was an indication that hundreds of people in Edmond did not approve of the manner in which CSC was expanding.

The removal of about 400 homes from around the school's campus greatly increased the institution's square acreage. By 1968, school officials began construction on a new classroom building, a student union, and acres of parking lots.

Garland Godfrey, making several tough and controversial decisions during the socially turbulent 1960s, ensured his institution's continued prosperity. His dedicated efforts and wise resolutions to assert the right of eminent domain and to utilize federally subsidized urban renewal funds, led to his successfully providing a brighter future for all students attending Central.

President Garland Godfrey giving the dedication speech for the opening of the new student center on October 15, 1967. The new student center housed meeting rooms, a snack bar, a barber shop, a beauty shop, a cafeteria, a ballroom, study lounges, and a campaign center on the main floor for campus elections. *Courtesy Archives and Special Collections, UCO Library.*

BELOW: Professors Terry Harrison and Ethel Derrick, members of the biology faculty, worked together in the 1960s. *Courtesy Archives and Special Collections, UCO Library.*

ABOVE: During a time of great change on campus, key administrative leaders (left to right,) Wilma Armstrong, Dean of Women; Joe C. Jackson, Dean of the College; Charles Richmond, Dean of Students; and E.C. Hall, Graduate Dean; provided stability and vision. *Courtesy Archives and Special Collections, UCO Library.*

Faculty Needs

Temporary quarters provided classroom space and faculty offices during the construction and renovation of buildings on campus in the 1960s. The size of a class was determined solely by the size of the classroom, with little regard to quality of instruction or special needs. Faculty loads, in terms of hours and students, greatly exceeded what accrediting agencies recommended. Funding for the college, which determined salaries and the number of personnel, always was based on the previous year's enrollment.

Growing by 1,000 or more students each year meant that Central State always was behind in terms of employing enough people to accommodate the increase. There was little adjustment of new staff after the school terms began. Godfrey was also concerned with Central State's need to recruit new faculty with doctorate degrees to accommodate accreditation requirements of North Central and also meet the needs of the growing student population. At one time, the school was 100 short of the recommended proportion. But Godfrey and his administrators recruited heavily. The faculty increased to 310 in 1970, with 40 percent holding a doctorate.

Competitive faculty salaries were also an issue at Central State. On a positive note, CSC received an increase in appropriations from the state regents for higher education in June, 1963, which allowed for faculty raises averaging $200. Godfrey hired 13 new instructors and two administrators. The Central State faculty received a second pay increase of about $300 to $500 per year for most instructors in 1966. But salaries at CSC were still below par. On average, OU faculty received an annual salary of $10,200 in comparison to the Central faculty average of $9,328. "I think that two Ph.D.s, each doing the same work at the two schools, should be paid equally," Godfrey said in a speech to the CSC chapter of the American Association of University Professors in December, 1967.

Cold War Curriculum

In the bipolar world of the Cold War, the federal government poured millions of dollars into higher education in an effort to compete with the educational system of the Soviet Union. Especially following the launch of the Sputnik satellite in 1957, the National Defense Education Act provided student loans and additional curriculum requirements for mathematics and science. Reba Collins, editor of *The Vista* during the late 1950s, produced a special edition of the newspaper about Sputnik. "Sputnik, which was the first object in space controlled by the Russians and they sent it up," Collins said in an oral history interview in 2004. "And here we were in the United States sitting over here and we didn't have a space program yet. And it disturbed us all. We really had the feeling that we had been left behind. So we really got on the ball and a lot of people changed majors to science."

President John F. Kennedy continued such support and added special education to it. Then federal support for education was a major trademark of Lyndon B. Johnson's presidency and the quest for the "Great Society."

Division of Education and Psychology

The public demand for certified teachers continued to soar during the 1960s, and the School of Education charted a deliberate course to provide excellent teacher training programs. CSC also developed new programs in special education, speech and hearing, and reading.

The faculty grew quickly from 118 in 1960 to 301 by 1968. Old North, the original building and symbol of teacher education since the territorial days in Oklahoma, underwent renovation in two phases to house these new programs and new faculty. The first phase, completed by 1963, prepared offices and classrooms for special education and the reading clinic on the first floor and the speech and hearing clinic and classrooms on the second floor.

New faculty members in the division of education secured a series of grants to fund new programs in speech and hearing and special education. Dr. Lillian Ivey, director of the speech and hearing clinic, and her colleagues, began the speech and hearing program with four students in Old North. Booths were set up for testing hearing. Dr. Ivey took the program from four students to a level where both B.S. and M.S. degrees were offered in the discipline.

Other grants provided funding for teachers of children with special needs. Throughout the 1960s and 1970s, Dr. William Van Osdol served as director and then chair of the Department of Special Education. Under Van Osdol's leadership, grants exceeded $1 million and provided funding for undergraduate and graduate students to become certified as special education teachers. The funds also provided

Long lines were common during fall enrollment in the original Student Union. *Courtesy Archives and Special Collections, UCO Library.*

Staff distributed ID cards to students during fall enrollment week. *Courtesy Archives and Special Collections, UCO Library.*

additional faculty and staff, professional development, equipment, and instructional materials.

In the late 1960s, the 1,300 special education majors made up nearly one fifth of the college. Van Osdol said, "We moved the whole state into special education. After our programs and certifications were approved, the other universities picked up what we started."

In addition, grants from the State Department of Education supported programs in early childhood education and adult basic education. A member of Cooperative Urban Teacher Education, a federally-funded program, Central State prepared teacher education majors to work in schools with a high concentration of minority students.

The training school was an integral part of Central's education program and lasted from 1901 until 1962. The children who attended the program helped to pack in anticipation of the program's end in May 1962. *Courtesy Archives and Special Collections, UCO Library.*

Students Diversify Majors

Though firmly grounded in the tradition of a teacher-training college, Central State's students gradually shifted from teacher education to other majors. In the early 1960s, less than half of the students enrolled in the teacher education program, while the other half studied liberal arts, pre-professional, and vocational programs. Popular majors included teacher education, business and commerce, social sciences, English and journalism, and biological sciences.

In the Cold War era, Dr. Whit Marks, a physics professor at Central from 1955 to 1988, mentored ten students who went to work for the National Aeronautics and Space Administration (NASA). One of his students, Milt Heflin, graduated from UCO in 1966 with a double major in physics and math. Employed by NASA since the 1960s, Heflin served as flight director for 20 space shuttle flights.

Other new degree programs included funeral service education, nursing education, computer science, safety education, home economics, journalism, library science, psychology, sociology, political science, school counseling, and preprofessional training in medicine, nursing, dentistry, dietetics, medical technology, engineering, law, veterinary medicine, osteopathy, and optometry.

Business

Office space was scarce and scattered around campus for the 18 business school faculty members. Travis Hyde's office was a makeshift location shared with David Landrum and John Smith on the balcony of the Auditorium. Business moved into the new Business Building during Christmas break in December, 1962. The Business Building contained 13 classrooms and labs, conference rooms, a faculty lounge, and office space for staff. It was a welcome sight to faculty and to the more than 1,100 business majors who comprised almost 25 percent of the total CSC enrollment. Business also offered graduate courses and the Master of Business Administration (MBA) by the early 1970s.

Business became one of the fastest growing majors during the 1960s. In the fall of 1960, the B.S. in Business Administration expanded to allow students an area of emphasis in General Business, Marketing, or Management. Dr. Milton Bast, department head of business education, said the areas of emphasis were created because they had been requested by students for years. *Courtesy Archives and Special Collections, UCO Library.*

New course offerings in computer science reflected the technological developments of the era. In 1960, Cal Guthrie, a new faculty member who worked at Tinker Air Force Base as a data processor, designed a course on the operation of electronic computers. The class also visited Tinker to observe the utility of computers. "Computing science started in the math department," Guthrie recalled, "and I guess I was the one that started it. It was just a course or two as it started, and it developed into full-time computing science for me, until I objected. And then they put me back in mathematics. It was changing so rapidly, and they wanted you to teach sixteen hours of computing science, and you couldn't keep up without taking off and going back to school."

By 1969, the Department of Mathematics, Computer Science, and Statistics, formerly called the Department of Mathematics, offered a computer science major and statistics minor. The department offered evening courses to attract non-traditional students. During the fall, 1969, semester, more than 500 students were enrolled in computer science, a 250 percent increase from the previous spring.

Math department professors Cal Guthrie, Francis Olbert, and Nettie Brorsen enjoyed a shared session in the Math Building. *Courtesy Archives and Special Collections, UCO Library.*

Funeral Service

Two new departments, Funeral Service Education and Nursing, were established in the 1960s. The initial program in Funeral Service Education was developed by John H. Cage who joined the faculty in 1964. He served as department chair until his retirement in 1986. The new Department of Funeral Service Education was first housed in Howell Hall in the Chemistry Department. For a brief period, funeral service enjoyed spacious accommodations of more than 4,000 square feet when CSC acquired the "Vannoy House" in 1968 and remodeled it for instruction.

Within nine months, however, Funeral Service Education was moved to the basement of Evans Hall. When Central received university status in 1971, Funeral Service Education became part of the School of Special Arts and Sciences. In 1984, the Departments of Funeral Service Education and Nursing moved to the newly completed Coyner Health Sciences Building. Since 1988, the programs have been part of the College of Mathematics and Science.

Nursing

CSC's pressing need for a B.S. program in Nursing began in the late 1950s. However, not until 1966 did the Oklahoma State Regents for Higher Education authorize CSC to begin development of a program to meet the increasing need for baccalaureate-trained nurses in Oklahoma. Due in large part to the efforts of Joe C. Jackson, CSC developed a partnership with Baptist Hospital in Oklahoma City. Students took classes at Baptist and on Central State's campus.

In January, 1968, M. Elizabeth Wiebe, Director of Nursing Education at the Baptist Hospital School of Nursing was appointed chairperson of the Department of Nursing at CSC. Wiebe held the B.S. degree from the University of Colorado and the Ed.M. degree from OU. With Weibe's leadership, a committee of CSC nursing faculty designed the nursing curriculum. The B.S. program in Nursing received full approval by the National League of Nursing one month prior to graduating the first class of 18 students in 1972.

After Wiebe retired in 1978, Dr. Barbara Henthorn was appointed chairperson of the department and held that position until her retirement in 1991. By fall, 1991, the number of faculty had increased to 19 full-time members, and nearly 1,000 students had earned the B.S. degree in Nursing.

Dr. Pat LaGrow, a nursing student at Central during the 1970s, returned as a professor of nursing in the early 1980s. During her doctoral program, LaGrow specialized in nursing research and theory. "We had a philosophy in the nursing department at that time," LaGrow has recalled, "that it's good for faculty members to continue working on the weekends or in the summers to keep their skills updated, to keep their knowledge updated about what's going on in nursing and the health care industry, and to be able to provide up-to-date and current information to the students in the classroom."

Graduate Program

During the 1960s, leaders of the graduate program at Central State discussed the possibility of expanding beyond the Master of Teaching degree, later called the Master of Education degree. President Godfrey, Dean of the College Joe C. Jackson, and Graduate Dean E.C. Hall met with Oklahoma Higher Education Chancellor E.T. Dunlap to discuss broadening the graduate program to include the Master of Arts and the Master of Science degrees.

The graduate council considered three programs—the M.A. in English, the M.S. in Biology, and the MBA—and decided to move forward with the English and business programs. In 1968, the North Central Association denied preliminary accreditation to the M.A. in English and MBA programs, citing inadequate library collections, the need for additional qualified faculty, and heavy teaching load. The first attempt to offer graduate programs outside the field of education failed.

The first graduate assistants at Central began classroom work during 1961-1962. Policies were established regarding teaching and enrollment load. Although graduate assistants were used in laboratory type courses, their number was small. The administration and faculty took pride in the fact that classes at Central were taught by full- time, qualified faculty, not graduate assistants. However, with the implementation of graduate degrees other than education, graduate assistants began to teach freshman level courses more frequently.

Graduate assistantships provided well-qualified graduate students with financial assistance and professional experience. In 1990-1991 there were 50 graduate assistants. In 2007, the graduate college coordinated more than 60 graduate and research assistants.

Although Stan Hoig worked at Central State University during turbulent times nationally and locally, he remained active professionally and tackled contentious issues in *The Vista*. He retired from Central in 1986. *Courtesy Archives and Special Collections, UCO Library.*

Dr. Stan Hoig

By Erica Johnson, B.A. in History, 2005

Born in Duncan, Oklahoma, in 1924, Stanley "Stan" Hoig spent his childhood in Gage, Oklahoma. After graduating with a class of 17 students from Gage High School in 1942, he served as a sergeant in the United States Army Air Corps from 1943 to1945. He completed his B.A. degree in English at Oklahoma State University in 1949. Hoig taught briefly at OSU, but quickly accepted an opportunity to work as a technical writer for Douglas Aircraft in 1953. In 1956, he became editor of publications for Baroid Lead Company in Texas. Returning to Oklahoma, he earned a M.A. degree in journalism from University of Oklahoma in 1964.

During the mid-1960s, the Central State College Journalism Department—headed by Dr. Ray Tassen—hired Hoig as an Assistant Professor and Coordinator of Publications, to supervise *The Vista*, the *Bronze Books*, and the alumni's *Newsletter*. Hoig's experience as a sponsor for the school newspaper at OU during graduate school made him a solid candidate for the position.

While working at Central State University, he earned his doctoral degree in Higher Education from the University of Oklahoma in 1971. In 1975, he wrote the lyrics for 16 songs for the bicentennial musical pageant and a book entitled *Oklahoma, U.S.A.* with Dr. Robert Dillon, for which they received the first Songs of Oklahoma Heritage Award from the Oklahoma Heritage Association.

Hoig's passion always has been writing, and he has received many awards for his publication achievements and contributions to the history of the University of Central Oklahoma, state and local history, American Indian history, and western history. Because he has never received a degree in history, Hoig defines himself as a "journalist-historian" who reports on what happened in a particular period.

In 1958, he published his first of more than 20 books, *The Humor of the American Cowboy*. In 1987, he wrote a series of Edmond history articles for the *Edmond Sun* entitled "Peek at the Past." He was inducted into the Oklahoma Hall of Fame in 1989 and the Oklahoma Historical Society has honored him several times.

Chapter Six Timeline

1960

- John F. Kennedy elected President of the United States
- Garland Godfrey became President of CSC

1961

- Construction of the Berlin Wall
- Bay of Pigs
- Freedom rides
- The use of graduate assistants at Central was approved

1962

- Cuban Missile Crisis
- Completion of dormitories, East and West Halls, and the Math Building
- Howell Hall doubled in size
- Central Cafeteria and married student apartments constructed
- Central Football team won the NAIA national championship

1963

- Martin Luther King, Jr. delivered "I Have a Dream" speech in Washington, D.C.
- President Kennedy assassinated, Vice President Lyndon B. Johnson assumed office
- Betty Friedan published *The Feminine Mystique*
- Henry L. Bellmon became Governor of Oklahoma
- Completion of Hamilton Field House and Lillard Administration Building

1964

- Tonkin Gulf Resolution
- Civil Rights Act
- Free Speech Movement at Berkeley
- Margaret Chase Smith, of Maine, became the first woman nominated for President of the United States by a major political party, at the Republican National Convention in San Francisco
- The Beatles first appeared on the Ed Sullivan show and sparked "Beatlemania"

1965

- President Johnson signed the Voting Rights Act
- Malcolm X assassinated
- Anti-Vietnam War Movement began
- Chicano Movement began
- Edmond voted on urban renewal to expand CSC

1966

- Cultural Revolution in China began
- Black Panther Party formed
- Oklahoma Regents approved the development of a nursing program for Central

1967

- Arab-Israeli War
- Hippie "Summer of Love"
- Dewey F. Bartlett became governor of Oklahoma

1968

- Tet Offensive
- My Lai Massacre
- Robert Kennedy assassinated
- Martin Luther King, Jr. assassinated
- Richard Nixon elected President of the United States
- American Indian Movement began
- Asian American Political Alliance established
- Students hold peaceful march in honor of Martin Luther King, Jr. death
- A campus chapter of the Afro-American Student Union was formed
- Central approved ROTC program for the campus

1969

- Apollo 11 landed on the moon
- Gay Liberation Movement began
- Woodstock music festival
- American Association of University Professors (AAUP) censured CSC following an investigation of Benz's termination
- Home Economics and Liberal Arts buildings completed
- Faculty Senate created at Central

Central's band marched through downtown Edmond for the 1968 Homecoming parade. *Courtesy Archives and Special Collections, UCO Library.*

Left to right, Hilary Brinlee, Melanie Reser, Natalie Taylor, and Jeri Berger celebrate following graduation from the College of Education with majors in Early Childhood. *Courtesy Archives and Special Collections, UCO Library.*

CHAPTER SEVEN

The 1960s
Central State College

I walked into my first class and approached the podium. About a dozen students, many of them African American,
got up and walked out. After the dust had settled, we got down to business and everything went along fine.
Professor Paul Lehman

We had a great spirit among the faculty. Actually, we always had a few dissenters that didn't think
the school was run properly. They wanted to be the ones that would make the final decision on things.
You can't have that, you know. Somebody's got to say "the buck stops here."
President Garland Godfrey

You may be acquainted with a song called "Good Ole Central Blue."
In my third year at Central as football coach, we had a player by the name of Harry Boyd.
He was a running back/defensive back who composed a team song called "Good Ole Central Blue."
We sang it after a victory. We were back in the locker room and there would be family and friends outside
the locker room and we would burst out into "Good Ole Central Blue."
That is such a fond memory for us. I think it is still continued to this day.
Coach Phil Ball

Campus Protest and Activism in National Context

Central did not experience as much campus unrest in the turbulent decade of the 1960s as other colleges and universities in Oklahoma and in other parts of the nation. Discontent with America's involvement with the war in Vietnam caused sometimes destructive demonstrations on many campuses.

In speaking to several Central faculty and administrators from the 1960s, they all maintain that Central did not experience much campus unrest. Some said it was because of the 30 miles separating Edmond from Oklahoma City. Others said it was because Central was a commuter campus and many students worked—they did not have the time or resources for such protest. Another theory is that administrators and support staff on campus controlled and protected the student body in such a way that unrest did not occur, and if it did, the press did not cover it.

Some student demonstrations took place at OU and OSU, but never to the degree of movements at Berkeley or other campuses on the West and East coasts. Students for a Democratic Society (SDS) organizers did attempt to create a stir at Central during the 1960s, but Dr. Charles Richmond, Dean of Students, quickly ended it. But quelling controversy was a duty of the administration—the community expected it and the parents demanded it—and Central State was no exception. Speaking at a meeting of public university presidents, Dr. Lewis F. Powell, president of the Virginia State Board of Education and a past president of the American Bar Association, expressed the sentiments of administrators throughout the country in the latter half of the 1960s. "These extremists and the faculty members who support them have forfeited any rights to remain as members of a university community," he stated. "The sooner they are expelled from student bodies and dismissed from faculties, the sooner our campuses will resume their historic roles as centers of reason and intellectual pursuit."

Students gathered on North lawn of the Student Center for a Peace Rally. The peace movement was often marked by men's longer hair and psychedelic clothing and was based upon the cry of many students for love and peace. A common sign at demonstrations throughout the land read, "Make love—not war!" *Courtesy Archives and Special Collections, UCO Library.*

George Benz and Bernard Lax

While the Vietnam War did not spark much protest on the Central campus, the treatment of two professors did. In February, 1966, President Godfrey notified the two faculty members that they would not be recommended for continued employment.

George Benz, assistant professor of economics, also was the president of the Central State chapter of the American Association of University Professors, and had taught at Central State for seven years. He identified himself as a political liberal and had run unsuccessfully for city council in Edmond the year before. In addition, Benz had helped organize SDS activities and helped create the first African American fraternity on campus.

Bernard Lax was an assistant professor of psychology and had taught at Central State for three years. Shortly after receiving the letter, Lax resigned his post. For Lax, it was a personality conflict within his department. "The president told me it was not a question of my ability," Lax stated, "but rather one of a serious personality clash." He had planned to stay at Central State for only another year before returning to the University of Texas to complete his Ph.D.

Benz, however, announced his intent to appeal his dismissal. President Godfrey said the decision to dismiss the professors was taken after consultations with their department chairs and a long tussle with his professional conscience. "It is not a pleasant task to dismiss any teacher," Godfrey said, "but there are times when it must be done for the ultimate good of the school."

In protest, a group of students circulated a petition challenging the administration's decision to dismiss Benz and Lax. The students perceived that the dismissals were due to "nonconformity." One of the first students to sign the petition, Sandy Moon of Guthrie, said the dismissals were "discriminatory" and declared that both instructors were dismissed because they were "nonconformists." The petitions described both instructors as professors of the "highest caliber" and said that their dismissals would create "an intellectual vacuum" on campus.

Benz requested an appeal hearing before the Board of Regents for Oklahoma Colleges, with the assistance of the AAUP. The six-hour hearing was held in the Oklahoma Supreme Court chambers at the State Capitol. Witnesses for Benz, three professors and three students, noted that he was a competent instructor, though a rigorous grader.

Conversely, Central State officials characterized Benz as arrogant and uncooperative with faculty and the administration. The most damaging testimony came from Dr. Joe C. Jackson, academic dean. After tracking a number of student complaints by date, Jackson responded, "I have nothing against Mr. Benz personally." But the attorney for Benz, Barry Albert, pressed the issue and asked the dean for his professional opinion of Benz's competence. After a pause, Jackson replied, "Mr. Benz is not a fit and competent teacher to teach on the staff of Central State College."

President Godfrey did not question Benz's knowledge of economics. Instead, for Godfrey, class decorum and language appeared to rest at the heart of the matter. Benz used language such as "hell and damn" during class discussions, but he stopped at the request of President Godfrey. In addition, Benz required students to read a book entitled, *Viet Nam*. Benz told the board he purchased 20 copies of the book at 66 cents each and sold them to his students for 65 cents in a small book shop he operated off campus.

In Godfrey's letter to Benz, he cited "troubled relations with both faculty and students" and "discriminative grading" as cause for dismissal. In a unanimous decision, the regents upheld President Godfrey's decision to dismiss Benz. Following the decision, Benz said he had no plans to further the appeal. President Godfrey and Benz shook hands after the ruling, each expressing "no hard feelings, personally." "It was a fair trial," Benz told President Godfrey, "and you probably could have been a little rougher on me than you were."

After the Benz hearing, the AAUP decided to censure Central State College during the Godfrey years. In a joint House-Senate Committee on Education in October, 1969, representatives of the AAUP and President Godfrey were present. When copies of the AAUP report on censure action against CSC due to the Benz firing were passed around, Representative C.H. Spearman, Jr., of Edmond asked permission for Godfrey to speak. "This AAUP report is not fair, in fact and in conclusion," Godfrey declared.

Also in the late 1960s, psychology students at Central voiced their concern when three psychology professors, Kenneth Dick, Joe Griggs, and David Bennett, resigned their positions. Students, five men and four women, issued a statement, "We feel that the loss of these three qualified teachers and their replacement with people holding lesser degrees will damage the psychology program at Central State, and the quality of future education will suffer." They suggested the Board of Regents review the issue. The three professors had written letters of resignation that reportedly told the students they would stay and teach at Central State "if things could be worked out." The issue, the students maintained, was that the three professors held Ph.D.s and were replaced by Ed.D.s.

President Godfrey defended the move, saying that in a teacher-training institution, it was not necessary to have all faculty with Ph.D. credentials. Griggs, associate professor of educational psychology, said he and two other professors were leaving the psychology department and three professors were leaving the business department. Griggs, highly critical of Central administration, said his decision to leave was based on "deteriorating conditions in the academic climate" and "clear and outrageous violations of students' rights."

In a letter to President Godfrey, Griggs called the student disciplinary committee a "kangaroo court" and called the school's tenure policy "apparently meaningless," in a reference to the dismissal of George Benz. In a prepared statement, President Godfrey responded, "We are always sorry when a faculty member takes the opportunity to indict the college when he is leaving."

Another faculty member squabbled with the administration and resigned, or was fired, depending on perspective. Dr. Joe Walker, director of student teaching at Central State, had only been at his post for 18 months. "I didn't resign, my termination has been through the office of the president," Walker said. "Dr. Walker resigned today," said President Godfrey. "We urged him to stay on, but he was adamant. We did accept his resignation," Godfrey added.

Walker came to Central State from the Women's Job Corps Center at Guthrie in January, 1968. One campus source had said Walker became angered in a committee meeting at what he regarded as administrative harassment of two unidentified students. Another report said personality clashes within the department triggered the decision to quit his post.

Faculty Senate Created

With the Benz case as the backdrop, the local chapter of the AAUP pressed for creation of a faculty senate on campus, an idea that received tentative administrative approval in April, 1968. John Cage, AAUP chapter president, said a faculty senate could "fill an existing communications gap" between the faculty and the administration. In May, 1969, faculty at Central State approved the creation of a faculty senate. The faculty vote was 184 in favor and 18 against, with 100 members not voting.

Following faculty approval, the drafting committee prepared the constitution of the faculty senate and presented it to President Godfrey and the Board of Regents. The committee included Alvin Alcorn, Mike Bachi, Kathleen Black, Bob Ford, Alvin Frieberger, Herman Fulgraf, George Guess, Sam Hanke, Gene Hodges, Joe Jackson, Bobbye Persing, Verlin Richardson, and Loren Smith.

Elections for the first faculty senate took place in the fall of 1969. Recalling his experience as one of the founding members of the faculty senate, Herman Fulgraf said, "I was not one of the organizers, but one of the enthusiasts. When asked about some of the issues that the senate dealt with, one of the big things was how do you hire, do the committees recommend, and will the recommendations be forwarded up the line in a clear kind of way, and will departments have a voice in who is hired?"

Students marching in funeral day walk across campus in honor of Dr. Martin Luther King, Jr., April 1968. *Courtesy Archives and Special Collections, UCO Library.*

Desegregation and Campus Unrest

At Central, as on other college campuses in Oklahoma, the enrollment of African American students increased during the 1960s. By the late 1960s, "minor racial disturbances" occurred on some Oklahoma college campuses. At the same time, as historian Stan Hoig has noted, African American athletes were actively recruited to Oklahoma colleges and universities.

At Central State, two specific incidents concerning race led to the suspension of four students and a more active role for the newly-formed Afro-American Student Union. On the day of Martin Luther King, Jr.'s funeral, April 11, 1968, approximately 70 African American students at Central participated in a peaceful march around campus. They began at the Administration Building and walked to the College Center and into the Oklahoma Room singing "Amen," "We Shall Overcome," and "Give Me That Old Time Religion."

Marchers returned to the College Center for an 80-minute discussion on racial discrimination and civil rights. One student remarked that this was the first time that African American students had gathered together in peaceful protest on campus. Another student charged that African American students did not receive grades above a "C" at Central due to discrimination. One student put it this way, "Don't give us nothing because we're black, but hell, don't deny us nothing because we're black." Central administration had planned a brief memorial service for King that morning, but classes were not dismissed. *The Vista* reported a "brief scuttle" in the College Center during televised funeral services for King.

In May, 1968, about 50 undergraduates organized a campus chapter of the Afro-American Student Union and elected Muskogee, Oklahoma junior Gary Royal as temporary chairman. Student suggestions for positive action included helping new students, finding more African American students to help tutor those needing academic assistance, working through "friendly persuasion" to get more high school and college courses in African American history, and building a positive image of the black student body.

A constitution for the new group was adopted and presented to the student senate for approval. Dean of Men Alvin Frieberger volunteered to serve as temporary sponsor of the new student organization.

In October, 1968, the Afro-American Student Union held a forum urging Central to hire African American professors. Sixty-five black students attended along with a dozen white students and several faculty members. At the time, Central had a faculty of some 300 white instructors, but no African American professors. Dean of Students Dr. Charles Richmond pledged that within the next year, Central would hire one or more qualified black professors. "We will hire 30 to 60 new faculty next fall," Richmond, said. "These posts will be filled by qualified people, whatever their race."

In November, 1968, two racial incidents occurred on campus and four students received suspensions. In the first case, a fight broke out at lunchtime on a Friday in the cafeteria involving about a dozen African American and white students. One black student, Paul Burleson, sophomore business major from Edmond, was involved in the fight and had a chair thrown in his face, losing two teeth in the process.

Campus Police Chief Jim Dunn arrived at the scene and handcuffed Burleson. Students attempted to intervene and block the officer's path—including Guin Greene, sophomore history major from Hillsboro, Texas. Burleson was taken to the Edmond police station first and then to a local clinic to treat his injuries. Dean Frieberger confirmed that both races were involved. Burleson, and the white student, Gary Shuffield, a freshman from Edmond, were suspended for 30 days.

In many ways, the second incident was an outgrowth of the first. Two African American women students, Guin Greene and Mattie Butler, junior English major from Lawton, also were suspended following an incident between African American and white students in the West Hall women's dormitory. The two students appealed their 30-day suspension and won a rehearing.

At a rehearing, the Dean of Students suspended all four students for 30 days. The students then appealed their cases to the committee on student conduct, and the committee upheld the original decision.

However, there was a larger issue. It seemed to some observers that sanctions against black students were far more severe than for white students. White students had been involved in both incidents, yet only one was suspended.

The day after the student disciplinary committee met to hear the four students appeal their suspension, approximately 30 students, African American and white, staged a peaceful demonstration in the east end of the Administration Building. Three representatives of the group presented a list of grievances concerning student rights to President Godfrey. Their chief concern was that the suspension, particularly the suspension of the two women students, was "too strict." Other grievances on the list included the denial of legal counsel for the suspended students during their appeals to the committee.

President Godfrey verified there was denial of counsel, and said the college had ample legal guidelines on the issue. He pointed out that any student appealing college discipline

African American Student Union

By Shbrone Brookings, M.A. in History, 2007

Central State College became formally integrated in 1954 when Mrs. Addie Lee Jordan became the first African American student to enroll. Many other black students followed, creating a small but noticeable atmosphere of diversity. As this minority population grew, the need became apparent for a university-wide organization to unify people of color and help individuals cope with existence on a campus steeped in white culture. The Afro-American Student Union (AASU), established on campus in 1968, quickly became a mouthpiece for all Central students involved in the battle for human rights.

Within months of forming, the AASU lodged a peaceful protest, urging the reinstatement of four students, two of whom were African American women, suspended following an incident in the women's dormitory. The protesters claimed the administration was inconsistent in enforcing university rules, especially toward black students. The demonstration aroused public sentiment, and within a week, the students were reinstated and given a new hearing in which they would receive proper representation.

Over the next two years the organization incorporated more than 115 members, and sponsored a Black Lecture Series that included prominent civil rights activist Clara Luper and State Representative Archibald Hill, Jr. The AASU served as the education vehicle through which the culture and heritage of African Americans could be transmitted. The organization set as its goals the encouragement of academic excellence and promoting a good reputation and public image on campus. AASU annually sponsored Black Heritage Week, which included activities such as the Brother – Sister of Blackness contest, Miss AASU Pageant, a lip sync contest, talent show, and the Gospel Extravaganzas.

The Afro-American Student Union grew into an organization that not only focused on the needs of students at the university, but the larger Edmond and Oklahoma City communities. The organization maintained an active relationship with the NAACP and the Urban League. In the 1980s the AASU, one of the largest representative forces of black students on campus, served its members and the general populace as an information source regarding African Americans at Central as well as a forum for discussing issues that were vital to the well being and self image of black Americans.

It gave members a chance to become involved with on-campus activities and socially interact with other students and faculty members. "Getting involved and being more than just a student is what it is all about," stated Jeanette Brown, former AASU President. In conjunction with the Black Peer Center, the group maintained a social and scholastic relationship between students of upper division or graduate standing with peers in lower divisions. The group supported a philanthropic agenda by continually sponsoring a child at the President's Club Christmas Parties for underprivileged children.

The 1990s brought a new name, the Black Student Association (BSA), but community-oriented activities remained. The BSA sponsored the "When I Grow Up Festival," a community activity for children in the Edmond area. The young participants had an opportunity to view the News 9 helicopter and listen to speakers from the Edmond police and fire departments. The BSA also sponsored educational seminars, such as police harassment panels, career and placement panels, alcoholism awareness, and the black family and gang panel discussion. The organization continued to play a vital role in the activities of Black History Month, the Martin Luther King Day Celebration, and the Miss Black UCO Pageant.

The AASU/BSA has served as a cornerstone for the unity and progress of African Americans at Central. It provided a platform for the preservation of cultural heritage and assurance of educational opportunities in the future. The BSA currently is the largest multicultural organization on campus and continues to promote unity, contact, and academic excellence among black students and the entire community.

A campus crowd gathered around Gerald Parks, president of the Afro-American Student Union, during a 1968 demonstration. *Courtesy Archives and Special Collections, UCO Library.*

may be accompanied into the hearing by his or her parent or a faculty member. "This disciplinary committee is set up to help the students, not punish them," Godfrey said. Green's attorney, Henry Floyd, said he was asked to leave a disciplinary committee meeting without finding out why his client was supposed to have been dismissed except that she was charged broadly with misconduct and destruction of property.

Green and Butler both filed suits in district court seeking readmission to Central so that they could resume coursework. They charged that the college had refused to give them a proper hearing and denied them the right to legal counsel. In response, Godfrey said, "I feel the problem is caused from a misunderstanding of our rules and regulations and misunderstanding concerning the disciplinary committee." The suits named the Board of Regents for Oklahoma Colleges, President Garland Godfrey, Dean Charles Richmond, and Dean Wilma Armstrong.

Then the Afro-American Student Union staged another demonstration—the second in a week. Responding to the suspension of Butler and Green, the student organization protested "the outdated school rules and the inconsistent administration of them." Gerald Parks, Edmond senior and president of the Afro-American Student Union, stood on his car outside the Administration Building and addressed the marchers. "We have a lot of influence in Edmond and right here on campus, so let's get with it and get these rules changed so they can be carried out the same way for both black and white students," Parks shouted. His statement drew loud cheering from the crowd.

"Kick the girls out of the dorm, not out of the school," Parks said, concerning the dismissal of the two women students. Parks then attacked the Committee on Student Conduct, which upheld the original suspension made by the Dean of Students. "This committee is not fair, there is not one student on the committee, so the group cannot know what is going on," Parks continued. "Put some students on the committee, like the president of the Student Senate or the president of the Association of Women Students, maybe even both. Then, the committee would be fair."

During the march, the students walked two-abreast while singing spiritual songs. President Godfrey was not available for comment. Earlier in the week, however, he defended the suspension of the two women students in an open letter, published in *The Vista*.

In district court, the two women students suspended were ordered reinstated by District Judge Harold Theus. He ruled that the women students be given a new hearing in which they would be allowed representation by counsel. Theus found that the students' constitutional right had been violated because they were not allowed to have an attorney present at hearings.

While the new hearing was being scheduled, the federal government became involved in the conflict. In December, 1968, Richard Dockery, the six-state regional director of the National Association for the Advancement of Colored People (NAACP), filed a request in the Dallas regional office of the Department of Health, Education, and Welfare (HEW) to investigate allegations of racial discrimination at CSC. Dockery said that Oklahoma's NAACP director, Reverend Wade Watts, had conducted an investigation of CSC's housing policies. "There is racial discrimination on that campus," Dockery charged, "and it is by design." Dockery charged that some African Americans had been asked to leave dormitories and find new housing in Oklahoma City.

HEW officials said that if evidence was found to support the allegations in the complaint, corrective action would be taken. Although there was not specific mention of freezing federal funds to the college, Carl Flaxman, regional director of the civil rights division of the Dallas HEW office, said such measures could be used if any discrimination was not eliminated.

The new hearing for the suspended students was held on December 3, 1968. The state attorney general's office provided counsel for CSC administration. W.J. Monroe, attorney for the Board of Regents, urged President Godfrey to consider the student disciplinary rules to include the right of students to have legal representation. Godfrey said that speedy action was important in the case. "The people are back in school. They have more or less flaunted authority and will continue to do so," he said. "If we satisfy due process, we satisfy the court order," he said.

After testimony was heard from 23 witnesses in the nine-hour hearing, the CSC disciplinary committee slapped a stiffer punishment on Mattie Butler than the original 30-day suspension she was appealing. The committee recommended immediate probation to the end of the current semester, followed by suspension from the college until the spring term of 1970. She would have to wait one year until she could enroll again at Central. Butler was told to move out of the dormitory immediately. She was deemed guilty of "interfering with campus officials who were attempting to maintain order and prevent violence." Guin Green's punishment was lessened. Her 30-day

Sex, Sexuality, and Sexism

By James Etzler, B.A. in History, 2005

The 1960s witnessed great change in American thinking and behavior. Many significant issues were addressed such as racism, poverty, voting rights, Vietnam, and sexuality. While many universities underwent drastic, and sometimes violent changes throughout the 1960s, Central remained relatively calm. Edmond was a conservative town that featured many churches, a predominantly white population, and largely Republican voters. During a mock election in 1960, the freshman class at Central overwhelmingly chose Richard Nixon over John F. Kennedy by a nearly 3-1 margin.

An examination of *The Vista*, the school-sponsored newspaper, provides understanding of student life at Central. Students attended classes during the day and attended social functions supervised by administrators during the evenings. Events included tea parties for women, smokers for men, and dinners often in mixed, but chaperoned company. In 1962, the rush motto for the Sigma Kappa Sorority was "Ah So! Confucius say Sigma Kappa is the sorority for you!" the Sigma Kappa parties featured Japanese themes that included a Kimono fashion show. Proper attire and decorum was "a must" at these student functions. A good college education included refinement lessons to help mold students into proper adult life.

The women's dorms were guarded vigilantly by dorm mothers Vivian Roofe and Elsie Whitacre. The watchful eye of the dorm mothers could not control the hearts and minds of their students, and a large expectation was placed on earning the "MRS. Degree." *The Vista* began 1960 with an article encouraging women to find a man, "That 'inner fire' burns as a result of the ever present thought in spinster minds 'Oh, boy, now's my chance.'" This chance was probably increased for Peggy Jo Alexander, the only female student in her economics class. *The Vista* described Alexander as a "Pert, vivacious 18 year old" and as "one distracting influence."

The Vista also featured a cartoon entitled "Little Man on Campus." It depicted sexist images often with predatory men pursuing unwilling women. One cartoon included a well-endowed woman wearing a bikini, sitting inside a cage with a trap door. The caption read, "Louise is a graduating senior—it's her last chance to catch a man." A letter to the editor written by a female student voiced her concern that Americans were not having enough children to keep up with "Red China."

While many students at Central believed that college

suspension was reduced to one-year probation. Guin Greene was accused of both physically interfering with authorities during the fight at the cafeteria as well as refusing to leave the dorm when ordered.

Following the ruling, defense lawyer Henry Floyd claimed racial discrimination existed on the Central State campus. That allegation sparked a local NAACP officer to ask HEW to cut off federal funds for both Edmond public schools and CSC. Speck Reynolds, vice president of

was the place to find a meaningful relationship, some women recognized that an education could provide women with satisfaction. Margaret Stout, a chemistry student, wrote an article in *The Vista* encouraging fellow female students to focus on course work based on their interests and desires. She encouraged women to become scientists, and attacked the stereotype that intellectual women were boring and drab.

A study at the College of William and Mary in Virginia found that 70 percent of college women said they wanted "someone to look up to," and the majority said they wanted a man to help them make important decisions. Most men believed they wanted a woman who would support their ambitions. Many women earned degrees in Home Economics, and learned how to decorate for social occasions, prepare food, and keep house.

Each student organization selected a woman student as their Queen, Playmate, or Calendar Girl. The *Bronze Book* dedicated many pages to these "honored" recipients. The practice of nominating Calendar Girls continued at Central into the 1980s. But times have changed. Today many women students attend Central with plans to earn the MBA rather than the "MRS. Degree."

the Edmond NAACP chapter, said there was only "token integration" in Edmond schools and in employment on the CSC campus. "I feel that federal money is being used to perpetuate a system of white separatism in Edmond," Reynolds said.

President Godfrey went on the offensive. He said HEW representatives, in an informal investigation at CSC the previous summer, were "highly complimentary" about the progress the school had made in employment of blacks. He said the school had four full-time and one part-time black teacher in a total faculty of 330. Although not sure of the figures on the staff, he said around 30 to 40 of the 300 to 400 staff members were black.

"We can't find qualified black applicants," Godfrey said. "We have no applications at this time from a qualified black person." He said the college required a Ph.D. or at least 60 graduate hours from its applicants.

Reynolds called for the employment of a minimum of 50 full-time black faculty members and 75 black staff members by June 1, 1971. He also requested a minimum of 30 black teachers in the Edmond public schools before the 1971-1972 school year.

Vietnam and Peace Demonstrations

After CSC's skirmishes with allegations of racial discrimination, the growing frustration of many students over the nation's involvement in Vietnam began to surface. There was no escaping the nightly news reports of massive anti-war demonstrations on many college campuses. There also was frustration expressed by many students over the assassinations of Martin Luther King, Jr., and Robert F. Kennedy.

The anti-war sentiment began striking close to home. Eighteen students at Oklahoma Christian College, also in Edmond, were expelled for holding a sit-in at the administration building.

College campuses across the nation participated in a one-day moratorium of classes in October, 1969, protesting United States involvement in Vietnam. OU and OSU organized teach-ins with United States Senator Fred Harris speaking at both institutions. Other schools also held events, including the University of Tulsa, Oklahoma Baptist University, Oklahoma City University, and Phillips University.

In contrast, none of the six regional schools canceled classes. "We're not ignoring the war—we're ignoring the moratorium," said Central State Vice President Steve Bradshaw. Central's student senate, in a narrow 18-16 decision, agreed with administrators not to participate in the national Vietnam War moratorium.

It was uncertain whether the student senate accurately reflected the feelings of the student body. Several students spoke out in *The Vista* in favor of the moratorium. David Priest said CSC should join the other 500 colleges and universities. He said, "The purpose of the moratorium would not be to disrupt the educational processes nor organize a student strike, but rather to set aside one day in October to unite with more than 500 college and university communities across the nation in expressing our opposition to the war."

Priest recognized that CSC was not organized to function as a political institution. "But times are abnormal," he said, "Those who have a desire to end the war have no choice but the engage themselves in the democratic process, to demonstrate at a time in which unity could prove most effective in expressing the hope of a nation."

Writing in *The Vista* against the moratorium, Bob Osborn wrote, "The teach-ins, preach-ins, and talk-ins which will be held tomorrow will do little to bring peace." He continued, "Much credit should be given to the CSC student senate for carefully considering the 'moratorium' proposal on its merits and not blindly following the examples set by the student governments at OU and OSU in asking for a day 'to discuss the war.'"

Many of the students who demonstrated on the CSC campus against the war in Vietnam on that day of moratorium were accused of being unpatriotic. Students distributing unauthorized flyers calling for support of the war moratorium were asked to leave the College Center. The Young Democrats, the only campus-sponsored organization to take an active part in the one-day protest, held a forum in the Liberal Arts auditorium. More than 125 students and 12 faculty members attended, including guest speakers John Tymmtz, history professor, and John George, political science and government professor. Later that evening, a group of Central State students joined 1,500 people in a peace rally at the State Capitol.

At least 200 Central State students held a candlelight peace observance in May, 1970, in response to the violent incident at Kent State University when the Ohio National Guard killed four students during a student demonstration. Wearing black arm bands as a symbol of mourning for the slain Kent State students, CSC students formed a huge circle on the lawn near the College Center.

In an open forum, speakers took turns responding to the tragedy. Campus and Edmond police were alerted for trouble, but the demonstration was quiet and non-violent. Students continued to respond to the tragedy by distributing pamphlets, staging demonstrations, and marching quietly through the Administration Building. Interestingly, OSU and Oklahoma City University did not report any demonstrations. The University of Tulsa, however, participated in the nationwide peace demonstration on May 16, 1970, in response to Kent State and President Richard Nixon's decision to broaden the scope of the Vietnam conflict to include Cambodia.

Students Continue to Press for Reform

In mid-May, Lieutenant Governor George Nigh met with students on campus for a two-hour "listening session" in the College Center coffee shop. Student complaints ranged from co-ed dorm regulations to Vice President Spiro Agnew. Several students wanted campus policemen disarmed. Some said the administration ignored student complaints and others protested being "treated as children." Asked by Nigh if they felt free to express opinions on campus, a majority of the group promptly expressed an opinion by yelling "No!"

Other students said they did feel free to speak out and another said he did not find dorm regulations irksome. One young man flatly declared that the administration discriminated openly against black students and "long-hairs." Another said he found the administration "very receptive" to complaints and suggestions by students. One student suggested that if the administration was truly interested in student thinking, the deans would be "on the front row here today." Nigh said he had specifically requested administrators to stay away from the exchange.

In many ways, *in loco parentis*, or university administrators, professors, and staff supervising and serving

Gerry Cherry

By Julie Bennett-Jones, B.A. in History, 2005; M.A. in History, 2007

Born in Dewey, Oklahoma, as one of five children, Gerry Cherry decided to blaze her own trail in life. All of her brothers and sisters went to college at Northeastern State University and she was "tired of being the baby sister."

Cherry began classes at Central in 1963. She recalls many fond memories of her time on campus. Her dormitory room in Murdaugh Hall overlooked the Student Union giving her "a bird's eye view of everything that went on in front of the Student Union. We could watch the students go in and out—we could see if anyone we knew was going in there and dash over if we wanted to visit."

Dormitory life for women students was regimented during the 1960s. There was a strict curfew and mandatory meetings. Women were required to wear dresses on campus at all times. One night, when she ran late for dinner, Cherry threw a raincoat over shorts she was wearing. The dean of women was inside the cafeteria at the time and suggested Cherry see her in her office. The dean threatened to call Cherry's mother and tell her about the incident. With the advent of the mini-skirt in 1964, Cherry recalled the increasing difficulty in dressing modestly when pants were not an option.

From the moment she arrived on campus, Cherry wanted to be a teacher and to follow in the footsteps of several of her siblings. "At that time," Cherry has recalled, "there were not many professions that were appropriate for women— teacher, secretary, nurse, housewife." She moved out of state with her husband before completing her degree in 1970 and launched a career in the newspaper business.

In 1996, primarily because of her background in journalism, she was hired as an administrative assistant in the UCO Office of Research. She was hired for the job on the condition she could work in small spaces. At that time, the Office of Research was comprised of Dr. S. Narasinga Rao and another assistant. All three members of the Office of Research, as well as books, desks, and filing cabinets, filled a small room in the Administration Building normally occupied by one person.

After a few months on the job, Cherry had her first experience in grant writing. She attended conferences, workshops, and schools to improve her skills. She became successful in writing grants for UCO. The grants of which she is most proud include the PFI Grant of 2001, that helped create a certification program and center for emerging technologies, and the Step Grant of 2004, a math and science grant. Both grants were from the National Science Foundation.

Cherry completed her M.A. in English with an emphasis in Creative Studies in 2001. She enjoys the classroom environment and intends to take more classes "just for fun." When asked about her experiences as a staff member at Central, Cherry replied, "I love it—the opportunities to see things, do things, and listen to people who are very knowledgeable in their fields. I love the campus climate, the inquiry. It's a good place to be."

As both a graduate and staff member of the University of Central Oklahoma, many of the experiences in Gerry Cherry's life relate to her time on campus. *Courtesy Archives and Special Collections, UCO Library.*

as surrogate parents for college students during their college years, was a tradition on college campuses. Such close supervision was a source of tension during the 1960s and 1970s, as college students were breaking away and searching for their own identities.

Dorm life, specifically separate curfews for men and women students, indicated the gender and social assumptions administrators made regarding campus life. At Central State, freshman women students living in dormitories had a 9:00 p.m. curfew Monday through Wednesday. The curfew was midnight on Thursday and Sunday and 1:30 a.m. on Friday and Saturday. Upperclass women in West Hall had a midnight curfew during the week and a 1:30 a.m. curfew on weekends. Men students did not have a curfew.

There were other rules. Visitors of the opposite sex were prohibited in dormitory rooms. At the time, students thought the curfews were strict. However, they were far more liberal than 20 years previously. Dr. Virginia Peters, professor and coach of women's athletics from the 1960s until the 1990s, remembered what curfew was like during the 1950s when she was a student at Central. "We had to be in the dorm in study hall from 8:00 p.m. to 10:00 p.m. For the next 30 minutes, you could go around and visit other people or take your shower or go to the bathroom. At 10:30, it was lights out. After hours, if women students needed more time to study, they sat in the closet with a flashlight, or put a towel at the bottom of the door so the house mother could not see light coming from the dorm room."

In December, 1970, the student senate considered revising the curfew policy. In a surprising move, the student senate rejected a resolution calling for abolition of the dormitory curfew for women. The vote was close, 19-16, and most no votes came from women senators, many of whom were dorm residents. President Godfrey was pleased with the outcome. He said most parents supported the curfew for women students. OU recently had disbanded curfew restrictions of women students in the residence halls, with parental consent. It appeared the women residents at Central did not want to change the curfew policy.

What Central Means to Me

Julio Pacheco, B.S in Physics and Mathematics, 1969

Four years had passed since I arrived in New York City to live with my mother and sister. We had moved to New York when the Guggenheim Foundation awarded a three year post-graduate Fellowship for painting to my mother. In January, 1961, I was four months away from graduating from Archbishop Molloy HS in Queens, NY, and in the process of selecting a college.

It was then that I received an unexpected letter from my cousin Gonzalo with very good news. He wrote that I could rent an apartment with him and a Cuban friend in Edmond and enroll in Central State College. I was very happy because Gonzalo, his brothers and I were very close while I lived in La Paz, as is common with most extended families in Bolivia. In his letter, he told me that he was in Edmond attending CSC, following the steps of other South American students, and was a pre-engineering major with plans to transfer to OU after two years to pursue a degree in Petroleum Engineering. I was also interested in Petroleum Engineering because it was the field where most of the science and technology jobs could be found in Bolivia and it was also a career that could be pursued anywhere in the world. Who knew that 46 years later I would witness geo-politics convert petroleum into the fuel of wars and see science prove the ill effects of petroleum on the health of our planet.

In August 1961, eight months after Gonzalo's letter from Edmond, I arrived for the first time in Oklahoma. I do not remember the ride from the airport, but I do remember the small, old house on Broadway and Ayres Street. Gonzalo and Jose had rented the bottom floor of the two-story house. It had three bedrooms and a combination kitchen, living room, and dining room. After one semester in that house, in the spring of 1962, we were all lucky to be able to move to Thatcher Hall, the men's dorm. If I am not mistaken, my first room in Thatcher is now the office of a professor in the College of Business.

Thatcher was a luxury after that house on Broadway. In the two or three semesters that I lived in Thatcher, we did not have to battle natural floods, only those caused by some unknown students. Another good thing about Thatcher was that there were no mice to chase out. Naturally, chasing a mouse is not the same as when a horse was stampeded down the third floor hallway in Thatcher! Worse than the mouse or the horse was that live skunk thrown through the window opening of one of the dorm room doors. Fortunately, it was not my door, nor my skunk, nor my horse. I do remember fondly the first couple of years in Edmond and CSC. It was a good time to share with good friends, be welcomed by warm and friendly people, learn from good teachers and be swept off my feet by some very lovely Oklahoma girls.

What I did regret was the fact that in Edmond there was practical isolation regarding the troubles brewing in the world and in the U.S. There was no real access to world news or news from Latin America. Because of the South American students at CSC and from my visits to New York, I was aware of what had occurred at the Bay of Pigs in Cuba and knew that Castro had his sights in Latin America. However I had no realistic knowledge of the violence being perpetrated against blacks and that we had started into the Vietnam misadventure. At that time there was no Internet and the only thing that you could do with computers were mathematical, statistical or accounting computations using Fortran and Cobol languages and a whole bunch of perforated cards or punched tape. Telex was high technology then. Long distance calls to other countries were practically impossible to make for technical and financial reasons.

The high cost of long distance calls to Bolivia is why I had the good fortune to meet Bertha and Allan Watson. Bertha and Allan, who lived on Hurd Street, just 1/2 block from campus, were both amateur radio operators who used their powerful equipment to contact other amateur radio operators in many parts of the world. They allowed many CSC international students to talk to their families for free. But their kindness did not stop there. They were wonderful counselors and Bertha would frequently invite international students to dinner. I still do not know whether they adopted me or I adopted them. In any case, Bertha, Allan and their three beautiful daughters became wonderful and dear friends. They are unsung American heroes who established friendship and respect between the U.S. and

dozens and probably hundreds of students from all over the world. When I returned to Edmond in 2001, I have been delighted to have made contact with Allan and especially with Becky, their youngest daughter, who is now a university professor at OSU-Okmulgee, teaching graphical design. When I decided to stay at CSC continuing my studies in Physics and Mathematics and not transfer to OU, one of my fellow students with whom I had many classes was Milton Heflin, one of UCO's Legends who has had an exemplary career at NASA. We became friends because we were both hired as Physics Lab Assistants by Dr. Whit Marks, the Chair of the Physics Department and partnered in our senior-year research project. Regarding Dr. Marks, he together with the Watson family, has been and is another great ambassador of the U.S. Dr. Marks has always treated international students with interest, respect and friendship. I was very fortunate to have him as a teacher and I am fortunate now to have him as a friend.

Julio Pacheco

After I graduated from CSC, I lost touch with my Edmond friends for quite a while, but I was fortunate to re-establish contact with Milt, when I worked at NASA Headquarters in Washington, D.C., in the 1990s. It was during that period that I returned to Oklahoma for two short visits and reestablished contacts with Dr. Marks. In 2001, it was Dr. Marks, who made me aware of a position in the Title III program and recommended me to Dr. Rao. This resulted in my return to Edmond after having lived in La Paz, Santa Cruz, the Netherlands and Washington, D.C. My wonderful daughter, who now lives in Washington, D.C., with her very smart husband and my fabulous granddaughter, has come to visit and love Edmond, UCO and my friends.

The main part of my job for the Office of Information Technology is to work with the faculty and I also teach a Physical Science course for the Department of Engineering and Physics. Since last year, I have also taken advantage of a benefit available to employees of UCO and I am enrolled in a Masters degree in the College of Education. That means that I am a UCO alumnus, staff, faculty, student and a fan of the fantastic UCO Women's Soccer Team. Go Bronchos!

But a few days later, as reported in *The Daily Oklahoman*, a petition by nearly 700 dormitory students requesting closed-door visitation hours was presented to President Godfrey. Student Senator Gerald Atkins took the petition to Godfrey's office on behalf of approximately two-thirds of the dormitory residents at the college. The president indicated there would be no fast action on the request. If granted, the petition would have radically changed dormitory rules which prohibited room visitation between the sexes to any degree.

In a statement released through the school's information office, Godfrey said, "I do not dictate policy on housing. Such decisions are made by the students and faculty working together. But these changes would concern many other people, parents as well as others, and I feel that it must be studied carefully." Student promoters of the petition, sophomores Brent Cunningham and Tom Power, said that they could have obtained more signers but were barred from such activities in Murdaugh Hall, the freshmen women's dormitory.

Road from College to University

By 1970, the majority of CSC's 10,600 students were commuters and the average age was 24.6. Central's plans to become a university had started two years before the name change became a reality. Students, faculty members, and administrators worked endless hours under President Godfrey's leadership, completely restructuring programs. Under the new structure, the administration created three vice president positions for administration, academics, and student services. Schools led by deans, overseeing departments led by chairs, replaced the older division structure. Deans would report directly to the vice president of Academic Affairs. Five undergraduate schools— Education, Business, Liberal Arts, Mathematics and Science, and Special Arts and Sciences—were created. The sixth was the Graduate School under Dean Roy Valla. President Godfrey and Dr. Joe Jackson already had given considerable study to reorganizing the new university. Jackson, Dean of the College since 1951, became Vice

Before the ink was dry on the new law that would make Central State College a university, the pattern for becoming a university was already underway. *Courtesy Archives and Special Collections, UCO Library.*

Central students at the local Sonic Drive-In located on Broadway in Edmond, 1961. *Courtesy Archives and Special Collections, UCO Library.*

President for Academic Affairs in 1969, and Alvin Alcorn who had been business manager or comptroller since 1960, was named Vice President for Administration. Representative C.H. Spearman, Jr., introduced a bill in the state legislature to upgrade CSC to university status. On January 23, 1967, Spearman successfully moved his university status bill for Central State through both houses of the state legislature, but Governor Dewey F. Bartlett vetoed the measure.

Spearman won re-election to the State House of Representatives in 1968 and he pledged to win university status for Central State in the next legislative session. From time to time, a delegation of Central State students visited the state capitol to encourage legislators to change the name of their school from college to university. In the 1969 legislative session, Spearman's bill passed 78-13. In his appeal to the State Senate Education Committee prior to a vote, Spearman said, "This is not designed to hurt OU or OSU, or any school. It is to help higher education in Oklahoma. If any college has grown in size, stature, and excellence to where it deserves university status, that college is Central State."

When word reached campus that the bill had passed both houses of the legislature, there was much celebration. The missing piece was Governor Bartlett's signature. Dean

Jackson saw nothing but positives as a result of the name change. "I can see us recruiting staff and faculty now who just would not have been interested before. This is the opportunity for us to become a major institution of higher learning," Jackson maintained.

Students organized a letter writing campaign to encourage Governor Bartlett to sign the measure. A week earlier, Central State had received a federal grant in excess of $3 million for its urban renewal program to double the size of the campus. But this enthusiasm quickly waned when, only four days later, Governor Bartlett vetoed the Central State College university bill again.

During the gubernatorial campaign of 1970, Democrat David Hall of Tulsa promised to support legislation to make CSC and other regional colleges universities. When Hall upset Bartlett in the November, 1970 general election, university status was one step closer for CSC.

Under the leadership of Spearman in the House of Representatives, and CSC graduates Bryce Baggett and Cleeta John Rogers in the Senate, the bill was again introduced and passed by both houses. On April 15, 1971, the governor signed the bill, and CSC became Central State University. The bill-signing ceremony took place in a packed ballroom with thousands of students, faculty members, and citizens of Edmond.

Chapter Seven Timeline

1960

• John F. Kennedy elected President of the United States

• Garland Godfrey became President of CSC

1961

• Construction of the Berlin Wall

• Bay of Pigs

• Freedom rides began

• The use of graduate assistants at Central approved

1962

• Cuban Missile Crisis

• Completion of dormitories, East and West Halls, and the Math Building

• Howell Hall doubled in size

• Central Cafeteria and married student apartments constructed

• Central football team won the NAIA national championship

1963

• Martin Luther King, Jr. delivered "I Have a Dream" speech in
  Washington, D.C.

• President Kennedy assassinated, Vice President Lyndon B. Johnson
  assumed office

• Betty Friedan published *The Feminine Mystique*

• Henry L. Bellmon became governor of Oklahoma

• Completion of Hamilton Fieldhouse and Lillard Administration Building

1964

• Tonkin Gulf Resolution

• Civil Rights Act passed

• Free Speech Movements began at Berkeley

• The Beatles first appeared on the Ed Sullivan show and sparked
  "Beatlemania"

1965

• President Johnson signed the Voting Rights Act

• Malcolm X assassinated

• Anti-Vietnam War Movement began

• Chicano Movement began

• Edmond voted on urban renewal to expand CSC

• Completion of the Hamilton Fieldhouse and Chambers Library

1966

• Cultural Revolution in China began

• Black Panther Party formed

• Oklahoma Regents approved the development of a nursing program at
  Central

1967

• Hippie "Summer of Love"

• Dewey F. Bartlett became governor of Oklahoma

1968

• Vietcong Tet Offensive

• My Lai Massacre

• Robert Kennedy assassinated

• Martin Luther King, Jr. assassinated

• Richard Nixon elected President of the United States

• American Indian Movement began

• Women's Liberation Movement began

• Students hold peaceful march in honor of Martin Luther King, Jr. death

• A campus chapter of the Afro-American Student Union formed

• Central approved an ROTC program for the campus

1969

• Apollo 11 landed on the moon

• Gay Liberation Movement began

• Woodstock music festival

• Home Economics and Liberal Arts buildings completed

• Faculty Senate created at Central

Larry Anderson, Acacia sophomore, in "Tug-o-war"
activities during Sadie Hawkins week. *Courtesy
Archives and Special Collections, UCO Library.*

LEFT: 1961 Summer Graduation in the Music Amphitheater. *Courtesy Archives and Special Collections, UCO Library.*

BELOW: The United Nations float, built by students for the 1963 Homecoming Parade, coming down Broadway in Edmond. *Courtesy Archives and Special Collections, UCO Library.*

BELOW: Students walking by Y-Chapel during the 1960s. *Courtesy Archives and Special Collections, UCO Library.*

Central

CHAPTER EIGHT

Becoming a University

Central State University

We became a university and it opened the possibility for development and growth.
I was really proud of the spirit on campus—the spirit of going somewhere, doing something.
President Garland Godfrey

Not very many people get the opportunity to take a four-year college and develop it into a university.
Joe C. Jackson

Growth of Edmond

During the 1970s, Edmond became one of the fastest growing cities in Oklahoma. The city population more than doubled during the decade, from 16,600 in 1970 to more than 34,000 by 1979. When United States District Judge Luther Bohanon ordered the forced integration of Oklahoma City schools through crosstown busing, many families voted with their feet and moved to Edmond. "White flight," or white families electing to move away from urban centers such as Oklahoma City to suburbs such as Edmond, helped boost Edmond's growth.

"Edmond's public school system already had an excellent reputation," Edmond historian James Crowder noted, "and the availability of new homes added to the environment of a relaxed college town became a selling point that no marketing expert could have manufactured."

One pressing problem for Edmond during the 1970s was traffic. After two Central State students died in automobile accidents at Second Street and Bryant, Second Street was widened in 1974 to meet the demands of increased traffic. By the mid-1970s, the city established the Parks and Recreation Commission and launched plans for a huge city park east of Bryant. In 1976, when the park opened, the city council named it for former CSC sports star E.C. Hafer. Hafer attended the dedication of Hafer Park in 1979. Edmond also attracted new residents when Kickingbird Golf Course opened in the early 1970s.

An aerial view of Central State's campus as it looked in 1978. In the years following Central's name change, the campus expanded with the construction of new educational facilities.
Courtesy Archives and Special Collections, UCO Library.

Spring enrollment in 1971 at newly-named Central State University (CSU) crossed the 10,000 threshold, and Old North Tower was listed on the National Register of Historic Places. *Courtesy Archives and Special Collections, UCO Library.*

Alvin Alcorn replaced Neal McCaleb as head of the Edmond Chamber of Commerce. Business boomed as building permits reached a record $3 million. The Second Street underpass finally opened, ending a traffic problem that had existed for decades. Politically, Edmond shifted from a Democratic to Republican town in 1972 when Democrats Spearman and Baggett were defeated by Republicans Jan Turner and Phil Watson, respectively.

From College to University

Enrollment at Central during 1971 was 10,678, only a slight increase from the previous year. The period of rapid growth during the 1960s slowed, due largely to the establishment of Oscar Rose Junior College in Midwest City and South Oklahoma City Community College. These institutions offered lower division work to many students who would otherwise have attended Central State.

In addition, nearby Oklahoma Christian College, a private Church of Christ institution, transitioned from a junior college to a four-year college. The growth that did occur at CSU in the 1970s was primarily at the graduate level. In fact, there was a gradual decline in undergraduate enrollment in Teacher Education which was offset by an increase at the graduate level with the creation of new programs and the expansion of older ones.

The decline during the 1970s was the result of demographic and economic conditions, and it followed national trends. Nationally, there was an oversupply of teachers. Enrollment in public and private schools across the country was declining, and fewer teachers were needed. There were increased opportunities for college graduates in business and the computer industry. Those programs saw increased enrollment during the 1970s.

By 1972, enrollment at CSU reached 11,300. Students commuting to campus were concerned about the world oil embargo and soaring gas prices. CSU administrators considered offering a shuttle between Edmond and Oklahoma City for commuters but the experiment was quickly dropped. Even with the high price of gas—by 1979 the price of gas was more than $1 a gallon for the first time in Edmond history—students enjoyed the flexibility and freedom of driving their own vehicles to campus.

Students were also exploring issues of sexuality in the campus newspaper, in class discussions and student groups, and in the "streaking" craze. In a public display of nudity, streakers appeared on campus in the mid-1970s, in many ways part of a larger national trend on college campuses. Even the commencement in the spring of 1977 had a streaker.

International Students and Growing Diversity on Campus

Beginning in the 1970s, Central experienced a surge in international student enrollment. Nigerian students flocked to Central during the first half of the 1970s due to CSU's low tuition rates for international students and the "open admission" policy of the MBA program. Several tuition increases during the 1970s and a gradual tightening of the admission requirements for the MBA program resulted in fewer international students.

In 1978, the 500 Iranian students at CSU conducted a fundraising campaign to assist other Iranians who had been arrested in a demonstration in Oklahoma City. The following year, Edmond residents watched with the rest of the world as the drama in Iran unfolded. The Tehran airport was clogged with fleeing Americans as the Shah's pro-American government was overthrown. With the release of 52 hostages held 444 days in Iran, Central students organized a special ceremony and tied a large, yellow bow around the Old North Tower. Vietnamese refugees also began arriving in the Oklahoma City area in 1979 and many enrolled at CSU.

President Godfrey and the Transition from College to University

President Godfrey was realistic in his approach to Central State's transition from college to university status. "People from OU and OSU would say, 'That's the silliest thing, they're not a university,'" Godfrey reflected in an interview in 2004. "Well, I answered them very well I think, I said, 'Well neither was the University of Oklahoma when it became a university. You grow into a university and that's what we're going to do.'"

"The day after we were made a university," Joe C. Jackson recalled, "Dr. Godfrey called me in and said, 'Dean Jackson, I know and you know, we're no different today than

BELOW: "My dad is my hero," UCO pre-med student Nassim Houshmandi said, "and he called his studies at Central the 'golden time' of his life." Nassim Houshmandi was born in Edmond in 1978, while her father, Karem Houshmandi, from Shiraz, Iran, was an undergraduate and graduate student in mechanical engineering at Central. The family returned to Iran shortly after her birth and the completion of her father's degree. Nassim Houshmandi returned to UCO in 2003 to study pre-med and prepare for medical school. She is pleased with her decision, but it comes at great personal cost, for she has not visited her family in four years. *Courtesy Nassim Houshmandi.*

we were yesterday. We were not a university yesterday and we are not a university now. We're Central State College, although our name is Central State University.'" Godfrey told Jackson, "I want you to do what's necessary to organize the faculty and make us a university. It means hiring about 50 more people, most of them with doctorate degrees. We have to change the curriculum. We have to reorganize the school—we have to make it a university."

With such an inspirational mandate, Jackson and faculty committees added new programs and broadened the curriculum. The organizational structure on campus changed, and divisions became schools with deans.

Twelve members of the Central State University delegation posing in the rotunda of the Oklahoma State Capitol while attending the fall session of the Oklahoma Intercollegiate Legislature in the 1970s. *Courtesy Archives and Special Collections, UCO Library.*

Faculty

Central State University faced many challenges regarding students and faculty. Traditional and non-traditional students sat side by side in classes, and minority and international students attended Central in record numbers. The majority of students commuted to campus. In addition, faculty recruitment and retention were pressing issues for the administration. The number of full-time faculty increased from approximately 100 in 1959 to 335 in 1971.

This was an era of pacesetting change on campus—new buildings, unprecedented enrollment, and the brisk hiring of new faculty—reminiscent of a similar pattern on campus during the 1960s. In the School of Education, for example, only four of the 48 faculty had been employed by the university before 1960. Many of the new faculty members altered the direction of the school and university for the next two decades. With the influx of faculty, it also meant a large turnover again in the 1980s and early 1990s as the professors from the 1960s retired.

School of Business

The School of Business launched Business Day in the 1970s, an opportunity for business recruiters to meet graduating CSU students. Keynote speakers for Business Day included Dan McGurl, Jr., of IBM, Eric M. Hilton of Hilton Hotels, Marilyn Neimark of Arthur Andersen Company, and Henry Bellmon, United States Senator from Oklahoma.

Dean Frank Finney

By Dr. Paul Lehman, Professor of English, B.A. in English/Speech, Central State College, 1969; M.A. in Language Arts Communication/English, Central State University, 1971; Ph.D. in English, Lehigh University, 1976

When thinking about the late Dr. Frank Finney, Dean of the College of Liberal Arts, many descriptive words come to mind—words like scholarly, kind, compassionate, efficient, and dedicated. For me and my relationship with Dean Finney, three words readily come to mind–teacher, mentor, and friend.

I first met Dean Finney in 1967 when I enrolled in his graduate class on Hemingway. One of the course requirements was a critical paper on one of Hemingway's works. Upon returning the graded papers to the students, Dean Finney asked if I would mind reading my paper to the class and field questions from the class. I agreed and did as he requested. A few days later, Dean Finney asked if I could stop by his office for a visit.

As my professor, Dean Finney would spend the time during our visits to talk about a range of topics from Hemingway's works to sports. After several weeks of visits, Dean Finney asked me if I would consider teaching a few classes of freshman English. My initial response was no. We continued our visits and after a few more weeks had passed, he asked me a second time. Again I answered no. Dean Finney was not a person to give up on a challenge. He would not let me "off the hook," so to speak. Eventually, I relented and agreed to teach two classes.

English professor and the first Dean of Liberal Arts Dr. Frank Finney helped students decorate the department's Christmas tree during the 1960s. *Courtesy Archives and Special Collections, UCO Library.*

Once I had agreed to teach the courses, I realized this activity would be a new experience for me. Dean Finney realized it too, and met with me on an almost daily basis to answer all my questions. In addition, he would offer advice or allay feelings of dismay. In effect, he became my mentor. Being the insightful person he was, Dean Finney knew the best way to get me to teach was to first establish a friendly relationship with me.

Although the idea of creating a relationship with me seemed fairly easy, the fact of the matter was that Finney was in for a lot of negative feedback from a variety of home fronts. Central State College had never hired an African American as an instructor. I was the first, and Dean Finney was responsible for that action. One reason he developed a close relationship with me was he knew there was no one else I felt comfortable turning to for help or comfort. He knew he had to be that person for me, and he was.

Dean Finney's encouragement meant very much to me. One incident I recall that impacted him negatively involved the election of the English department chairperson. Over a period of days, several of my colleagues approached me to consider running for department chair. I was reluctant to run, and personally had no real desire to be chair. However, after discussing the matter with Dean Finney, he suggested that I run. I decided to throw my hat into the ring.

Unfortunately, some members of the department felt they did not want to be represented by an African American, so they organized a campaign against me. I had no knowledge of this until I was told by a member of another department.

Dr. Paul Lehman was the first African American to be hired as an instructor at Central State University. Through the encouragement of Lehman's mentor, Dean Frank Finney, Lehman went on to become the Dean of the Graduate College. *Courtesy Archives and Special Collections, UCO Library.*

Nevertheless, I stayed in the running with one other colleague as my opponent.

When the vote was finally taken and the results presented to the faculty by Dean Finney, he appeared before the department with red eyes and a serious look on his face. After reading the results, which overwhelmingly gave my opponent the victory, Dean Finney stated that this vote was the most blatant display of racism he had ever witnessed at Central. He hurriedly exited the room slamming the door behind him.

One year later, Central held a national search for dean of the Graduate College. Dean Finney encouraged me to apply. Unfortunately, he passed away before I assumed the position of dean but I know he was proud of me. After all, had he not pushed me into teaching, I may never have pursued a career in education.

As more women students enrolled as business majors during the mid-1970s, faculty created new seminars such as "Bringing Women into Business." The Business Day theme for 1976 was "A Salute to the Academic Year of the Woman." By the spring of 1979, 33 percent of CSU's enrollment was in Business. Coincidentally, the School of Business produced 20 percent of CSU's credit hours but had only 14 percent of the faculty.

New Graduate Programs in the 1970s

Graduate enrollment continued to increase during the 1970s, from 1,027 students in 1970 to 3,503 in 1984. With the development of new junior colleges in Oklahoma City, CSU created a Master of Education degree in Junior College Education in 1972 under Dr. Stewart Beasley. In 1975, Dr. Ben Duncan, who had been a faculty member at Oscar Rose Junior College in Midwest City, directed the program.

In the 1960s, Central offered one graduate degree in education, but after a few accreditation snags, North Central granted preliminary accreditation and then full accreditation for master's degrees during the 1970s. In June, 1970, Dr. E.C. Hall retired as graduate dean and was replaced by Dr. Bill E. Fisher, professor and director of student teaching, and registrar and director of admissions for 11 years.

The MBA program began in the fall of 1972 with 91 students. By 1973, 167 students were enrolled in the MBA program and 44 were in the M.A. program in English. By the late 1970s, the first graduate program in Mathematics and Science was the M.S. degree in Industrial and Applied Physics. The first students graduated from the program in 1982. By 1979, Central State offered four master's degrees. Two other graduate programs were developed in the 1970s.

In response to a request from professors at the new dental school at the University of Oklahoma Health Sciences Center, a Master of Education degree for Professional Health Occupations was designed and approved in 1977.

In 1978, Central offered the Standard Elementary School Principal Certificate. By 1980, Central added the Standard Certificate for Secondary School Principals. With the approval of these certificates, the School of Education had three programs, including the School of Psychology, which required work beyond the master's degree.

Athletics

CSU hosted the Oklahoma State Special Olympics each May on campus. In 1973, 800 Special Olympians attended the event and by 1978 the number of participants soared to more than 1,650.

The football program experienced some highs and lows during the 1970s. Coach Phil Ball led the football team to a berth in the NAIA playoffs in 1972. By 1976, Ball resigned as football coach and was replaced by Gary Howard. In 1979, the Bronchos were the top-ranked NAIA team until they were defeated in the final regular season game by Northeastern. The record in 1979 was 11-2-0. Still, the Bronchos advanced in post-season play, winning their way to the Palm Bowl at McAllen, Texas, where a last-minute pass interception and ensuing 100-yard run caused their defeat by Texas A&I University, Kingsville.

During the late 1970s, CSU men's basketball stars were Wesley Clark and Terry Anderson. In 1977, Mark Winters resigned at the end of the basketball season after 16 seasons, and Eddie Evans became coach.

"My first year," Dr. Gerry Pinkston recalled in an interview in 2006, "I taught nine classes in the fall and nine classes in the spring, and coached two sports in the fall and two in the spring. I don't know how I did it, but I loved every minute of it." *Courtesy Archives and Special Collections, UCO Library.*

Former Edmond High wrestling coach Sherman Tyler helped CSU reinstate its wrestling program. CSU wrestlers captured the NAIA crown in 1978-1979. They defended their crown the following season, with five All-Americans and one national champion returning under Coach Eddie Griffin. David James, a senior from Del City, became the first four-time All-American in Central State history.

In women's athletics, Virginia Peters recruited Gerry Pinkston and Karen Dowd. During the mid-1970s, Coach Pinkston pursued graduate studies at Central and worked as a graduate coach for volleyball, basketball, and softball. One year later, Peters encouraged Pinkston to apply for a full-time position in women's athletics. Pinkston served as an essential member of women's athletics at Central for more than 30 years and retired in 2006.

President Bill Lillard (1975-1992)

In 1975, Garland Godfrey retired as president of CSU after serving for 15 years. Before stepping down, he had the privilege of officiating at the mortgage burning signifying the university's last payment on all land purchased under the urban renewal program. Godfrey provided steadfast leadership during a period of significant growth on campus. Student enrollment climbed from 3,968 in 1960 to 12,736 in 1975. The campus expanded from 20 acres to more than 200 acres. University faculty and staff presented him with a new Ford Bronco at the retirement dinner.

Dr. Bill Lillard served as Central's seventeenth president from 1975 to 1992. During his time at Central he encouraged the beautification of the campus. *Courtesy Woody Gaddis.*

The new president, Bill Lillard, long-time superintendent of public schools in Oklahoma City, succeeded Godfrey. Born in Wilburton in eastern Oklahoma in 1925, Lillard completed high school at age 15. He joined the United States Navy at age 17 and served three years during World War II. After the war he attended Southeastern State College in Durant and graduated at age 22. His wife, Mary Helen Lillard, graduated from Central State during World War II at age 19.

Bill Lillard taught in the Oklahoma City Public School system and took graduate courses in education in the summers. He later received his Ed.D. from OU and much practical experience as assistant principal, principal, and superintendent of the state's largest public school system.

When he arrived, President Lillard noticed "not a single paved parking lot, nor a single flower bed" on campus. His administration initiated a campus beautification program, especially along Second Street, with trees and flowers. By 1978, the parking lots on campus were paved with improved night lighting.

When assuming the helm at Central, Lillard announced a five-point plan. He wanted to establish an Indian Hall of Fame—reflecting his Choctaw heritage and interest in preserving American Indian history in Oklahoma. Other goals included improving academic excellence, construction of a performing arts theater, building an efficient alumni foundation, and obtaining accreditation of a doctoral program.

According to Lillard, the political scene in Oklahoma deterred Central's hopes for doctoral programs. Lillard wanted a Doctor of Business Administration degree. Even though neither OU and OSU offered such a degree, higher education leaders would not allow CSU to enter the doctoral program arena. Lillard argued that CSU also should be allowed to offer at Doctor of Education degree. He said, "We had a much better education faculty and better qualified than the education faculty at OU, yet they offered the Ph.D. and Ed.D. and we couldn't get it." The request was placed "under study" by state regents. Lillard said, "under study" became a political term which meant the idea would never see daylight again." He continued, "We had people leaving the comprehensive universities in education coming to Central State because we had a better education program."

President Lillard inherited an experienced and dedicated administrative staff and faculty. Dr. Joe C. Jackson, Vice President for Academic Affairs, had held the post of Chief Academic Officer for 24 years. Alvin Alcorn, Vice President for Administration, had served for 15 years. Alvin Frieberger, Vice President for Student Affairs, had been Dean of Men from 1960 until being named vice president in 1971.

Growth, in terms of numbers of students and campus facilities, had slowed. Initially, Lillard's major challenge was to maintain and build on the growth which had occurred during the Godfrey years.

Women's Athletics and Title IX

By Hillary Grange, B.A. in Social Studies Education, 2005; and Virginia Peters, B.S. in Physical Education and English, 1957, M.S. in Health and Physical Education, University of Colorado, 1962, Ph.D. in Physical Education, Florida State University, 1968

During the late 1970s and the early 1980s, key individuals at CSU battled to comply with Title IX and provide equal opportunities for women athletes. However, with its teams competing in separate leagues, in separate facilities, and the coaches receiving vastly different salaries, many wondered how Title IX could be defined. While some only called for the same number of programs, others called for "substantially equal per capita expenditures." In either case, all questioned where they fit into the grand scheme of sports equality.

Dr. Bill Lillard, the university president, was very supportive of the men's athletic program and he indicated an interest in increasing the emphasis on women's athletics. Charles Murdock, Director of Men's Athletics, and Dr. Virginia Peters, Director of Women's Athletics, had dual responsibilities of coaching and teaching in the Department of Health and Physical Education. For example, Murdock taught one class in addition to his athletic administrative duties. In contrast, Dr. Peters coached the women's basketball team, chaired the Department of Health and Physical Education, and taught three or four classes in addition to her athletic administrative duties.

In many cases, though not all, coaches of men's sports received pay for coaching and a reduced academic assignment. The coaches of women's sports did not. For example, Paul Parent, head coach of men's track and field and men's cross-country, taught two or three classes. In 1984, Coach Parent also coached the women's track and field and cross-country teams. His class load remained the same – much like his pay. When Dr. Gerry Pinkston was hired in 1975, she taught nine classes and coached four of the women's sports teams. In the 1980s, Pinkston taught four or five classes and was the head coach of women's volleyball and women's softball.

Once Title IX arrived at CSU, administrators and coaches began to look at the governing bodies for the athletic teams. The men belonged to the NCAA and NAIA while the women belonged to the AIAW. In 1979, there was a proposal to merge the men's and women's athletic programs at CSU into one athletic department with a membership in only one of the governing bodies.

Dr. Peters and the coaches of women's sports feared that the consolidation would take away the decision making voice in women's athletics and cause the standards of the women's program to be lowered. They did not want to accept the philosophy, policies and practices of the NCAA and NAIA which they felt would change the emphasis on women's athletics from educational values to winning, financial and public relations gain for the university, and exploitation of women athletes. They feared that this proposed merger would cause the women's program to fall into a second-rate status.

President Lillard, Murdock and the coaches of men's sports believed that a merger of men's and women's athletic departments would benefit the women's teams and their opportunities to compete. They believed that having a combined athletic department under one governing body would provide women greater assistance through athletic scholarships. President Lillard stated that while NCAA and NAIA did place stronger emphasis on recruitment, the final score and winning, rewards would come to the women athletes for success on the court or on the field in the form of publicity they would receive in the press. The maintained that recruitment was a vital part of a "winning" program and that coaches must find prospective athletes rather than post flyers and await for the return they felt the coaches of women's sports were doing.

Other areas of concern for equality for the men's and women's athletic teams were athletic training opportunities and playing facilities. The women athletes were not allowed to use the training facilities and did not have access to the services of a trainer during their competitions at home or away. Women athletes still practiced and played in the old, outdated Wantland Hall gymnasium and on improvised fields. As the softball coach, Dr. Pinkston took issue with the inadequacies of the softball field. Although the university eventually provided a "new" field riddled with rocks and ant hills, Dr. Pinkston was the only one maintaining the field while the men's baseball coach had student assistants to maintain the baseball field. Eventually, the Lady Bronchos basketball and volleyball teams played their games in the newer Broncho Fieldhouse and, finally, practice there.

In another major area of perceived inequality, coaches of women's teams called "foul" when it came to compensation for their coaching responsibilities. They claimed that the coaches of men's sports had salaries based primarily on their coaching responsibilities and not on their academic credentials. Salaries for women's coaches were based on academic credentials and the faculty pay card with nothing extra figured in for coaching. Dr. Peters presented this concern to President Lillard and requested that coaches of women's sports receive pay for coaching, just as the coaches of men's sports did. President Lillard researched the issue and indicated that the coaches of women's sports would benefit from the same pay once they shared the same duties of recruiting and competition and the scrutiny involved in wins and loss records.

Through all the interpretations of Title IX and the many promises to comply with it, women athletes and coaches still faced inequities. The coaches of both men's and women's sports presented their beliefs and arguments. Those coaching women's sports believed in equal pay, equal facilities, and equal opportunities for men and women athletes. Those coaching men's sports reasoned that equality came with the idea of sharing the same responsibilities and the same pressures to compete and to win. In 1993, a Title IX investigation at Central initiated some changes for women's athletics including improved facilities, more scholarships, and larger budgets.

Evans Family Legacy

By Brandi Bullard, B.A. in History, 2009

Eddie Evans attended Central and earned his Masters of Secondary Administration degree in 1973. In 1978, he became head coach of the men's basketball team. Not only was it his first collegiate head coaching position, it was also the first time Central hired an African-American coach to head the program.

Eddie brought with him proven coaching techniques and a spirit of perseverance. For Eddie, coaching basketball came quite naturally. He had been an All-State player at Douglass High School in 1959 and a three-year starter for the University of Oklahoma. He was head coach at three Oklahoma high schools where he won two state titles.

Eddie saw racial discrimination first hand in high school and college. On road trips, he often had to stay in a different hotel and eat at different restaurants than his white teammates. Rather than become bitter, Evans determined in his heart to display his athletic talents to the best of his ability and overcome the discrimination based solely on the color of his skin.

Eddie found a coaching home at Central. He was so comfortable that he brought his eight-year-old son, Terry, to the gym almost daily. He included his son in team meetings, took him on road trips, and allowed him to sit on the bench during games. Terry did not just observe his father as a coach, but as the only African-American coach in the conference at the time. Often, racial slurs were heard from opposing teams or fans. Despite facing adversity, Terry watched his father continue to coach with his head held high until his retirement in 1992.

With his father as his model, Terry began his athletic career as a member of three state title teams at Millwood High School and started all four years at the University of Oklahoma, receiving Player of the Year honors on the Academic All Big Eight squad three times.

After college, Terry embarked upon his own coaching journey. He led Midwest City High School to three state titles in four years. But the stellar career at the high school level left Evans wanting more. In 2002, Terry became the second African-American head basketball coach in Central's history. He led the Bronchos back to the national tournament after a four-year drought and continues to set goals for himself and for the team.

Today, Eddie proudly watches his son coach the Bronchos from the stands in Hamilton Field House. On the bench is a little boy named Tre, looking up to his father, and learning what it is to coach and be a coach. The Evans Family Legacy continues.

For Eddie (on left) and Terry Evans (right), the family basketball coaching tradition continues at Central. *Courtesy Eddie Evans.*

ROTC students used the University Center to practice their repelling exercises in the 1980s. *Courtesy Archives and Special Collections, UCO Library.*

The 1974 Army Blades, the women's auxiliary of the ROTC, with their banner. The Blades march in parades, present the colors along with the ROTC at all home football and basketball games, and support the ROTC in all of their activities. *Courtesy Archives and Special Collections, UCO Library.*

ROTC

By Oliver Leo Pettry III, B.A. in History/Museum Studies, 2007

I am the future— the future warrior leader of the United States Army. May God give me the compassion and judgment to lead and the gallantry in battle to win. I will do my duty.

—Creed of the Broncho Battalion

The cadets of the University of Central Oklahoma Reserve Officers Training Corps (ROTC) have exemplified this creed for nearly 40 years. Chartered in 1969 at Central State College under the command of Lieutenant Colonel Robert E. Osbourn, the Army ROTC program is a series of elective courses offered in the Military Science Department.

The program combines courses in military science with leadership instruction to train men and women to become officers in the United States Army. The military science program instills leadership, discipline, and enhances regular college studies.

Thatcher Hall was home to Naval Aviation Cadets and Air Force students prior to the inception of the Army ROTC program. Thatcher Hall has been the headquarters of the UCO Army ROTC since 1969. The ROTC program is responsible for commissioning hundreds of cadets to the rank of second lieutenant in the United States Army Reserve and the Army National Guard. The Army ROTC program assumed the name of Marauders until 1986 when the name was officially changed to the present Broncho Battalion.

UCO Cadets are required to participate in a six-week Leadership and Development Course during the summer following their junior year. They attend supplementary training in Airborne and Air Assault schools and officer apprenticeships at military installations located in Korea, Germany, and the United States.

Cadets have organized and participated in many social, professional, and community service events. The Spring Formal Military Ball has been the pinnacle event each year since its inception in 1970. The first UCO Military Ball Queen, Janie Hurst, was recognized as Honorary Cadet Colonel.

The Broncho Battalion has made significant strides in recent years. The UCO Army ROTC detachment garnered first place finishes in the 2004 Oklahoma National Guard Governor's Twenty and Major Subordinate Command Rifle Matches. The Broncho Battalion made the National Commissioning Mission in 2004, for the first time in the previous five years. Under the present command of Lieutenant Colonel Stuart Jolly, the UCO Broncho Battalion will continue the tradition of military excellence on campus.

Members of the Central State ROTC program performing drills near Thatcher Hall in the 1970s. *Courtesy Archives and Special Collections, UCO Library.*

In 1976, Charles Murdock was hired as the new athletic director for Central State. *Courtesy Archives and Special Collections, UCO Library.*

In 1976, Dr. Joe Jackson and Dr. Asbury Smith, Dean of the School of Special Arts and Science, retired after decades of service to the institution. Dr. Smith served as dean in 1971 when the schools were organized. He was chair of the Department of Industrial Arts for many years. He had played a major role in the planning and construction of the new buildings during Godfrey's tenure. Also, retiring that same year was Dale Hamilton who had been coach, athletic director, and chair of the Department of Men's Physical Education for 40 years. Combined, the three of these men represented 102 years of service to Central State. After consultation with faculty, Lillard recommended Dr. Norman Russell to replace Dr. Jackson, and Dr. Lucille Patton to succeed Dr. Smith. Dr. Patton became the first woman to be named to a major administrative post. Charles Murdock became the new athletic director.

Affirmative action was a major task faced by President Lillard's new administration. Civil rights legislation, passed in the 1960s, was just beginning to impact college and university campuses. Lillard had already experienced new laws in the Oklahoma City public schools as he worked with court-ordered busing of students to achieve racial balance in the schools, and the need to employ minority teachers and staff members. His job was to develop a plan of affirmative action that would comply with the law and pass inspection of the Office of Civil Rights. The record shows that he met that challenge successfully.

Tight budgets caused Lillard to ask all departments to eliminate positions. He eliminated his assistant's position. He recalled, "Here I was the president of a university with 15,000 students and no assistant, but I had three vice presidents. Dr. Dudley Ryan, former Dean of Students, as Vice President of Student Services, Joyce Mounds had been a Director of Personnel Services and became Vice President of Administration, and Dr. Clyde Jacobs became Vice President of Academic Affairs. So when I walked into a meeting that dealt with integration and desegregation, the state regents always pointed to Central State University as an example of what could be done without lowering standards. My vice presidents were the most competent people in the world."

Lillard also focused on improving faculty salary, hiring quality faculty, and reducing class size. "We had great faculty and we paid them well," Lillard said. At one time during the Lillard administration, the average faculty salary was "within $500 annually of OU, and greater than OSU."

George Nigh also has attested to Lillard's commitment to faculty salary increases and the connection to academic excellence. "When President Lillard was here," Nigh recalled, "I think there were six classifications of professor salaries in the State of Oklahoma. Under his leadership, UCO had the highest average salary of a professor in five of the six classifications."

The quality of faculty was extremely important to President Lillard. For example, he hired five new faculty members with doctorates and high school teaching experience to teach freshman composition. Lillard said, "The last thing a freshman needs is to sit in a class of 300 to 400. We received great support from parents who appreciated the fact that CSU wanted to teach basic subjects in a much smaller class setting."

Lillard embraced Central's significance as the largest of the regional universities, but also an intimate place where professors knew their students and the classes remained small. "Not only do they educate students in their classrooms," Lillard said, "but they know them by name and say hello to them when they walk across campus."

Dr. Elaine Bartgis

By Kim Penrod, B.A. in History/Museum Studies, 2005; M.A. in History/Museum Studies, 2007

While serving as an executive secretary in the regional office of Arkla Gas Company, Elaine Bartgis realized she wanted to attend college and pursue a different career path. She had grown up in a family of modest means in Oklahoma City. She began attending classes at CSU in 1970 with her initial focus in nursing. With changes in her personal life, she needed to find employment at night.

As a result, the Edmond Police Department hired her as a new dispatcher. This change influenced her to redirect her educational focus to law enforcement and criminal justice at CSU. Bartgis recalls, "By this time, I was a single parent and my daughter was here with me frequently. It truly was a family atmosphere, there were many nights she waited for me in the hallways or in the classroom coloring."

In 1973, women were allowed for the first time to serve as police officers in Edmond, and Bartgis was hired as Edmond's first woman police officer. "There were a few bumps in the road," Bartgis said. "I felt I had to do more to be accepted. Many of us in the 1970s thought we were pioneering and thought we had to prove ourselves so that women coming after us would have an easier road. I don't think it made it easier for women coming after us. It's still tough and there are still issues." She graduated from Central in 1984.

She has 15 years experience in law enforcement; first as a police officer in Edmond, and then as an agent with the Oklahoma State Bureau of Investigation. She attended the FBI National Academy in 1980. In late 1988, while working for OSBI in southeast Oklahoma, her daughter called and said she was ready to attend college but that Bartgis made too much money for her to receive

financial assistance. Both women decided to return to school and lived together in Norman. Bartgis began her graduate work at Central State, while her daughter attended OU. With bills to pay, Bartgis worked nights for the CSU Campus Police.

In 1994, Bartgis completed her Ph.D. at the University of Oklahoma. Her dissertation focused on researching policing in education and why police officers get a degree when it is not a requirement for hiring or promotion. For ten years, Dr. Bartgis was a professor in the School of Social Science at Fairmont State University in West Virginia, until she became homesick for Oklahoma.

In 2004, she was hired as a professor of criminal justice in the Department of Sociology, Criminal Justice, and Substance Abuse Studies. Bartgis continues to research the issue of the "brass ceiling," the lack of women attaining higher positions in law enforcement such as chief of police. "With women making up only 12 percent of the nation's law enforcement positions," Bartgis said, "there is still more work to be done." Dr. Bartgis continues to work with students to do research and projects beyond the classroom. "If women are interested in a law enforcement career in my classrooms, then I do my best to encourage them."

In 1973 Dr. Elaine Bartgis was the first female officer in the Edmond Police Department. Bartgis started working in patrol, became a detective, and then later served as an undercover narcotics officer. In addition, her career included working for the Oklahoma State Bureau of Investigation until 1988. *Courtesy Elaine Bartgis.*

NCATE Accrediting Team and Review

Teacher education underwent numerous changes in the 1970s. There was a national concern about education that focused on the preparation of teachers. The federal government had continued, throughout the 1960s and 1970s, to put money into special programs for training teachers to work in inner-city schools and with minority students. Colleges were accused of not preparing teachers for such assignments.

Affirmative action and school integration were court ordered and enforced by the Office of Civil Rights. Against the backdrop of a general national feeling of inadequate teacher preparation, the National Council for the Accreditation of Teacher Education (NCATE) was in the process of writing rigorous standards to answer criticisms and deal with the challenges. CSU, as a member, was preparing for its regular ten-year review.

Since a campus-wide review by the North Central Association of Secondary Schools and Colleges was also scheduled for 1979, it was decided to ask for a joint visit by the two accrediting agencies. The review by NCATE and North Central occurred in March, 1979. Generally, teacher education programs passed inspection. All programs were approved until September 1, 1986.

In a letter to President Lillard dated July 9, 1979, NCATE identified weaknesses in the area of governance, clinical experiences prior to and during student teaching, placement services for graduates, and support and utilization of media and curriculum materials. In addition, team members concluded that the graduate faculty was not engaged in sufficient scholarly activity, especially publishing in professional journals.

The North Central Visiting Committee was not quite so kind. Their report noted a number of shortcomings, particularly faculty participation in governance. CSU was given two years to make improvements.

Bicentennial

In the post-Vietnam era, people throughout the nation enjoyed watching American astronauts, led by Oklahoman Thomas Stafford, link up in space with Soviet cosmonauts. The movie "Jaws" became a national sensation. In 1975, Edmond received an award for civic achievement from Governor David Boren.

In 1976, America's Bicentennial brought a much-needed renewal of patriotism all across the country. In Edmond, a special bicentennial pageant, "Oklahoma, USA," created by two CSU professors, Dr. Stan Hoig and Dr. Robert Dillon, joined the traditional Fourth of July parade. "That was really a remarkable experience in my life," Hoig has recalled with fondness, "to be acquainted with people in other professions. I had a chance to write the book and sixteen or seventeen songs for the pageant. And what I did was write the words, and Bob Dillon wrote the music. It was a matter of the chorus practicing with the songs, and the orchestra doing the music, and recording it, and putting on a soundtrack. It was really a very interesting experience for the vocalists, and it was a lot of fun."

During the Bicentennial year, a new fire station located at Second and Bauman began operations, as did the Edmond Racquet Club, the improved Kickingbird Tennis Center, Sequoyah Middle School, and plans for the Metrochurch's new 900-seat auditorium. Alvin Alcorn was selected Citizen of the Year.

When Jimmy Carter defeated Gerald Ford in the 1976 presidential elections, Ford signed a bill before leaving office reauthorizing the building of Lake Arcadia. During the next few years, the Lake Arcadia Project would become a reality after a two-decade battle to build the water reservoir.

Also in 1976, Elaine Bartgis became the first woman detective on the Edmond police force. Today she is a member of the sociology faculty at Central. Edmond hired its first African American police officer, Elmer Allen, in 1979.

Playground of the Rich

An oil boom pushed the Oklahoma economy, population, building, and government revenues to record levels. By the late 1970s the "land rush" continued on Edmond homes with more expensive ones in the greatest demand. The first Oak Tree Golf Club lots were sold at $31,000 each. In 1979, Carl Reherman, a member of the city council and future mayor of Edmond, took offense at a statement by *Oklahoma Observer* editor Frosty Troy that Edmond had become a "playground of the rich." But with homes selling for $200,000 and above in such posh additions as Huntwick, Kickingbird, Oakdale Farms, and Oak Tree, it was difficult to dispute.

Shopping, golf, and new construction continued to reshape Edmond's look and feel in the 1980s. Quail Springs Mall opened in October, 1980. As an encouraging signal of growth, four new shopping centers were approved by the city council in the mid-1980s, but one at the corner of Southeast 15th Street and Bryant Avenue proved most controversial. First approved for commercial zoning, 84 acres were purchased by Trammel Crow Company. But development of the corner was halted by the courts in face of opposition from the Bryant Accord citizens' group.

The soaring local economy continued in the early 1980s. While construction sagged across the nation, it broke records locally. The 957 new homes topped the 1977 mark of 891. Commercial building was even hotter, and the mini-oil boom continued with 32 wells drilled during the year. Perhaps the saddest casualty of this new growth in Edmond was the demolition of the historic Wide-A-Wake Café. By 1985, Edmond included some 94 square miles with a population of 46,000. The city contained ten elementary schools, four secondary schools, and nine parks.

Local pro golfers Danny Edwards, David Edwards, Mark Hayes, Gil Morgan, and Doug Tewell were making a name for themselves and their hometown. Danny Edwards won the Oklahoma Open Golf Tournament at the Kickingbird course in 1979. Francis Baxter, the CSU women's tennis coach, helped organize the Avon Future Tournament, which brought several tennis champions to Edmond.

In the fall elections, Edmond joined the Republican Revolution that put Ronald Reagan in the White House and gave control of the United States Senate to the GOP for the first time since 1952.

Local news made national headlines during 1986. First, a tornado dipped down into the Fairfield neighborhood in west Edmond and destroyed 28 homes and damaged 131 more. No lives were lost, but damage was estimated at $15 million. On August 20, 1986, Patrick Sherrill, a discontented postal worker, pulled out a gun and began shooting his fellow employees. He killed 15 and wounded many others before taking his own life.

The biggest event for Edmond in 1988 was hosting the Professional Golfers' Association (PGA) tournament at Oak Tree. Promoters already called golf Edmond's silent industry.

Nearly 150,000 people attended the four-day event to see such legends as Arnold Palmer, Jack Nicklaus, Lee Trevino, Greg Norman, Ben Crenshaw, Tom Kite, Tom Watson, and Bob Tway and pull for the Edmond locals, Doug Tewell, Dr. Gil Morgan, David Edwards, and Scott Verplank. Jeff Sluman won the 70th PGA before the roaring crowds, but perhaps Edmond was the ultimate winner.

Mayor Carl Reherman hoped that the city's positive publicity during the last two days of ABC's coverage would help the rest of the country associate Edmond with golf, instead of the postal massacre. The Edmond Postal Memorial was dedicated on May 29, 1989, to honor those killed and injured in the tragedy.

Edmond's history was not forgotten during this era of growth. As Edmond prepared to celebrate its 100th birthday in 1989, city officials established the Edmond Trust for Historic Preservation, committed to preserving city history and overseeing the Edmond Historical Society. The Edmond Historic Museum and Edmond Historic Community Center both opened in the renovated Old Armory in 1985.

In 1989, Edmond celebrated its centennial in many ways. The Knights of Columbus from St. John the Baptist Catholic Church built a scale model of their original structure and Dr. Virginia Peters wrote a one-hundred-year history of the parish. The *Edmond Sun* boosted city pride with its series of articles on historic institutions and people. Edmond honored 101-year old Pearl Cartmill, who made the Run of 1889 to a homestead west of Edmond when she was a baby in her mother's arms. Edmond citizens held an "old fashioned social" at Stephenson Park with a 587-foot-long birthday cake that earned a place in the *Guinness Book of World Records*.

Chapter Eight Timeline

1971

• President Nixon took the U.S. dollar off the gold standard

• Twenty-sixth Amendment passed changing voting age to eighteen

• David Hall became governor of Oklahoma

• CSC became Central State University (CSU)

• Demolition of Old South at CSU

1972

• M*A*S*H debuted on television

1973

• Peace agreement ended the Vietnam War

• Oil crisis in the United States

• *Roe v. Wade* legalized abortion

1974

• Resignation of President Nixon

1975

• Second Indochina War ended

• David L. Boren became Governor of Oklahoma

• Bill Lillard became President of CSU

1976

• Jimmy Carter elected President of the United States

1978

• First "test-tube baby" born in England

• Bakke v. University of California limited affirmative action programs

1979

• Iranian Revolution

• Soviet invasion of Afghanistan

• National Energy Crisis

• George Nigh became Governor of Oklahoma

LEFT: Students make lifelong friends at UCO.
Courtesy Archives and Special Collections, UCO Library.

RIGHT: The Central State choir performing in a 1970s Christmas program. *Courtesy Archives and Special Collections, UCO Library.*

LEFT: Central students Kevin Matthews and Audrey Renee Winston, taking part in the Queen of Hearts Dance in the 1970s. *Courtesy Archives and Special Collections, UCO Library.*

LEFT: Eating tables in the student center served as a perfect place for playing chess before an attractive audience. *Courtesy Archives and Special Collections, UCO Library.*

CHAPTER NINE

The 1980s

Central State University

UCO is probably one of the best kept secrets in Oklahoma, because students coming to UCO can get a quality education from some of the best minds in education. We've been very fortunate to attract a very high caliber of professors in a variety of disciplines and I think UCO's record will speak for itself.
Dr. Paul Lehman

When I was a student here, I had a great time. I enjoyed my classes and I enjoyed the faculty that taught the classes. And I guess my desire is to be that type of person with my students. I want to be relaxed, but at the same time I want them to learn from the experience. I want them to not just learn from me but from each other.
Dr. Elaine Bartgis

Though Edmond business remained healthy during 1983, the weakened state economy caused severe problems in education. Although enrollment was up at CSU, President Lillard faced the need to freeze salaries, cut staff, and restrict travel due to a reduction of nearly $1 million in the annual budget.

During the 1980s, graduate and undergraduate courses were offered in the evening to embrace the growing need to accommodate students who worked full time and had family responsibilities. In the School of Business, for example, it was possible for a student to complete a degree without taking a day-time course. By the spring of 1982, Business began offering an evening MBA program at Tinker Air Force Base. Later, CSU also offered undergraduate courses at Tinker. Both programs served military and civilian personnel and dependents at the base. The Tinker offerings continued throughout the 1980s.

Need for New Mission Statement and Sense of Purpose

The Lillard administration experienced several clashes with faculty and the Edmond community over a number of issues. Shortly after becoming president, Lillard moved CSU's athletic teams into a higher competition level—National Collegiate Athletic Association (NCAA), Division II, rather than the NAIA level for small colleges. Some faculty members criticized Lillard for what they perceived was his emphasis on athletics over academics.

Graduates of the 1980s make the traditional walk through the campus past Old North to the football stadium. *Courtesy Archives and Special Collections, UCO Library.*

On October 14, 1980, *The Vista* director Dennie Hall and editor Tina Chavez accused President Lillard and his administration of censoring the newspaper. The front page of *The Vista* featured a letter by Weldon Watson, president of the Student Association, quoting the First Amendment and listing the charges against the Lillard administration. A copy of the letter was sent to each member of the Board of Regents. But in a 5-2 vote, the regents voted to renew Lillard's contract for the 1981-1982 year. Edmond newspaper publisher Ed Livermore, also a member of the Board of Regents, called for Lillard's removal and Hall resigned his position as director of *The Vista* in protest of censorship.

Reshaping CSU's Image

An alarming headline in the *The Daily Oklahoman*, "Identity Crisis Cited at Central State," captured the sentiment of Lillard's critics. A management audit said CSU's major problem was "a critical need for a redefined mission statement," a need which has resulted in an "identity crisis" believed to "be at the heart of much of the frustration on campus."

During a two-month period, 78 people were interviewed to register their feelings about 24 areas of university operations. More than 300 hours were spent interviewing administrators, deans, chairpersons, faculty senate representatives, and other staff members.

Mary Lou Bond and the Special Collections and Archives Department

By Diane Rice, Archives and Special Collections

The Special Collections and Archives Department in the Max Chambers Library of the University of Central Oklahoma owes its development in large part to the driving energies of Mary Lou Bond, archivist of the collection from the inception of the "Oklahoma Collection" in 1981 until her retirement in 1995.

The department began with the creation of the library's Oklahoma Collection Development Committee, which held its organizational meeting on January 22, 1981, under the chairmanship of Dr. John Lolly, Director of Library Services. Members of the committee met with President Bill Lillard and Vice President Cassens on January 28, 1981. Lillard and Cassens strongly supported the development of an Oklahoma research collection. As a result of the January 28 meeting, an Executive Committee, chaired by Dr. Donald Green, was established to oversee development of the project. Members of the

committee included Dr. Stan Hoig, Dr. John Lolly, Dr. Richard Peters, Royce Petersen, and John Purdy.

In a grant application submitted in October, 1981, for funds to establish the collection, Dr. Lolly said the Oklahoma Collection would benefit both students and members of the community and would serve as a research facility to provide primary research materials for graduate students in the university's Southwest History program. His intent was to use grant funds to acquire an initial opening day collection of books, periodicals, microforms, and manuscripts relevant to Oklahoma history and the history of the American Southwest. By February 1982, construction on a special area to house an "Oklahoma Collection" on the second floor of the library was underway. The official opening took place on April 22, 1982.

Mary Lou Bond's involvement in the library's Oklahoma Collection Development Committee led to her position as the collection's administrator, a role she performed with great energy and enthusiasm. As the collection grew and materials were donated or collected, Bond generated publicity for the collection by providing information describing the acquisitions in articles in *Old*

Mary Bond, a former director of the University of Central Oklahoma Archives and Special Collections, helped excavate a time capsule from the Y-Chapel, which is now in storage in the archives. *Courtesy Archives and Special Collections, UCO Library.*

North Magazine, The Vista and the *Edmond Sun.*

In 1989, when the scope of the collection expanded and it became the Archives/Special Collections Department, Bond supervised its move to historically renovated Evans Hall, and saw that appropriate measures were taken to preserve the many rare and delicate materials the collection contained.

By the time Bond retired as director of Archives and Special Collections in 1995, she had built a collection that included nearly 1,300 linear feet of manuscripts, 7,000 volumes of books, 176 microfiche units, approximately 1,100 reels of microfilm, more than 1,000 periodicals, and over 20,000 photo images. Today, her legacy is a collection that preserves and provides access to primary and secondary sources for scholars interested in Oklahoma's local and state history, Western history, and the history of the university. It is a legacy that connects the past, the present, and the future—and one that will benefit generations of students and researchers.

The audit called for a new marketing image to accompany a new mission statement. "The future success in such areas as a doctoral program, and other expanded activities at Central State University, will rest on the acceptability of this institution by the public and by the leaders of the state of Oklahoma," the report said. There was also a conclusion in the report that the school lacked academic leadership.

The management audit did have some points of praise. The university budgetary process, the libraries' "quality of excellence," increased research support, and the operation of the physical plant were positives in the report. Three of five academic deans said the school should go back to a more centralized system giving the office of the president more support than it received under the decentralized system. Seventy-five percent of the people interviewed said the faculty handbook was of little use to them and thought it should be revised.

Rewards and benefits in the form of merit awards were recommended throughout the audit. In response to the report, Lillard announced a merit system plan to include ten percent of all full-time professors and associate professors. Bonuses of $1,000 would be included in the paychecks of those selected for the honor by their peers.

Schools Become Colleges

As part of administrative restructuring, schools became colleges at Central State University in 1984. For example, the School of Business became the College of Business Administration. The Department of Economics transferred from the College of Liberal Arts to Business, reflecting national trends to integrate economics into business education. Later in the 1980s, the Military Science Department was housed under Business, though it remained relatively autonomous in operation.

The College of Mathematics and Science housed a host of departments including the newly-formed Department of Computer Science which had been part of the Department of Mathematics and Statistics. The division was the result of growth in the number of computer science majors and to the emergence of Computer Science as an independent discipline.

Dr. Bill Radke is the Provost of the University of Central Oklahoma. Courtesy Daniel Smith, UCO Photographer.

Two faculty members from the Department of Biology, Dr. William Caire and Dr. William Radke, had ambitious research agendas during the 1980s. Dr. Caire, well known for his work on bats, published two articles in the *Journal of Mammalogy* and also edited *Mammals of Oklahoma*. Radke took two sabbaticals during the 1980s to pursue his research. He spent 1982-1983 at the Wolfson Institute of the University of Hull in England and 1990-1991 at the University of Arizona. From his first sabbatical, he published two papers in *General and Comparative Endocrinology*, "Thyroid and Adrenal Responses of Ducks during Saline Adaptation" and "Dietary Sodium and Adrenocortical Activity in Ducks and Chickens."

Throughout the twentieth century, women's sports at Central continued to steadily develop, which resulted in an increase in participation and a rise in popularity. Today, the lady Bronchos are among the most competitive in the nation in a variety of sports. *Courtesy Archives and Special Collections, UCO Library.*

Campus Life

Dr. Karen Dowd, assistant professor of health, physical education, and recreation, was appointed assistant athletic director in charge of women's programs, a new position established in summer 1980 when Dr. Bill Lillard combined the men's and women's athletic departments. Combining the athletic departments raised a few eyebrows and many people expressed a fear that the women's department might suffer. She was determined it would not. "The women's athletic program has been growing for forty years," Dowd said, "having this program placed under the umbrella of the total athletic program cannot and should not eradicate the tradition and quality of this growth."

In 1982, CSU won NAIA championships in both wrestling and football while the cross country team won its second District 9 championship. The CSU women's basketball team won the AIAW Division II title. In 1986, Central State's wrestling team won its third straight NAIA championship. Charles Murdock resigned as CSU's athletic director.

In 1990, under the leadership of Coach Doug Duke, a professor of Mass Communication, the debate team ranked first in the nation at the Cross Examination Debate Association National Tournament. "Doug Duke is debate in Oklahoma," said Todd Graham, debate coach at Northwest Louisiana State University. Duke served as debate coach from the mid-1960s through 1997.

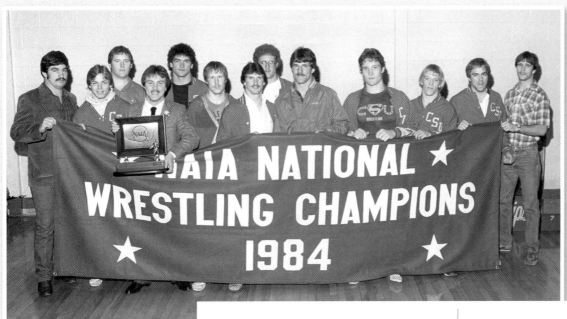

ABOVE: Throughout the 1970s and 1980s, Central State University's wrestling team won multiple NAIA National Wrestling Championships. *Courtesy Archives and Special Collections, UCO Library.*

ABOVE: Football coach Gary Howard with Daric Zeno and Mike Tasby who won the NAIA outstanding offensive and defensive player awards in 1982. The Central football team also captured the NAIA National Championship the same year. *Courtesy Archives and Special Collections, UCO Library.*

LEFT: UCO debaters Steve Donald, left, and Jason Russell earned multiple debate awards. Their coach, Doug Duke, served as the head of the debate program at UCO for more than thirty years. *Courtesy Daniel Smith, UCO Photographer.*

Nigh Institute of State Government

Since leaving the governor's office in 1987, Nigh had been connected with UCO as a distinguished statesman in residence at the Nigh Institute of State Government. Carl Reherman, Edmond mayor from 1979 to 1989, was the director of the Nigh Institute. The institute was instrumental in creating a partnership between UCO and the University of Puebla in Mexico.

Marching bands, along with many other participants, are always warmly welcomed in the annual Christmas parade in Edmond. *Courtesy Daniel Smith, UCO Photographer.*

Carl F. Reherman

By Jessie K. Hopper, M.A. in History/Museum Studies, 2006

Service is the hallmark of Carl Reherman's life. After a 90-day stint in the Oklahoma oil fields, Reherman joined the United States Army in 1959. The military took him across the globe, spending time in South Korea, Spain, Germany, and Washington, D.C. The threat of Vietnam led him to return to Oklahoma and enter Central State College in 1966. He majored in political science and found a mentor in the department who gave him the opportunity to teach as an undergraduate.

Upon graduation in 1969, CSC asked him to stay on and teach for $1,000 a month. He agreed and began a nearly 30-year career at the school. He continued his education at OU, earning the M.A. in Public Administration in 1970. He recalled the terror he felt when he taught his first class, "All they told me was, 'Here's the book. If you have notes, that's fine, but here's the book!'"

Reherman taught political science at UCO until 1997. He also served as director for the Bureau of Government and Public Services in the political science department from 1975 to 1980 and as chairman of the University Research Council from 1978 to 1981.

His teaching experiences led Reherman to a new career in public service. Tired of hearing him talk about what needed to be done in politics, his students told him to run for an open city council seat in 1976. He won and then went on to serve five terms as mayor of Edmond from 1978 to 1989, working to ensure the growth of both the city and the university. He never stopped being a teacher, bringing real life problems he encountered as mayor into the classroom, and giving his students the opportunity to integrate the theory they learned with the reality of governing. "The give and take on the reality side," he said, "helped me be a better professor."

From 1980 to 1986, Reherman moved into administration, working as executive assistant to President Bill Lillard, and dealing with faculty issues from the other side. Due to his friendship with former Governor George Nigh, he also served as Director of the Nigh Institute of State Government from 1992 to 1997. In addition, Reherman served as Director of the Urban Studies graduate program and Director of Urban Outreach, overseeing continuing education, KCSC Radio, global education, and community outreach programs, the English Language Institute, and Town and Gown.

Reherman retired in 1997, ready to move on to new challenges. Not wanting to rest on his laurels, he was elected mayor of his hometown of Chandler, Oklahoma.

Carl Reherman's career has provided a major link between Edmond and the University of Central Oklahoma. Serving both the school and the city, he has helped each to grow and prosper, leaving each a better place.

Classroom in the Casket Room

CSU public relations director Linda Jones recalled a time during the Lillard administration when the economy slumped and thousands of people lost their jobs and returned to college. What this meant for Central was a significant enrollment surge. "We literally had people in broom closets," Jones said. "Wherever there was a space big enough to put a teacher and five or six students, we created a classroom."

The need for classrooms was so great, some interesting things happened. The funeral service program had a room in Evans Hall that contained caskets. The room was made into a classroom and the caskets were lined up around the walls on their ends. A math class was held in the room. Jones thought the story was compelling enough to interest local media outlets. Not only did Oklahoma City television stations cover the story, it made the national news.

Jones said, "Every television station in Oklahoma City was on campus shooting video of math students sitting with all these caskets lined up behind them. It's not very often you have a story like that."

In 1988, CSU recorded the largest number of students ever. History seemed to repeat itself as the administration had to rent classroom space from a Methodist church to accommodate some of the more than 14,000 students.

Preparations for Centennial Celebration

In the late 1980s, planning commenced for Central's Centennial celebration in 1990-1991. The College of Business launched a plan to construct a courtyard immediately south of the main Business Building. Funds for this project were donated by faculty, students, alumni, and business organizations. Dana Palmer, an advertising major, submitted the winning logo design in a contest to develop a new logo and motto for Business. The winning motto was "Learning Today—Leading Tomorrow," submitted by Delena Lang, a Decision Sciences major and a charter member of the Decision Sciences/APICS Club.

CSU began its hundredth year with a record enrollment of 14,245 students.

Chapter Nine Timeline

1980

• Iran-Iraq War (1980-1988)

• Ronald Reagan elected President of the United States

• John Lennon assassinated

• CSU nicknamed "Condom State University" when President Lillard refused to allow condom distribution on campus

1981

• Sandra Day O'Connor appointed as the first woman United States Supreme Court Justice

• AIDS recognized and named

• MTV and CNN began broadcasting as cable channels

1982

• Israel invaded Lebanon

• *E.T.* hit the box office

1983

• United States and Caribbean Nations invaded Grenada

1984

• Madonna hit Top Ten List with "Borderline" and began her famous career

1985

• Gorbachev declared Glasnost and Perestroika

1986

• Nuclear accident at Chernobyl, Soviet power station

• Iran-Contra hearings began

• War on Drugs began

• Space shuttle Challenger disaster

1987

• World stock market crash

• Henry L. Bellmon became Governor of Oklahoma

1988

• Benazir Bhutto became first woman elected President of Pakistan

• George H.W. Bush became President of the United States

1989

• Berlin Wall opened to West Germany

• Tiananmen Square demonstration in China

• Colin Powell became first black chairman of the United States Joint Chiefs of Staff

• "Reality" Television initiated with the show COPS

Central students Lisa Danser Moore and Mike Seager promoting the musical *Hair* performed by members of the campus theatre program in the early 1990s. *Courtesy Daniel Smith, UCO Photographer.*

Miss CSU 1983 Jennifer Fowler, center, with her attendants, Joni Billinger, left, and Alicia Megehee, right. *Courtesy Daniel Smith, UCO Photographer.*

Central

CHAPTER TEN

Educating Generations

University of Central Oklahoma

When students leave this university, we want them to take with them a first class education that positions them for a career.
We also want them to understand what it means to be a leader.
President Roger Webb

Being president of UCO was one of the most fun, most rewarding, most successful projects of which
I've ever been involved.
President George Nigh

We produce the cream of the crop when it comes to teachers. But the School of Business,
the School of Math and Science—all the colleges—there's so much to be proud of here.
It's not just a little sleepy community with a little teacher's college anymore.
Donna Nigh

No Edmond Without CSU

"Without CSU, there would be no Edmond, Oklahoma, as we know it today," announced Paul Walters, Edmond Mayor and Central graduate, in an official proclamation celebrating Central State University's centennial of 1990-1991. As the city's largest industry, CSU generated $120 million annually for Edmond. During the early 1990s, Central employed 1,500 full-time and part-time workers with a budget of $40 million, roughly 75 percent for salaries.

With more than 50,000 residents in 1990, Edmond was a prosperous bedroom community of Oklahoma City. Edmond was one of nine cities in the state to receive "Certified City Status" for capitalizing on its economic development goals. The city's population boom continued to put pressure on the local school district that expanded to three high schools, four middle schools, and 13 elementary schools. Currently, Edmond's population estimate approaches 75,000.

Edmond's greatest challenge remains preserving its small town origins and sense of community during a time of unprecedented growth. In fact, Edmond calls itself "a great place to grow," and continues to be a place of change. Cars once drove through the center of Edmond on US-66 and US-71, but now bypass town on Interstate 35.

Residents today tend to identify their address less often by street name than by addition such as Oak Tree, Huntwick, Cheyenne Ridge, or The Trails. Recreation has become a big part of life in Edmond. Kickingbird Golf Course and Tennis Center provides physical activity. Hafer Park is the place to go in summer to watch Edmond All Sports Association ball games or enjoy a picnic at a Shakespeare in the Park production.

In 1987, Lake Arcadia was completed offering nearby outdoor recreational opportunities as well as a solution to Edmond's growing water problems.

Centennial Celebration

With much pageantry and excitement, Central continued its centennial celebration with a name change. On July 1, 1991, Central State University became the University of Central Oklahoma. State Representative Ray Vaughn and State Senator Mark Snyder, both of Edmond, helped secure legislative approval for the name change.

President Lillard initiated a host of projects for the Centennial, including a Centennial fountain and garden near Old North. He also wanted to eliminate bonded indemnities, and raise $250,000 for student scholarships.

The dedication of the Morrisett Centennial Fountain located in front of Old North took place in 1991. The estate of Stella Jo Wantland Morrisett, wife of Lloyd Morrisett, made the fountain possible. Lloyd and Stella were both longtime Central alumni and graduated from the school in 1913. *Courtesy Daniel Smith, UCO Photographer.*

The *Edmond Sun* featured a series of articles written by Linda Jones marking Central's Centennial and highlighting interesting aspects of Central's history. "I don't think that people realize that UCO is as old as it is," Linda Jones has said. "And actually the University of Oklahoma, and UCO, and OSU, were created by the territorial legislature in 1890, but we were the first ones to hold classes and Old North is actually the oldest collegiate building in Oklahoma."

One memorable Centennial event for Linda Jones was opening the time capsule from the Y-Chapel of Song

that had been deposited there 50 years earlier. Physical plant personnel knocked a hole in the wall of the Y-Chapel and retrieved the time capsule, a small metal box. Those who created the time capsule guarded against fire with an asbestos lining, but they did not plan for possible water damage.

During the half century, water had poured into the box, and every item in the time capsule was soaked. The archivist at the time, Mary Bond, salvaged what she could from the time capsule, but what should have been a rewarding time capsule opening was a major disappointment.

Edmond's Shannon Miller

Shannon Miller, 15-year-old, four-foot seven-inch gymnast won two silver and three bronze medals in the Summer Olympics held in Barcelona, Spain in 1992, the most medals won by an American athlete. She came home to an Edmond parade that drew at least 10,000 cheering fans. During the 1996 Olympics, she won two more gold medals, making Miller the most-decorated gymnast in history.

Edmond embraces this heralded woman athlete. Shannon Miller Parkway is located along Interstate-35 between Danforth Road and Memorial Road. As one enters Edmond on Second Street, the "Welcome to Edmond" sign calls out, "Home of Shannon Miller." Her father, Dr. Ron Miller, is a physics professor at UCO.

Gymnast Shannon Miller celebrated her Olympic medals with the citizens of Edmond in1993. *Courtesy Daniel Smith, UCO Photographer.*

Governor George Nigh gave the last commencement speech to Central State University graduates before the university officially became the University of Central Oklahoma in 1991. *Courtesy Daniel Smith, UCO Photographer.*

President Bill Lillard and Dr. Reba Collins, president of the Alumni Association, look on as deputy speaker of the Student Association, Todd Dealy raises the first UCO flag on campus in 1991. *Courtesy Daniel Smith, UCO Photographer.*

Edmond City Seal Controversy

In 1992, the American Civil Liberties Union (ACLU) attacked the city's seal because it had a cross in one quadrant representing the heritage of churches in the building of the town. The ACLU charged that the Christian cross violated the constitutional law theory of the separation of church and state and sued to have it removed.

The seal had been adopted in the 1960s when Frances Bryan won a contest with two designs that were combined into one seal. The seal showed the merging of the railroad and petroleum industries with the land run, Central State College, and the role played by churches in the founding and early years of the town.

The original design of the Edmond City Seal was created by artist Frances Bryan in 1965. *Courtesy Archives and Special Collections, UCO Library.*

After two years of legal wrangling, a federal appeals court ruled that Edmond violated the First Amendment of the federal constitution by displaying the cross, and the cross was removed from the seal. While some residents suggested possible substitutes, the right-side of the city seal stayed blank so people would remember what had happened. Inspired by the municipal seal struggle, MetroChurch leaders went before the city planning commission to seek permission to build a 157-foot white cross on their property at Second Street and Interstate-35. With approval in 1997, the cross was allowed to be constructed 20 feet shorter than originally proposed.

Tall Chief History at UCO

By Russ Tall Chief, B.A. in Communication, 1995

My grandfather, George Tall Chief, attended Central State College from 1938 to 1940, earning a bachelor's degree in Education. He was the first of three generations to graduate from the school. Granddad met my grandmother, Marion Russell, at a mixer in the old gymnasium while she was earning a teaching degree and also studying piano. "The men walked around the gym in one direction while the women walked in the other direction," Granddad explained. "I was walking with my friends, Luke Thompson and Tex Ritter. When I got to Marion, I said to my friends, 'this is the one.'"

After the mixer, Granddad took my grandmother to Royce's Cafe on Main Street for a sandwich and a Coke. However, when they returned to campus past curfew time, he said he inadvertently got grandmother into some trouble. "I was banged up in a rodeo the week before in Memphis riding bulls and broncs," he said. "So I was limping along and made us 10 minutes late back to campus. Marion was 'campused' [grounded] for a week as a result," he said laughing apologetically. They were later married at St. Mary's Episcopal Church on University Street.

Granddad said that he very much enjoyed playing football in a leather helmet at CSC for Coach Dale Hamilton. Granddad later utilized teaching strategies and philosophies he learned from Coach Hamilton while coaching numerous junior high and high school teams across the country. "I admired his confidence in me," Granddad said. "I didn't weigh 140 pounds, which is small for a center. And yet he gave me a scholarship to play football. Most importantly, Coach Hamilton taught me that desire is more important than size. The philosophy stayed with me all of my life and helped me in everything from coaching, to serving as superintendent of schools in Montana, and later serving as Chief of the Osage Nation."

After a divorce, Granddad earned his Master's degree at Pacific University in Oregon in 1958. Marion later married Dwight Davis, chair of the English Department at CSC. She also earned her master's degree at CSC and a doctorate degree at the University of Oklahoma before she died in 2005.

Michelle Wilson Tall Chief attended Central from 1967 to 1972. During her time on campus, she was featured on the KCSC radio station. *Courtesy Russ Tall Chief.*

My father, Tim Tall Chief, attended the university from 1966 through 1971, earning his bachelor's degree in psychology, with minors in business administration and health and physical education. He later earned a master's degree in education in counseling psychology. However, in addition to going to college at Central, he also attended the school during his elementary years in Old North Tower in the laboratory school.

"The university has touched our lives in so many ways," he said. "I recall when my mother was wheelchair bound after contracting polio during the 1950s. Before the school was handicap accessible, I would help carry her up the stairs to her classes that she attended and also taught." Each semester, the elementary classrooms had a student teacher in addition to the regular classroom teacher. Dad said that all of the teachers were some of the most compassionate people he can remember. "We received the newest and latest teaching methods, which broadened our views of new possibilities in everything from teaching and learning to life," he said. "Because many of us were faculty children, it also was good to have our parents in the same vicinity. Students that came out of that program are now university presidents, doctors, and other truly outstanding national, state, and community leaders."

My mother, Michelle Wilson, married Dad while she attended the university from 1967 to 1972. Mom studied speech and hearing, and served as on-air talent for KCSC Radio. She was named Broadcaster of the Year in 1968. "Max Davis was my mentor in broadcasting and encouraged me despite the fact that I had no training in the business," Mom said. "In speech pathology, Dr. Lillian Ivey encouraged excellence and perfection in voice and diction. I particularly admired her techniques in visual learning." Amy, my sister, and I, were born while Mom worked on her master's degree in early childhood education at the university. Although Mom is retired, Dad currently serves as the Deputy Commissioner for Administration for the Oklahoma State Department of Health.

I earned my bachelor's degree in communication from UCO in 1995. Like Mom, I also had airtime on KCSC, presenting two morning newscasts on weekdays and anchoring and reporting on the Broadcasting Department television program, "The Edmond Report," and guest hosting "About Edmond."

Kelly Dyer hired me to work as a student writer in the Office of Communication and Publications where I began publishing articles in university publications, and other newspapers and magazines. Kelly also employed me to write the student recruitment catalog and a fundraising video for President George Nigh's multi-million dollar fundraising campaign to renovate the campus. Little did I know what a positive professional impact Kelly would have on my career.

That experience helped me earn my position as the head of Public Affairs for the Smithsonian Institution's National Museum of the American Indian in New York City. The writing experience I gained while working in the Communication and Publications office also led to my position as Art Galleries Editor for *Native Peoples Magazine* based in Phoenix, Arizona.

After completing work toward a master's of fine arts degree in dramatic writing at New York University's Tisch School of the Arts in New York, I later finished my master's degree in English at Bemidji State University in Minnesota. I also completed work toward my doctorate at the University of Toronto at the Centre for the Study of Drama before returning to Oklahoma. I am currently the Director of the Jacobson House Native Art Center in Norman and in my sixth year as Galleries Editor for *Native Peoples.*

While attending UCO, I felt a tremendous sense of pride carrying on a family tradition that spanned three generations and nearly 60 years. Because I was born while my parents attended the university, I came full circle—like my father before me—when I returned to campus to get my undergraduate degree.

George Nigh (1992-1997)

As early as 1990, George Nigh was considered a leading candidate to replace President Lillard. The transition from the Lillard to Nigh administrations had several interesting sidebars. Nigh was working on campus with the Nigh Institute and had already brought greater visibility to Central. President Lillard had been Donna Nigh's vice-principal when she was a student at Capitol High School in Oklahoma City. Both couples had known each other for quite some time. In fact, both first ladies had attended Central during their undergraduate years. Mary Helen Lillard had attended Central during World War II and Donna Nigh attended Central for one year after high school.

At age 65, George Nigh was the oldest person ever hired as a university president in Oklahoma. Interestingly, in his long career, he had been the youngest teacher in McAlester, Oklahoma's youngest legislator, and the youngest lieutenant governor in the nation. Nigh did not attempt to hide the fact that he was a public servant. He said, "I served in public office for 32 years, so I'm a professional politician. I grew up in a grocery store. I owned a grocery store. I taught school for eight years. I've done everything else, but I am the epitome of a professional politician. I believe in public service."

The regents set four primary goals for Nigh—establish a greater awareness of the university, develop a stronger tie

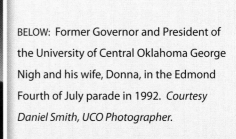

George Nigh served as the University of Central Oklahoma's eighteenth president from 1992 to 1997. During his time at Central, he earned the nickname the "Bricks and Mortar" president for his work to expand the university through construction and beautification. *Courtesy Bill Gooch, Curtis Studios.*

BELOW: Former Governor and President of the University of Central Oklahoma George Nigh and his wife, Donna, in the Edmond Fourth of July parade in 1992. *Courtesy Daniel Smith, UCO Photographer.*

with Edmond, create a greater multicultural awareness on campus, and establish a mission for the university. Nigh said, "I want to give you the facilities you need to do your job. I want former students to pull their diploma out of their drawer and hang it on the wall. I want Edmond and Oklahoma City both to think of this as their local university. And most importantly, I want never to hear again the reference 'Broncho High.'"

Many people within the Central community were happy with the decision to hire Nigh as president, but some were not. Some faculty were concerned with his lack of academic qualifications. He provided a deft response to his scholarly critics, "If you don't like it because I don't have a doctoral degree, just think how it's going to affect you when I remind you I don't even have a master's degree." He called on faculty to give him some time to serve as president of UCO. "Judge me when I leave," he told the faculty, "not when I start."

President Nigh launched a series of meetings with UCO faculty and administrators to develop a team concept for improving the physical plant and the classroom teaching programs of the university. The concept was patterned after the highly successful cabinet approach he used to manage state government.

During the weekend prior to assuming the presidency on July 1, 1992, Nigh and 43 faculty members and administrative staff attended a retreat for two days to discuss plans for UCO's future. Nigh was described as "a man in a hurry." He knew he would be at UCO only a few years, and needed to respond quickly to university needs.

As president, Nigh did not want to tinker with academic programs. It already was superb, he believed. But UCO needed greater visibility, and this was an opportunity for Nigh to lend his expertise to bolster UCO's image. "UCO is unrecognized by most people," Nigh said, "but it has an outstanding academic program." He wanted to provide the institution with the tools with which to teach—updated buildings, more parking spaces, bringing business people to campus, enhancing scholarships, raising faculty salaries, and raising funds for the university.

In retrospect, it was a good fit. "When I was hired," Nigh explained in an interview in 2004, "one of the leaders of the AAUP said it would be the worst thing that ever happened to UCO. When I retired, the president then of the AAUP said I was the best thing that ever happened to UCO."

Donna Nigh's Contributions

Donna Nigh's contributions included restoring the University House across from campus as a lunchtime restaurant for faculty. She oversaw renovation of the facility and acquired period furniture. In the evenings the house could be rented for social gatherings. "A lot of fundraising went on in that house," Donna Nigh recalled. "George would hold meetings and things and invite people to raise funds for the university. But that was a fun project for me. I worked on that for a couple of years."

Donna Nigh Art Gallery

When the University Center was expanded and remodeled during the Nigh years, the Donna Nigh Art Gallery was a wonderful addition to the fourth floor. Donna Nigh was instrumental in exhibiting art from Special Olympics. When the Nighs were in the governor's mansion, the art was exhibited at the State Capitol. When they assumed their leadership position at Central, they sponsored the Special Olympics Art Exhibit each year. With Donna Nigh as the driving force, the couple was instrumental in bringing the campus buildings up to code for individuals with special needs. She continues her work with the Donna Nigh Foundation, dedicated to helping individuals with special needs.

Massive Building Program

In the history of every institution, one observes the ebb and flow of trends. During the Godfrey years, Central experienced a swell of new faculty hires and unprecedented growth in campus buildings. During the Lillard years, the administration focused on raising the stature of academic programs and raising faculty salaries. During his five years as president, Nigh returned to a massive building program not seen since Godfrey.

Nigh was a quick study and learned that of all the institutions of higher education in Oklahoma, UCO received the lowest per capita allocation. As Nigh put it, "UCO's being at the bottom of the funding ladder was a problem. That's why we had gravel parking lots and un-air conditioned buildings. It was terrible. Yet, the academic program at this university was fantastic."

Members of the UCO administration gathered to celebrate the groundbreaking of the Education building in 1994. *Courtesy Daniel Smith, UCO Photographer.*

Dr. Marilyn Govich

By D. Keith Lough, M.A. in History, 2008

"I am an Oklahoman, born and bred," claims Dr. Marilyn Govich, Associate Professor of Music and coordinator of the vocal studies area at the University of Central Oklahoma. After graduating from Marlow High School, Govich attended the University of Oklahoma on a President's Scholarship. She earned bachelor's degrees in music education and vocal performance and received a Master's degree in vocal performance from OU. Govich returned to her alma mater in 2002 and completed a DMA in Vocal Performance.

Govich began teaching voice as a graduate student at OU and accepted a part-time position at Oklahoma Baptist University before becoming an adjunct professor at UCO in 1985. She received the UCO Hauptman Fellowship for research and creativity in 2002 and the OU School of Music further honored Govich for her outstanding achievements, naming her the recipient of the 2002 Gail Boyd DeStwolinski Award. OU recognized her dissertation, "Michael Heads Light Opera, Key Money: A Musical Dramaturgy," with the 2002 Provost's Dissertation Award. The dissertation was a co-winner in a national opera association competition in 2005.

Beginning with the lead role in a fifth-grade musical at Marlow Elementary, Govich has enjoyed a successful performing career appearing in the Lyric Theatre of Oklahoma productions, recitals for the Oklahoma Collegium Musicum, and the National Association of Teachers of Music regional conferences. Opera roles include Rosalinde in *Die Fledermaus*, Constanza in *Abduction from the Seraglio*, Dorabella in *Cosi Fan Tutte*, Alice in *Falstaff*, Madame Flora in *The Medium*, Miss Baggott in *The Little Sweep*, Lola in *Gallantry*, and Ann Putnam in *The Crucible*. Govich has performed in numerous musical theatre roles: Aldonza in *Man of La Mancha*, Winnifred in *Once Upon a Mattress*, Nancy in *Oliver*, Margot in *The Desert Song*, Ethel in *Footloose*, and Domina in *Forum*. The opportunity to perform influenced Dr. Govich to continue teaching voice at UCO. She held recitals for the National Association of Teachers of Singing and the Oklahoma Collegium Musicum, and served as adjudicator and clinician for vocal contests and workshops.

Students studying under Govich also have achieved great success in the performing arts on Broadway, regional theater, cruise line engagements, and as recording artists. Govich considered the accomplishments of former students among her greatest achievements. She said, "I have some honors, but my joy has been the success of my students—not just those who have performed on Broadway—but those who are teaching in public schools. I also enjoy hearing about my students who did not pursue music full-time, yet music has a special place in their lives."

And so the building projects began. Under Oklahoma law, an institution can issue bonds, but it must have a source of revenue to pay off the bond. As Nigh explained, UCO graduate Tom Thompson—the soccer field at UCO bears his name—was in the bond business. Thompson identified a revenue source for UCO to repay the bonds, but the plan appeared to be contrary to state law. He encouraged Nigh to appeal to the legislature and the state bond oversight committee to approve the plan.

Nigh used his political connections and received formal approval. A two-year $54 million capital-improvements master plan officially kicked off on April 22, 1994. Known as "The UCO Plan," other institutions of higher education in Oklahoma also have relied on the innovative funding idea. The revenue sources for the millions of dollars worth of bonds at UCO included student fees, parking fees, school land commission fees, and other fees.

Many construction projects were conceived, executed, and completed under President Nigh. A new central plant provided heating and cooling to university buildings. Placed alongside Old North, the new Education Building provided 30 classrooms, meeting rooms, and offices. Additions were built for the university library, Howell Hall, the business building, and the University Center. Additional parking,

Dr. Govich was married to the late Bruce Govich, a voice professor at OU and accomplished performer. Their three children, Milena, Mateja (Mat), and Nikola, graduated from UCO and were outstanding performers while on campus. Milena has appeared in numerous Broadway musicals, including the lead role in *Cabaret* in the touring company and on Broadway. Milena's talents have taken her to Europe, Canada, and China, and her acting skills landed several parts in television dramas, culminating in major roles on *Conviction* and *Law and Order* in 2006.

Mat also appeared in *Cabaret* on Broadway and has performed other musical productions and appeared in television commercials and dramas. Nikola, a theater major at UCO, did not pursue a professional performance career, but participated in musicals and dramas while attending UCO. A collection of photographs dedicated to the careers of her children adorns a wall in Dr. Govich's UCO studio.

Soon after graduating from OU in 1971, Dr. Govich performed Aldonza in *Man of La Mancha* for the Lyric Theatre. Twenty-six years later, Milena appeared on the same stage as a young actor, playing the role of Antonia. In 2004, mother and daughter shared the stage in a Lyric presentation of *Jekyll and Hyde*.

Her children and teaching manifest the passions of Dr. Govich. Describing her love for teaching, Govich said, "Oh, it's the greatest job. I love to come to work every day. I get to hang out with some of the greatest composers who ever lived, with the results of their work, and I get to work with young people who are aspiring to improve themselves and achieve something artistic."

Dr. Marilyn Govich, left, with her children Nikola, Milena, and Mateja. The theater remains a special place for Govich, especially when she shares it with her children. *Courtesy Marilyn Govich.*

landscaping, parks, and Broncho Lake were completed under the master plan. In addition, UCO donated land for a new Edmond Area Chamber of Commerce Building.

George and Donna Nigh have been pleased that they changed the physical look of the campus with campus beautification projects such as Broncho Lake. "It was fun because George came here with a mission," Donna Nigh reflected on her husband's tenure as president. "He knew he was not an academician. He wasn't going to come here trying to change how things were done. He basically came here to change the look of the campus and to get the community more involved with the school so they could work more closely together."

The Max Chambers Library after its new addition in 1997. *Courtesy Daniel Smith, UCO Photographer.*

Ringing of the bell tower in 1996 at the dedication of the newly-completed Education Building. *Courtesy Daniel Smith, UCO Photographer.*

Scholarships and Fundraising

President Nigh was instrumental in strengthening partnerships between Oklahoma businesses, foundations, and UCO. "The endowment of the Alumni Association when I became president," Nigh explained, "was just over $1 million. That's abysmal. And so we reinvigorated the foundation and the alumni and raised private funds." That renewed interest in funding the future of UCO has continued.

In August, 1994, President Nigh announced a $150,000 gift from Edith Gaylord Harper, secretary emeritus of The Oklahoma Publishing Company. The donation was matched by the university. Annual interest from the $300,000 was designated for use for faculty and staff development under the Edith Gaylord Harper Endowment Fund.

For three years while Nigh was president of UCO, Richard Burpee, retired lieutenant general, served as vice president for development and community relations and directed major fund raising efforts on behalf of the university. Under Burpee's leadership, significant gifts were added to the UCO Foundation. The school's first-ever private fund raising campaign surpassed its goal of $4.5 million. Burpee also headed Tinker Task Force 95, increasing visibility of UCO at Tinker Air Force Base in Midwest City.

President Nigh in the Classroom

President Nigh wanted the flexibility to engage students in the classroom with his knowledge and expertise on subjects ranging from Oklahoma history and government to handling a press conference, but he did not want to be tied down to the daily commitment and recordkeeping of teaching a formal course. "What I didn't want to be was the teacher, the instructor of record," Nigh said. "I didn't want to have to give tests and grade papers. But I would come in, for example, and lecture classes on press conferences and

Students, staff, and faculty "doing the Marcarena" at the urging of President George Nigh around the newly-completed Broncho Lake. *Courtesy Daniel Smith, UCO Photographer.*

how to do interviews and how to ask the right questions." Nigh also brought to the campus many nationally-known speakers from JCPenney, Sonic Corporation, Kerr-McGee Corporation, and other business and government institutions.

Campus Life

As in previous generations, student life sometimes led to controversy on the campus. On October 15, 1992, *The Vista* was accused of cutting out portions of student letters printed in the newspaper. The editor denied the accusations saying that the only time *The Vista* would ever cut parts of a letter would be to save space.

On October 11, 1994, gay and lesbian students held the first annual Gay and Lesbian "Coming Out" Day. The Gay and Lesbian Alliance Student Support, also known as GLASS, sponsored the event.

Murrah Bombing, 1995

On April 19, 1995, world attention turned to Oklahoma City and the bombing of the Alfred P. Murrah Federal Building. The blast could be heard in Edmond, and everyone would remember the half shell of the bombed-out building, the frantic rescue efforts, and the image of the firefighter holding the lifeless body of a child. Of the 168 people who perished in the worst terrorist attack in American history prior to 9/11, 21 were from Edmond.

Eight nursing faculty members and 51 students at UCO responded to the tragedy by providing triage stations at the federal building, volunteering with the American Red Cross, and serving in hospitals throughout the Oklahoma City area. "After 29 years of practicing disaster drills," Dr. Linda Steele, professor of nursing, said just weeks after the bombing, "it was good to see that we could actually respond and do a good job."

Edmond Growth

In 1995 new restaurants led all commercial development as Edmond Economic Development Authority Director Steve Kreidler reported that national chains began seriously evaluating the local market when Edmond's population reached 60,000.

Clintons Visit UCO Campus

On April 5, 1996, President Bill Clinton spoke to a crowd of 10,000 people in front of Old North on the UCO campus. The appearance was almost a year after the bombing of the Murrah Federal Building in Oklahoma City. President Clinton named President Nigh to the Oklahoma City Scholarship Fund Advisory Board to raise funds for the education of the surviving children of victims of the bombing.

Bill Clinton has visited the Central campus twice—once when governor of Arkansas and the second time for the Murrah bombing memorial. When President Clinton visited, Linda Jones recalled, it was "quite an experience." National media came to campus to cover the presidential visit—and a room in the basement of Evans Hall became the press room.

Tara Hodges, left, and Whitney Wheeler of Alpha Gamma Delta Sorority planted a tree on campus to remember those affected by the Alfred P. Murrah Federal Building bombing in 1995.
Courtesy Daniel Smith, UCO Photographer.

President Bill Clinton spoke in front of Old North when he visited the campus in 1996 to meet individuals who had survived the Alfred P. Murrah Federal Building bombing. *Courtesy Daniel Smith, UCO Photographer.*

Just west of the Y-Chapel of Song, the Heartland Plaza, a park dedicated to peace and reflection, opened in April, 1997, on the second anniversary of the Murrah bombing. Four markers are placed at the perimeter of the plaza, each containing messages of peace and healing from dignitaries, including President Bill Clinton and Reverend Billy Graham. A variety of trees, Caddo Sugar Maple, Possum Haw, Staghorn Sumac, and Sawtooth Oak, line the area. In 2004, with funding from the American Democracy Project and the College of Art, Media and Design, a sculpture entitled "Breathe," by alumnus David Thummel has been added to the plaza.

Downtown College Consortium

President Nigh saw two-year colleges in the Oklahoma City metropolitan area as feeder schools for UCO. He directed administrators to send UCO counselors to the community colleges to make certain students would not lose credit hours by later transferring to UCO. An innovative step in higher education was taken in 1995 when UCO and four other institutions opened a downtown Oklahoma City "college consortium" to offer college-level classes.

Nigh spearheaded a private fund raising drive to renovate classroom and administration space in the First National Center. Other schools participating in the consortium were Rose State College, Oklahoma City Community College, Oklahoma State University-Oklahoma City, and Redlands Community College.

In early 1996, Nigh announced he would retire from UCO on June 30, 1997, completing five years of service at the university, and a half century of public service.

In describing his sculpture, "Breathe," UCO alumnus David Thummel said, "Freedom embraces our arrangement as a civil society, allowing us to decorate our character as we wish. So breathe deep, because at the bottom of every breath, the opportunity to make a difference waits for you." *Courtesy Daniel Smith, UCO Photographer.*

W. Roger Webb (1997-present)

In 1997, W. Roger Webb, president of Northeastern Oklahoma State University for nearly 20 years, officially became the new UCO president. President Nigh described President Webb as a "mixture of the academician and the facilitator—a great marriage in one person."

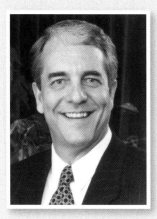

In 1997 W. Roger Webb became the University's nineteenth president. Since then, he has encouraged the growth of the student population and continues to strengthen academic programs on campus. *Courtesy Archives and Special Collections, UCO Library.*

President Webb had his work cut out for him from the outset. Enrollment had decreased during the previous three years, resulting in financial shortfalls in the operating budget, and prompting a vigorous advertising campaign for new students.

Born in Heavener, in eastern Oklahoma, Webb loved to read at an early age. During high school, he was active in sports and student council where a memorable civics teacher encouraged him to pursue government and leadership. Webb was the first member of his family to attend college and he felt a great sense of responsibility.

Webb enrolled at Oklahoma State University and studied history and political science. He graduated in 1964. Three years later, he secured his law degree from the University of Oklahoma. When asked in an interview if he wears orange or crimson, President Webb responded, "I wear blue."

By the late 1960s, Roger Webb had worked in Washington, DC, for a time and returned to Oklahoma and worked his way up the ranks in the Oklahoma Department of Public Safety. Appointed by Governor David Boren to serve as Commissioner of Public Safety, Webb was only in his late 20s.

Drawing on his political experiences, his knowledge of the law and his commitment to education, Webb became president of Northeastern Oklahoma State University at Tahlequah in 1978 at age 36. Prior to his appointment, no

President W. Roger Webb in a parade with his wife, Jeanie, and daughter, Anna Grace. *Courtesy Daniel Smith, UCO Photographer.*

one had served as president outside of public education. He was the first college president to hold the JD.

He served as president for 19 years and transformed a rural college into a university that was providing quality educational programs in eastern Oklahoma. Under Webb's leadership, for example, Northeastern partnered with the Cherokee Nation to develop a School of Optometry.

Dr. Jeanie Webb balances her professional career as Vice President of Student Affairs at Rose State College with her responsibilities as UCO's first lady. "Somehow Jeanie finds time to do it all," President Webb has said, "as well as be a great mom to our daughter, Anna Grace. Beyond serving as official hostess for many campus functions, she can often be found on campus lecturing on leadership, etiquette and other student-interest subjects."

Football and Wantland Stadium

In 1997, the winning football program helped bring greater visibility to UCO and attracted more students. The Bronchos ended the regular season as the top-ranked NCAA-Division II football team in the nation. The team made it to the second round of the Division II playoffs before falling to the University of California at Davis 26-7 and finishing the year at 9-3.

In 1998, the UCO Bronchos won their first ever Lone Star Conference football crown with a perfect 11-0 record. In 1999, the Bronchos had another successful football season by winning their first eight games with a number two ranking in the NCAA's Division II before fading at the end. Recently, campus improvements such as the renovated Wantland Stadium and the new Wellness Center have revitalized campus culture and residential life.

UCO star running back Joe Aska with Mike Kirk, 1995. Aska was a finalist for the Harlon Hill trophy, the NCAA Division II's equivalent of the Heisman. *Courtesy Archives and Special Collections, UCO Library.*

RIGHT: Basketball player Ton'Nea Cox, right, led the Lady Bronchos in the 1991-1992 season. The Lady Bronchos had a great year winning the Lone Star Conference in post season play. *Courtesy Daniel Smith, UCO Photographer.*

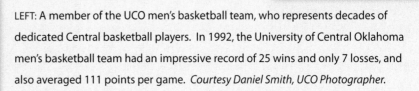

LEFT: A member of the UCO men's basketball team, who represents decades of dedicated Central basketball players. In 1992, the University of Central Oklahoma men's basketball team had an impressive record of 25 wins and only 7 losses, and also averaged 111 points per game. *Courtesy Daniel Smith, UCO Photographer.*

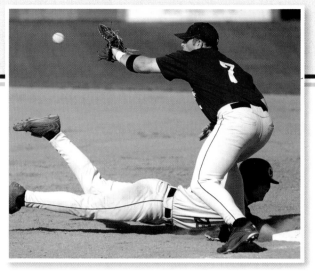

The relationship between the Bronchos and baseball dates back to 1896, and has come a long way from winning the conference championship for most original uniforms to becoming a nationally-recognized team. *Courtesy Daniel Smith, UCO Photographer.*

Fight Team, Fight for UCO

By Tim Cook, B.A. in History Education, 2007

As the athletes and coaches of the University of Central Oklahoma proudly stride onto the fields and courts throughout the Edmond campus, they walk into a place that many hold as a sacred location. While national recognition continues to grow at UCO, there are still many who have yet to experience the tradition that the Bronchos know so well—a tradition of excellence and achievement. Whether it is the first-class facilities, the loyal bronze and blue clad fans, or the endless enthusiasm through good times and bad, the University of Central Oklahoma has been, and will always be, an institution held in the highest regard by its peers.

In the past few decades, under the leadership of Athletic Directors Charlie Murdock, John "Skip" Wagnon, and Bill Farley, the University of Central Oklahoma has competed successfully in both the National Association of Intercollegiate Athletics (NAIA) and the National Collegiate Athletic Association Division II (NCAA II), and soon may be positioned for the NCAA Division I. Unlike some schools, UCO is not known for just one sport. In fact, athletes have excelled in a number of sports throughout the years.

When wrestling first returned to Central in the early 1970s after a thirty-year hiatus, the Bronchos were unique in that they sported an "All Oklahoma" roster, in other words, every member of the team came from Oklahoma. This team and the teams to follow experienced incredible success by proving themselves over and over again on the national stage. The wrestling teams at UCO won the NAIA national championship in 1979, six consecutive titles in 1981 through 1987, and again in 1989. From 1973 to 1989, the Bronchos placed second, third, and fourth multiple times. During the 1990s, UCO became a member of the NCAA II. In this era, the Bronchos won four national championships from 1992 through 1995, and won two more in 2002 and 2003.

Although there have been many people throughout the years that have contributed to wrestling at UCO, one man stands out among the rest. David James, a former wrestler and the Bronchos current coach, remains a positive influence on the sport. Coach James, a 1980 graduate of Central, was one of the best wrestlers ever to compete at

the university and finished his career with a 116-16 record for a winning percentage of .879. He was an NAIA Hall of Fame member, earned All-American honors each of his four years in competition, and was a two-time National Champion. As a coach, James also received multiple "Coach of the Year" honors.

In football, Chuck Langston was hired as the head football coach in 2002, and immediately took the Bronchos to the NCAA Division Playoffs. Coach Langston has a reputation for being a well organized, creative and hard-nosed football coach with an equally strong commitment to building character in his players.

Another thriving sport at UCO is women's golf. The current women's golf coach, Patty Coatney, had a very successful background in golf for more than four decades, including four-time Oklahoma Women's Amateur Champion. Hired four years ago to start the women's program at UCO, her team immediately won their first two Lone Star Conference Championships. She also coached two individual champions as well.

With its latest renovation, Wantland Stadium is now one of the premier football stadiums in Division II. *Courtesy Daniel Smith, UCO Photographer.*

Dax Johnston, former national championship golfer at Central Oklahoma, coaches the men's golf program. In just six years, the enthusiastic young coach has developed the program into one of the best in NCAA Division II.

The UCO women's soccer team also has had great success. With Major League Soccer and the World Cup, soccer has been growing in popularity in the United States, and soccer has found a home with the Lady Bronchos and their coach, Mike Cook. Since 2000, when women's soccer achieved a national ranking of sixth, the Lady Bronchos have finished in the top 25 four years in a row, they were the Lone Star Conference regular season champions five years, and the Lone Star Conference champions four years.

Other sports at UCO are accomplished as well. It seems that every year since Coach Wendell Simmons has taken over the baseball team, UCO is competing for conference and national championships. In 2006, Coach Ginny Honea and the UCO women's softball team won conference and regional titles, and were invited to the women's national softball tournament.

Terry Evans, one of the top young coaches in the United States, leads the men's basketball program. A former UCO athlete and graduate, Gary Hardaker, coaches the women's basketball program and the forecasts are very promising for this program. Women's volleyball, under Coach Jeff Boyland, is becoming a marquee sport on campus and there is new optimism about the prospects of women's tennis and cross country.

Athletic facilities help athletic programs compete. "Wantland Stadium has experienced an extreme makeover," President Roger Webb said. "It is a total new look paid for by students, and it gives us the finest football stadium in Division II." Significant improvements have been made to upgrade the soccer, softball and baseball fields. With first-class facilities, exceptional coaches, and superior athletes, the athletic programs at the University of Central Oklahoma have strong traditions and an exciting future.

BELOW: In recent years, the UCO women's soccer team has experienced a great deal of success on the national stage. *Courtesy Daniel Smith, UCO Photographer.*

ABOVE: Nikki Vandever is proof that a small-town athlete can make it big in a national arena. In her high school, Vandever helped lead the Davenport Bulldogs to multiple state championships, and brought the same leadership and intensity to the Lady Bronchos. *Courtesy Daniel Smith, UCO Photographer.*

LEFT: Football has been a long-standing tradition in Edmond. From its humble beginnings at the Normal School all the way to today at the University of Central Oklahoma, football has been, and will always be, an integral part of Central. *Courtesy Daniel Smith, UCO Photographer.*

By 2000, Edmond's population surpassed 70,000 and the construction of gated communities, new restaurants, and shopping centers have continued unrestrained. The Edmond Historical Society asked Dr. Samuel Magrill, professor of music at UCO, to compose a historical opera on the history of Edmond. Entitled "Showdown on Two Street," the opera's overture became the official march of the City of Edmond.

Oklahoma Forensic Institute

UCO has been a leader in forensic science education for thirty years. Beginning with the B.S. in Forensic Science in 1975, the program grew to include the M.S. in Forensic Science approved by the Oklahoma State Regents for Higher Education in 2000. President Webb's previous experience in law enforcement and his dedication to undergraduate research came together in his vision for the Oklahoma Forensic Institute.

Collaborating with the Oklahoma State Bureau of Investigation, UCO has launched the Oklahoma Forensic Institute which, according to President Webb, "will become a national center for providing the highest level of learning to our students in this highly specialized field. The Institute will also become a national center for forensic training to law enforcement personnel, district attorneys, judges, Homeland Security personnel and others who use DNA and forensic findings in legal or medical cases." The first director of the Oklahoma Forensic Institute is Dwight Adams, former director of the FBI Forensic Laboratory at Quantico, Virginia. Dr. Adams, an international expert on DNA evidence, is attracting many of the top forensic experts to Edmond and UCO to participate in this landmark program.

Dr. Wei Chen

By Julie Bennett-Jones, B.A. in History, 2005; M.A. in History, 2007

Few professors are more respected in the area of physics than Dr. Wei Chen. Born in Shanghai, China, he received his B.S. degree from Shandong University in Jinan, China, in physics. He later came to the United States to earn his M.S. and Ph.D. degrees in physics from the University of Oregon and became an American citizen. He also took postdoctoral classes from the University of Oregon before coming to Oklahoma in 1990 to teach at the University of Central Oklahoma.

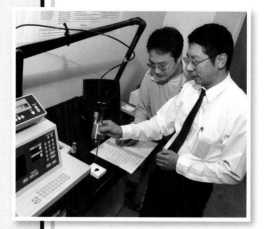

Dr. Wei Chen (right), Director of the Biomedical Engineering Program in the Department of Engineering and Physics at UCO. *Courtesy Daniel Smith, UCO Photographer.*

He began his career at the University of Central Oklahoma as a lecturer of physics in 1994. In 1999, he became an assistant professor of physics at UCO—a position he held until 2001 when he became an associate professor. Currently, Dr. Chen is the Director of Biomedical Engineering Program in the Department of Engineering and Physics Engineering at UCO. While holding this significant station, he also serves in other high-level positions as an adjunct associate professor in the School of Aerospace and Mechanical Engineering at the University of Oklahoma as well as an adjunct associate professor of Veterinary Clinical Sciences in the Department of Veterinary Clinical Sciences at the College of Veterinary Medicine at Oklahoma State University.

In the fall of 2000, Dr. Chen proposed the Biomedical Engineering undergraduate degree program at UCO which was approved by the Oklahoma State Regents for Higher Education. As a result, he created several classes including Principles of Biomedical Engineering I and II. Other classes developed by Dr. Chen included Medical Physics, Medical Physics Lab, and Modern Physics Lab. These are but a few of the 17 courses taught by Dr. Chen over the years.

Known for his cutting-edge research in laser cancer treatment, Dr. Chen is the recipient of no less than 15 University honors and awards as well as other commendations earned in his field. He continues to expand the current research in his field of study. The research Dr. Chen has conducted has led to numerous patents as well as extensive grants obtained from various sources such as the Office of Naval Research, the National Institute of Health, the Oklahoma Center for the Advancement of Science and Technology, and many others. Two research grants received from the National Institute of Health, in which he was the co-principal Investigator, totaled nearly $3.5 million.

Dr. Chen's writings have appeared in many publications. His journal articles can be found in publications such as the *Journal of Applied Research*, the *International Journal of Cancer*, the *Journal of Environmental Pathology, Toxicology and Oncology, Molecular Biotechnology, Cancer Investigation*, and a myriad of others. Additionally, he co-authored a chapter in *Fundamentals and Applications of Biophotonics in Dentistry*.

Undoubtedly, Dr. Chen's research has helped further not only an examination into essential topics such as cancer research, but also has increased the educational opportunities for the numerous students who have worked with him.

Stewardship and the Green Campus Model

Under the leadership and environmental initiative of Executive Vice President Steve Kreidler, UCO is the largest university in the country operating exclusively on clean energy and wind power. Sponsored by the Environmental Protection Agency and the Department of Energy, UCO joined other members of the elite Green Power Leadership Club as the first representative from Oklahoma in 2006. "We are using 100 percent wind energy in order to decrease our country's dependency on non-green energy sources and set an example for our students and community," Kreidler said. A pacesetter in the state as a Green Power model, UCO also has onsite bio-diesel production and continues to increase energy performance and efficiency on campus.

Under the direction of Dr. Bill Caire, the Selman Living Laboratory near Freedom, Woodward County, is a field station with opportunities for faculty and student research in the biology of western ecosystems, cave biology, astronomy and archaeology. *Courtesy Daniel Smith, UCO Photographer.*

Leadership for the Future

President Webb has infused his leadership style of the "3 C's"— community, character, and civility—into the University of Central Oklahoma's institutional culture. He believes that UCO has a responsibility to produce the next generation of Oklahoma's leaders. Building on the long tradition of providing quality learning and research experiences for students, UCO's outstanding and caring faculty and staff remain committed to educating the next generation of leaders for Oklahoma. UCO's mission statement is compelling and clear: Helping students learn so that they may become productive, creative, ethical, and engaged citizens.

From the new leadership minor and the American Democracy Project focus on civic engagement to the partnership with the U.S. Olympic Committee as an official Olympic training site, from the Selman Living Laboratory near Woodward to the academic programs offered on the Rose State campus, from a greater emphasis on undergraduate research and executive education to the Oklahoma Quality and Baldridge Quality Initiatives, the University of Central Oklahoma is emerging as a major U.S. metropolitan university.

In 2005, the University of Central Oklahoma was the first university in Oklahoma to receive the Oklahoma Quality Award. Governor Brad Henry presented the Oklahoma Quality Award to UCO administrators and regents. From left to right (top row): Dan Donaldson, Rocky Flick, Ed Cunliff, Chuck Hughes, Donna Guinn, President W. Roger Webb, Lon Denart, Governor Brad Henry, Cynthia Rolfe, Provost Bill Radke, Chris Markwood, Cheryl Steele, and Anne Holzberlein. Left to right (bottom row): Regent Jan Gordon, Jeanie Webb, Regent Belva Howard, Vice Provost Pat LaGrow, and Melinda Henderson. *Courtesy Daniel Smith, UCO Photographer.*

Bob Palmer, Muralist

By Megan McGregor, B.A. in History, 2005; M.A. in History, 2007

"You can change the feel of a space, whether that's a room or wall in a town, with a mural. And part of the thrill to me is bringing that space to life," said UCO art professor, Dr. Bob Palmer, on his life's passion. Born in Walters, Oklahoma, Palmer graduated in a class of forty-five people without having taken an art class. His teachers, however, began to take notice of his gift as he doodled on notebook paper. Soon, teachers asked him to create bulletin boards and decorate hallways. Despite these activities, Palmer's family was surprised when he decided to study art at the University of Oklahoma. After graduating from OU with a degree in Art Education in 1973, Palmer returned to Walters to establish an art department. Two years later, he decided to attend graduate school at East Tennessee State University in Johnson City, Tennessee, where he graduated with a Master's of Fine Arts in Painting and Photography. Palmer then returned to Oklahoma to teach at the university level, and simultaneously obtained his Ph.D. in Curriculum and Instruction from Oklahoma State University.

Dr. Palmer began teaching at UCO in the early 1990s, about the same time he started painting murals. Friends and neighbors frequently asked him to paint their kitchens or bathrooms, and he naturally gravitated toward constructing murals on large walls. In the mid-1990s, Palmer established a mural program in the Department of Art, one of the few programs of its kind in the nation. Palmer and his students completed murals in buildings across the UCO campus, including the Administration Building, Behavioral Sciences Building, and Howell Hall.

Dr. Palmer is especially proud of the work he and his students do in communities, not only to enhance their skills as artists, but as professionals in the public sphere. As of December 2006, Palmer

In 2000, the Oklahoma Art Educators Association named Dr. Palmer as the Outstanding Educator for Higher Education, and the same year the Arts Assembly awarded his work at the Oklahoma Capitol as the Outstanding Community Arts Effort for a group. In 2007, Dr. Palmer was selected as the state's overall Art Educator of the Year. Dr. Palmer continues to share his passion for murals with the art students at UCO, and communities across the world benefit from his talent. *Courtesy Daniel Smith, UCO Photographer.*

and his art students had completed more than 1,000 murals in Oklahoma communities, including Cushing, Drumright, Edmond, Hinton, McAlester, Stigler, Vian, Walters, and Yale. Palmer stated that these small town communities speak to him over and over. "Forgotten places pull me in and say, 'We are important! We need art too! We have a story to tell.'" Perhaps his most well-known murals, however, are located in downtown Oklahoma City. The business OKC Rocks commissioned Palmer to create the Oklahoma state flag on their 120-feet tall grain elevators, one of the most noticeable murals in the area. His newest project is a timeline of Oklahoma's history for the state's centennial, constructed in Bricktown alongside the Santa Fe railroad. Other murals in Oklahoma City include the Capitol Building and Pinnacle Fitness, which combines abstract art with images of extreme sports. Palmer and his students have also painted murals in Canada, Croatia, Macedonia, and Mexico.

My UCO

By Jill Sallee, B.A. in Geography, 2008

My favorite thing about the University of Central Oklahoma is watching the sun set on Old North from the second story of the Liberal Arts building. I have never seen anything more beautiful, and as I watch the sun race to the horizon I take the moment to stop what I am doing and think. I think about the things that remain unchecked on my to do list, the test I have the next day, and the friend I forgot to call. I think about the past and the future, about where I will be in ten years and the road that will take me there. I am just your typical college student. In my day, I go to class, work, eat, take a nap, do homework, and go to bed. I am still confused about life, love, school, work, family, and so much more. I try my hardest everyday to do what is right. No matter the good or the bad, the best or the worst, I would not change a moment of my life. I do not think I am special, talented, gifted or unique, but I have found my place at the University of Central Oklahoma.

As a wide-eyed senior in high school, I was overwhelmed with applications for colleges and scholarships. I applied for everything that I could get my hands on including the President's Leadership Scholarship. The day that I received the call that I had gotten the scholarship was the day I decided my future. I was going to be a University of Central Oklahoma "Broncho," even if it appeared to be misspelled. My scholarship required that I was in three organizations; however, before I had realized it, I had signed up for seven. I was meeting people, making friends, and planning events. In between organizations and homework, I did not have a lot of free time, but I liked it this way. I had received a 4.0 both semesters and I was very proud of my accomplishments.

I hit the ground running my sophomore year. I was already the officer of several organizations and even more involved than I was the year before. My biggest responsibility was the Speaker of the House in the Student Government Association. In the middle of the year, my best friend talked me into entering the Miss UCO pageant. I would be a great representative of my university because it

was my life. I had a passion for my school that the other contestants did not. I did not like wearing high heals and lipstick, but I pulled it off for one night. My love for UCO must have shown through because the night of the pageant, the crowd was surprised when I was crowned Miss University of Central Oklahoma. I did not realize how much extra work I would have to do with the title. I thought that the crown was just something pretty that I would get to wear in parades. However, I quickly found myself making appearances, filling out paper work, and raising awareness on my platform issue.

At this point in my life, I realized that my life was living me and not the other way around. I spent the entire day sitting next to Broncho Lake and decided that I had to rid my life of some of the unnecessary things. The only problem was that I did not want to quit anything. I love being involved because I wanted to give everything that I could to UCO. I started to think about the things that I would want to do with my life. I finally accepted the fact that I did not like my major, and my advisor showed me some other degree sheets that might be able to work with my schedule. Now the next sentence is not one that will win me a cool girl award, but I have loved maps since I was a little girl. I have always been fascinated with people and culture. I had taken some electives in Geography and talked to my professor about the career opportunities. Once I found out

Jill Sallee crowned Miss UCO 2006 by Miss UCO 2005 Kelee Bright. *Courtesy Jill Sallee.*

UCO has a long tradition of pageants on campus. Pictured here are all five Miss UCOs for 2006 (from left to right): Miss Asian UCO Umiko Akiba, Miss Black UCO Keondra Butler, Miss Oklahoma (then Miss America 2007) Lauren Nelson, Miss UCO Jill Sallee, Miss Hispanic UCO Erika Balderas. *Courtesy Jill Sallee.*

that I was right on track to graduate in the four years with the Geography degree, I switched right away. It took some reassuring to convince my parents that I had a future when it came to Geography. I felt as if this major switch was one of the hugest moments of my life because I was letting go of all of the things that I needed to.

When I moved back to campus for the start of my junior year I was sad to leave home. I had such an amazingly simple life in Bixby and I was afraid that I would get sucked back into the fast pace lifestyle that was typical of me. I surprised a ton of people because I did not run for offices or fill out leadership award applications. It was not until I realized that in losing the other, busy stuff, I was gaining so much more. I was able to invest my time into different people. I learned everything I could about my friends and their friends. I met the people in my classes who are also Geography majors. I took naps and watched television. I had my life back and I was able to do the things that I wanted to with it. I loved my classes this year, too. I guess it is true that you will enjoy what you are passionate about. Over Christmas break I went to a Christian conference. While I was there I decided that I wanted to spend some portion of my life China. When I came home I was thrilled to find out that UCO offered Chinese classes, and I enrolled. Because of my new Chinese class, I was exposed to even more culture, but that is not the best part. The class starts at 5:30 on Tuesdays and Thursdays. The professor always allows us a break at 6:30 because are minds are so

overwhelmed by the new sounds and words. I do one thing during this break and it had become the highlight of my week. I venture over to the large windows on the second floor of the Liberal Arts building and I watch the sunset.

I am so thankful for the time I have been able to spend at UCO. Everyday this place gives me so many opportunities and experiences that have allowed me to become the woman I am today. I am having the college experience that I have always dreamed about and I know that it would not be the same if I went to college anywhere else. I feel as though no task in future will be too hard because of what I have gained from my time here. I am unable to completely express the gratitude that I have for the University of Central Oklahoma and all that it has given me. I have laughed and cried, succeeded and failed, and loved and lost, but all of it has made me proud to be a Broncho.

Lauren Nelson, a sophomore music theatre major, brought national visibility to UCO when she became Miss America in January 2007. In back-to-back wins, Oklahoma transferred the title from Jennifer Berry to Lauren Nelson, a very special tribute during Oklahoma's centennial. *Courtesy Miss America Organization.*

Chapter Ten Timeline

1990

• Iraq invaded Kuwait

• Germany reunited

• Hubble Space Telescope launched

• *Home Alone* hit the box office

1991

• Operation Desert Storm and Persian Gulf War began

• David L. Walters became Governor of Oklahoma

• CSU became the University of Central Oklahoma (UCO)

1992

• Bill Clinton became President of the United States

• Rodney King verdict sparked rioting in Los Angeles

• George Nigh became President of UCO

1993

• Single European market began

• Terrorist bombing of the World Trade Center

• North American Free Trade Agreement (NAFTA)

1994

• Margaret Mandela elected president of South Africa

• *Pulp Fiction* premiered in theaters

• O.J. Simpson controversy

1995

• Bombing of the Alfred P. Murrah Federal Building in Oklahoma City

• Frank A. Keating became Governor of Oklahoma

President George Nigh with President Roger Webb on stage at the Lessons in Leadership Lecture (230 students enrolled). *Courtesy Daniel Smith, UCO Photographer.*

1996

• Dunblane Massacre in primary school in Scotland

• Whitewater Scandal

• Defense of Marriage Act

• Electronic Freedom of Information Act

• Completion of the Education Building at the UCO

1997

• Dolly, a sheep, successfully cloned

• Madeleine Albright became first female United States secretary of state

• Roger Webb became President of the UCO

• Completion of the Heartland Plaza at UCO

1998

• Europe declared continental currency, the euro

• Smoking banned in all California restaurants and bars

• Selman Living Laboratory established in Freedom, Woodward County, providing opportunities for faculty and student research

• *Saving Private Ryan* premiered in movie theaters

1999

• President Bill Clinton acquitted of impeachment charges

• Shootings at Columbine High School in Littleton, Colorado

• UCO Strategic Plan

• *Who Wants to be a Millionaire?* became a popular game show in the United States

Longtime Central athletics coach Dale Hamilton during the renaming of the Broncho Field House to Hamilton Field House in 1993. *Courtesy Daniel Smith, UCO Photographer.*

RIGHT: The relationship between Rose State and UCO began in the early 1990s. UCO now has a building on the Rose State campus offering degree programs in business administration, nursing and the Oklahom Degree Completion Program. *Courtesy Daniel Smith, UCO Photographer.*

ABOVE: Night of Champions including Nadia Comaneci, Shannon Miller, Jeanie Webb, Governor Brad Henry, and President Roger Webb. *Courtesy Daniel Smith, UCO Photographer.*

2000
- Mad Cow Disease panicked Europe
- Controversial Presidential election between George W. Bush and Al Gore
- George W. Bush designated President of the United States
- Vermont approved same-sex unions
- Reality Television revitalized its popularity with the show Survivor

2001
- Terrorists attacked World Trade Center
- United States military campaign in Afghanistan
- Patriot Act passed
- Anthrax scare panicked United States
- No Child Left Behind Act passed
- UCO Suites opened

RIGHT: Located on 5th Street in Edmond, the UCO Jazz Lab features outstanding student performances as well as leading jazz musicians including trumpeter Wynton Marsalis. *Courtesy Daniel Smith, UCO Photographer.*

2002
- UCO Jazz Lab opened
- Department of Homeland Security added to Presidential Cabinet
- Melton Legacy Collection
- Enron and WorldCom controversies
- Washington, D.C. snipers killed ten people

Emma Plunkett, shovel in hand, planted a tree at the dedication of the Emma W. Plunkett Garden located south of Wantland Hall. *Courtesy Khalid Awang, UCO Photographic Services.*

The historic Hazard House, built in 1910, became property of the University of Central Oklahoma in 1995. It was first used as a faculty and staff, dining and meeting place. Today it is the Alumni House. *Courtesy Justin Avera, UCO Photographic Services.*

2003
• United States' troops captured Saddam Hussein
• Wellness Center opened
• Space shuttle Columbia disaster
• Arnold Schwarzenegger became governor of California
• Brad Henry became governor of Oklahoma
2004
• Estimated 120 million voters set the record turn out for Presidential election
• College of Arts, Media and Design "Breathe" sculpture unveiled
2005
• Central Plaza
• Tsunami destroyed southern coast of Asia
• Oklahoma Quality Award
• Wantland Stadium renovation
2006
• Old North interior renovation begins
• Wireless Campus
2007
• Troy Smith donates $3 million to the College of Business

President Jim Cook of Rose State College and President W. Roger Webb of the University of Central Oklahoma signing the Rose State/UCO Agreement on July 21, 2005. *Courtesy Daniel Smith, UCO Photographer.*

Central

Conclusion

Teacher training remains at the heart of Central's mission. Families at the turn of the century would relocate to be close to Central's campus so that their children could attend school and receive a quality education. Kathryn Kunc, an art professor emeritus at UCO, recalls her mother and father making a deliberate decision to move to Edmond so that their four children could attend school at Central and grow up in a college town.

Beginning in 1928, Kunc attended the Kindergarten program at the training school at Central and continued her studies at Central through primary and secondary school and college. The teacher training program at Central benefited the college students training to be teachers and the children in the program. "We had all the advantages that anyone would want," Kunc said, recalling her days in the lab school. "We had swimming, dancing. They think skating is new, we skated on the campus. We had tennis. In grade school, we had an art teacher that was also a college professor. We had a gym teacher that was also a college professor. My history teachers, even in seventh and eighth grade, we had college professors and also, student teachers and all of them were outstanding. We were far above the average."

In many ways, as Central grew and developed from a teacher training institution to a college and then a university, Kathryn Kunc also grew up with Central. Her commitment to Central represents the deep commitment many people share with this special place – a place of memories, a place of learning, a place of relationships, a place of dreams.

As we prepare to celebrate Oklahoma's centennial in 2007, we also celebrate Central's vibrant past as inherently connected to the establishment of Oklahoma Territory, the uniting of Oklahoma Territory and Indian Territory at statehood in 1907, and the legacy and important place Central holds in the history of higher education.

Kathryn Kunc, fourth from left, and her classmates at the training school at Central, building furniture for a storybook house in their school, 1928. Kunc recalls lots of playground equipment near Old North for the children. *Courtesy Kathryn Kunc.*

Kunc attended college at Central from 1939 to 1942 and majored in home economics and art. During the next decade, Kunc gained teaching experience in public schools throughout Oklahoma and also pursued graduate study. In 1952, President Max Chambers offered her a position in the art department at Central State – and she remained a full-time faculty member until her retirement in 1986. Then she taught art classes at Central as an adjunct instructor from 1986 until 2004. *Courtesy Kathryn Kunc.*

BIBLIOGRAPHY

Archival Materials

Edmond, Oklahoma, Archives and Special Collections,
 Max Chambers Library, University of Central Oklahoma.

Vertical Files

Athletics
Bicentennial
Campus Maps
Central's Anniversaries
CSU Buildings Master Plan
CSU Centennial
Fraternity and Sorority Houses
History of UCO
Homecoming
Howell Hall
Jazz Lab
Mitchell Hall
Murdaugh Hall
Old North
Thatcher Hall
UCO Traditions
Y-Chapel

Oral History Interviews

Alcorn, Alvin. Interviewed by Brodie Pitts, 28 March 2006,
 Edmond, Oklahoma.

Alcorn, Alvin. Interviewed by Brodie Pitts, 20 April 2006,
 Edmond, Oklahoma.

Baker, James. Interviewed by Erica Johnson, 14 April 2005,
 Edmond, Oklahoma.

Ball, Phil. Interviewed by Oliver Pettry, 5 October 2004,
 Edmond, Oklahoma.

Bartgis, Elaine. Interviewed by Stephanie Shafer, 10 November
 2005, Edmond, Oklahoma.

Bond, Mary. Interviewed by Dianne Rice, 20 October 2005,
 Edmond, Oklahoma.

Cherry, Gerry. Interviewed by Felicia Harrison, 25 May 2006,
 Edmond, Oklahoma.

Collins, Reba. Interviewed by Jamie Martin, 27 October 2004,
 Edmond, Oklahoma.

Evans, Eddie. Interviewed by Brandi Bullard, 10 December 2004,
 Oklahoma City, Oklahoma.

Fulgraf, Herman. Interviewed by Kathi Nehls, 11 April 2005,
 Edmond, Oklahoma.

Galey, Conrad. Interviewed by Felicia Harrison, 4 April 2006,
 Norman, Oklahoma.

Godfrey, Garland. Interviewed by Kenny L. Brown, 11 September
 2004, Bella Vista, Arkansas.

Godfrey, Jocille. Interviewed by Nicole Willard, 11 September
 2004, Bella Vista, Arkansas.

Godfrey, Garland and Jocille. Interviewed by Erica Johnson, 11
 September 2004, Bella Vista, Arkansas.

Govich, Marilyn. Interviewed by Julie Bennett-Jones, 13 February
 2006, Edmond, Oklahoma.

Guinn, Donna. Interviewed by Amanda Cagle, 28 March 2006,
 Edmond, Oklahoma.

Guthrie, Cal. Interviewed by Melissa Brodt, 6 April 2006,
 Chandler, Oklahoma.

Guthrie, Peggy. Interviewed by Kim Penrod, 6 April 2006,
 Chandler, Oklahoma.

Hicks, Lee. Interviewed by Felicia Harrison, 9 March 2006,
 Oklahoma City, Oklahoma.

Hoig, Stan. Interviewed by Erica Johnson, 11 October 2004,
 Edmond, Oklahoma.

Howard, Gary. Interviewed by Jon Freeman, 29 March 2004,
 Edmond, Oklahoma.

Ice, Randy. Interviewed by Kathi Goebel, 4 April 2006,
 Edmond, Oklahoma.

Ivey, Lillian. Interviewed by Kim Penrod, 10 October 2004,
 Edmond, Oklahoma.

Jackson, Joe. Interviewed by Kathi Nehls, 17 November 2004,
 Edmond, Oklahoma.

James, David. Interviewed by Oliver Pettry, 2 December 2004,
 Edmond, Oklahoma.

Jones, Linda. Interviewed by Laura Lewis, 5 October 2004,
 Edmond, Oklahoma.

Jung, Walter. Interviewed by Lynn Brown, 30 March 2005,
 Edmond, Oklahoma.

Kidd, Juanita. Interviewed by Brandi Bullard, 14 October 2004, Edmond, Oklahoma.

Kunc, Kathryn. Interviewed by Leslie Dixon, 12 October 2004, Edmond, Oklahoma.

Kunc, Kathryn. Interviewed by Leslie Dixon, 16 November 2004, Edmond, Oklahoma.

LaGrow, Patricia. Interviewed by Julie Bennett-Jones, 17 February 2006, Edmond, Oklahoma.

Lehman, Paul. Interviewed by Laura Lewis, 8 December, 2004, Edmond, Oklahoma.

Lehman, Paul. Interviewed by Melissa Brodt, 20 February 2006, Edmond, Oklahoma.

Lillard, Bill. Interviewed by James Etzler, 1 October 2004, Edmond, Oklahoma.

Lillard, Mary Helen. Interviewed by Lisa Pham, 2 March 2005, Oklahoma City, Oklahoma.

Lower, Elaine. Interviewed by Michelle Byrd, 30 November 2004, Edmond, Oklahoma.

Lower, Gary. Interviewed by Michelle Byrd, 30 November 2004, Edmond, Oklahoma.

McGinnis, Patrick. Interviewed by Greg Zornes, 3 May 2005, Edmond, Oklahoma.

Naifeh, Saundra. Interviewed by Kim Penrod, 2 February 2006, Edmond, Oklahoma.

Nigh, Donna. Interviewed by Michelle Byrd, 28 October 2004, Edmond, Oklahoma.

Nigh, George. Interviewed by Stephanie Shafer, 28 October 2004, Edmond, Oklahoma.

Nigh, George and Donna. Interviewed by Stephanie Shafer, 28 October 2004, Edmond, Oklahoma.

Osborn, John. Interviewed by Ross Tripp, 11 April 2005, Edmond, Oklahoma.

Palmer, Bob. Interviewed by Shane Stansberry, 20 April 2006, Edmond, Oklahoma.

Peters, Richard. Interviewed by Erica Johnson, 2 May 2005, Edmond, Oklahoma.

Peters, Virginia. Interviewed by Michelle Byrd, 28 September 2004, Edmond, Oklahoma.

Peterson, Royce. Interviewed by Kim Penrod, 22 March 2005, Edmond, Oklahoma.

Pinkston, Gerry. Interviewed by Stephanie Shafer, 1 December 2005, Edmond, Oklahoma.

Pugh, Ed. Interviewed by Stephanie Shafer, 4 May 2005, Edmond, Oklahoma.

Radke, William. Interviewed by Kim Penrod, 23 February 2006, Edmond, Oklahoma.

Rao, S. Narasinga. Interviewed by John Barthell, 2 March 2006, Edmond, Oklahoma.

Reeder, Billie. Interviewed by Kim Penrod, 3 February 2006, Edmond, Oklahoma.

Reeder, Dale. Interviewed by Stephanie Shafer, 15 December 2005, Edmond, Oklahoma.

Reeder, Jimmie. Interviewed by Kim Penrod, 3 February 2006, Edmond, Oklahoma.

Reeder, Billie, Dale and Jimmie. Interviewed by Kim Penrod, 3 February 2006, Edmond, Oklahoma.

Reherman, Carl. Interviewed by Jessie Hopper, 28 March 2006, Edmond, Oklahoma.

Rice, Earl and Loree. Interviewed by Kim Penrod, 14 December 2004, Edmond, Oklahoma.

Ryan, Annette. Interviewed by Stephanie Shafer, 16 November 2005, Edmond, Oklahoma.

Van Osdol, William. Interviewed by Stephanie Shafer, 15 November 2004, Edmond, Oklahoma.

Warren, Cliff. Interviewed by James Etzler, 12 November 2004, Edmond, Oklahoma.

Webb, David. Interviewed by Erica Johnson, 8 April 2005, Edmond, Oklahoma.

Webb, W. Roger. Interviewed by Kim Penrod, 17 May 2006, Edmond, Oklahoma.

Williams, Bill. Interviewed by Leslie Dixon, 6 December 2004, Edmond, Oklahoma.

Newspapers

Daily Oklahoman, The

Edmond Sun

Edmond Sun-Democrat

Vista, The

University Publications

Annual Catalogue

Bowser Towser

Bronze Book

Central State Newsletter

Old North Alumni Magazine

Quarterly Bulletin

Books and Articles and Other Materials

Barde, Frederick S. "Shall Oklahoma Educational Institutions Be Kept Submerged in Politics?" *Sturm's Oklahoma Magazine* 6 (May 1908): 21-23.

Bennett, Henry G. "A System of Higher Education in Oklahoma." M.A. thesis, University of Oklahoma, 1924.

Burke, Bob. *Good Guys Wear White Hats: The Life of George Nigh.* Oklahoma City: Oklahoma Heritage Association, 2000.

Caraway, Suzzanne Kelley. "Guide to Historical Objects and Structures on the Campus of the University of Central Oklahoma." 2001.

Collins, Reba. "History of the Vista: Newspaper of Central State College." M.A. thesis, Oklahoma State University, 1959.

Crowder, James L., Jr. *Historic Edmond: An Illustrated History.* San Antonio: Historical Publishing Network, 2000.

Cunliff, Ed, et al. *Central State University Centennial Student Portrait.* Edmond: Central State University, 1990.

Davidson, Oscar William. "Education at Statehood." *Chronicles of Oklahoma* 28 (Spring 1950): 63-80.

Dickerson, L. L. "The Central State Normal School." *Sturm's Oklahoma Magazine* 5 (August 1907): 14-16.

Faulk, Odie, and William D. Welge. *Oklahoma: A Rich Heritage.* Sun Valley, CA: American Historical Press, 2004.

Fisher, Bill E. *A History of the Graduate Program.* Edmond, Central State University, 1990.

Fordice, Stella Barton. "History of Edmond, Oklahoma." M.A. thesis, University of Oklahoma, 1927.

Goble, Danney. *Progressive Oklahoma: The Making of a New Kind of State.* Norman: University of Oklahoma Press, 1980.

Hart, David M. *A Centennial History of Science and Mathematics at Central State University.* Edmond: Central State University, 1990.

Hoig, Stan. *The Early Years of Edmond.* Self-published, 1976.

_____. *Edmond – The First Century.* Edmond: Edmond Historic Preservation Trust, 1987.

_____. "A History of the Development of Institutions of Higher Education in Oklahoma." Ph.D. diss., University of Oklahoma, 1971.

Jones, Edna, ed. *Sixty Years at Central.* Edmond: Central State College, 1951.

Levy, David W. *The University of Oklahoma: A History.* Norman: University of Oklahoma Press, 2005.

Mullins, J. Dale, and Lucille Patton. *A Centennial History of the Education Program.* Edmond: Central State University, 1990.

Norris, L. David. *Southeastern Oklahoma State University Since 1909.* Durant: Mesa Publishing Company, 1986.

Norvell, George Eldon. "A History of the First Legislative Assembly of the Territory of Oklahoma." M.A. thesis, University of Oklahoma, 1946.

Nunn, E. Sherman. "A History of Education in Oklahoma Territory." Ed.D. diss., University of Oklahoma, 1941.

Nye, Harvey N. *A History of the College of Business Administration.* Edmond: Central State University, 1990.

Oakes, Francis Coram. "A Story of Central State College." Unpublished manuscript, Central State College, 1946.

Peters, Virginia Lee. "Emma W. Plunkett: Her Life, Career, and Professional Contributions." Ph.D. diss., Florida State University, 1968.

Ross, Walter L. "Edmond, Home of Central Normal." *Sturm's Oklahoma Magazine* 7 (December 1908): 84-87.

Rulon, Philip Reed. "The Founding of Oklahoma Agricultural and Mechanical College, 1890-1908." Ed.D. diss., Oklahoma State University, 1968.

Smallwood, James, ed. *And Gladly Teach: Reminiscences of Teachers from Dugout to Modern Module.* Norman: University of Oklahoma Press, 1976.

APPENDIX

University of Central Oklahoma Administration

W. Roger Webb
President

William J. Radke
Provost and Vice President for Academic Affairs

Steve Kreidler
Executive Vice President

Kathryn Gage
Vice President for Student Affairs

Anne Holzberlein
Executive Director, UCO Foundation

Myron Pope
Vice President for Enrollment Management

Cynthia Rolfe
Vice President for Information Technology

Cheryl Steele
Executive Director, Leadership Studies

Bill Wiseman
Director University Relations

Patricia LaGrow
*Vice Provost and
Associate Vice President for Academic Affairs*

John Barthell
Dean, College of Mathematics and Science

John Clinton
Dean, College of Arts, Media and Design

Richard Bernard
*Interim Dean, Joe C. Jackson College of Graduate
Studies and Research*

James Machell
Dean, College of Education

Michael Shirley
Dean, College of Business Administration

Pamela Washington
Dean, College of Liberal Arts

Members of the Regional University System of Oklahoma

Mark Stansberry
Chair

Sandy Garrett
Member and State Superintendent

Harold Jackson
Member

Belva Howard
Vice Chair

Jan Gordon
Member

Richard Ryerson
Member

Joe Anna Hibler
Secretary

Ann Holloway
Member

Mickey Thompson
Member

Presidents of the University of Central Oklahoma

FIRST	Richard Thatcher	1891-1893
SECOND	George W. Winans	1893-1894
THIRD	E.R. Williams	1894-1895
FOURTH	Edmund Dandridge Murdaugh	1895-1901
FIFTH	Frederick Howard Umholtz	1901-1906
SIXTH	Thomas Walter Butcher	1906-1908
SEVENTH	James Argyle McLauchlin	1908-1911
EIGHTH	Charles Evans	1911-1916
NINTH	Grant Bartholomew Grumbine	1916-1917
TENTH	James W. Graves	1917-1919
ELEVENTH	John Gordon Mitchell	1919-1931
TWELFTH	Malcolm A. Beeson	1931-1935
	Cliff R. Otto (*acting president*)	1935-1935
THIRTEENTH	John Ohlyer Moseley	1935-1939
FOURTEENTH	Roscoe R. Robinson	1939-1948
	George P. Huckaby (*acting president*)	1948-1948
FIFTEENTH	W. Max Chambers	1949-1960
SIXTEENTH	Garland Alonzo Godfrey	1960-1975
SEVENTEENTH	Bill Lillard	1975-1992
EIGHTEENTH	George Nigh	1992-1997
NINETEENTH	W. Roger Webb	1997-current

INDEX

B

J

Jackson, Enid 77

Jackson, Harold 201

Jackson, Joe C. xi, 67, 77, 82-83, 86-88, 112, 116, 123-135, 139, 141, 146, 150

Jackson, Rose M. 11-12

Jacobs, Clyde 150

Jacobson House Native Art Center 171

Jacobson, Francis 53

James, David 145, 182

Jamieson Dairy 1-4

JC Penney Company 178

Jeffries, Otto William 16

Jenkins, Roy Horace 17-18

Johnson, Charlie vii

Johnson, Erica vii, 11, 117

Johnson, Nina Eugenie 10

Jolly, Stuart 149

Jones, Edna 23, 58

Jones, Goldi Oldham 92

Jones, Linda 110, 164, 168, 178

Jordan, Addie Lee 93, 126

Journal of Applied Research 185

Journal of Environmental Pathology 185

Journal of Mammalogy 160

K

Kansas State Teachers Association 26

Kappa Alpha Psi 84

Kappa Sigma 84

KCSC Radio 163, 171

Kennedy, John F. 113, 128

Kennedy, Joyce 83

Kennedy, Robert F. 129

Kerr, Robert S. 55, 109

Kerr-McGee Corporation 178

Kibby, Minnie Morton 1, 11

Kickingbird Tennis Center 152

King, Martin Luther, Jr. 124

King's College 28

Kirk, Mike 181

Kitchen, Ida Waide 24

Klein, Edward G. 17-18, 29

Knight, Dale vii

Korean War 88-90

Kreidler, Steve vi, 178, 185, 200

Ku Klux Klan 48

Kunc, Kathryn 82, 101, 195

Kune, Kathryn Kerr 47, 67

L

Laboratory of Original Evidence 40

Lackmeyer, Wendy vii

Ladies Aid Society 2

LaGrow, Pat vi, 116, 186, 200

Lake Arcadia 152, 167

Landrum, David 114

Langston A & M College 13

Langston, Chuck 182

Laughton, Sadie 58

Lax, Bernard 122-124

Layton, Solomon Andrew 36-37

League of Nations 40

League of Young Democrats 57

Lehman, Paul vii, 97, 121, 142-143, 157

Lehr, Oscar J. x

Leonard, Lura 29

Letterman's Club 53

Letterman's Club for Women 53

Liberal Arts Building 106, 119

Lillard Administration Building 36

Lillard, Bill xi, 72, 145-153, 155-158, 167-169

Lillard, Mary Helen 67, 72-73, 145, 172

Livermore, Ed 158

Logan, Bryce vii

Logan, Mike vii

Logan, Owen vii

Lolly, John 158

Lone Star Conference 182

Lough, D. Keith 174

Lover's Rocks 78

Lower, Elaine 81, 95

Lower, Gary 81

Luidens, John 119

Luper, Clara 126

Lyceum Society 8, 18, 29, 38

M

Magrill, Samuel 184

Mammals of Oklahoma 160

Mann, Alice 17-18

Mann, Horace ix

Marks, Whit 114, 133

Markwood, Christopher L. 97, 186

Marland, E.W. 60-61

Martin, James 10

Mata, Julio vii

Mathews, John Joseph 60

Matthews, Kevin 155

Matthews, Rubye 5

Max Chambers Library 37, 105, 158-159, 176

McBurney, Laressa G. 17

McCaleb, Neal 140

McCarrel, Fred 50, 72

McCaskey, Ed vii, 30, 58

McCaskey, Kash vii

McCormick, Heather vii

McGill, Bob vii

McGinnis, Pat vii

McGregor, Megan vii, 187

McGurl, Dan, Jr. 142

McKendree College 5

McKinley, William viii, 14

McLane, Elmer 53

McLauchlin, James A. 28-30, 32

McNeiland, Stacy vii

Megehee, Alicia 165

Melton Gallery 85

Metropolitan Railway Company 27

Meyers, Carrie Wantland 42-43, 108

N

O